VINTAGE

A WHITE TRAIL

Haroon Khalid has an academic background in anthropology. He got his undergraduate degree from Lahore University of Management Sciences (LUMS), Pakistan, in social sciences with a focus on anthropology and history, and his graduate degree in anthropology from the University of Toronto, Canada. He has been a freelance journalist since 2008 and has written over 350 articles for numerous publications, including *Al Jazeera*, *CBC*, *MacLean's*, Scroll.in, Wire. in, TRT World, *Himal*, *Dawn*, the *News* and *Express Tribune*. He has travelled extensively around Pakistan and has written about minority rights, folk traditions, the politicization of history and heritage, nationalism and identity, and several other topics.

Haroon is the author of four books—*A White Trail* (2013), *In Search of Shiva* (2015), *Walking with Nanak* (2016) and *Imagining Lahore* (2018). He has also written a non-fiction short book called *The Enigma of Pakistani Identity* (2017) and *Beyond the Other* (2016). In his work, Haroon explores fluid identities, traditions and religious practices that challenge the notion of exclusivist identities, which defines communities in South Asia today. His writings have been translated into many languages, including Punjabi, Urdu, Hindi, Bengali, Gujarati and Italian. He is based in Toronto, Canada.

Celebrating 35 Years of
Penguin Random House India

ALSO BY THE SAME AUTHOR

In Search of Shiva: A Study of Folk Religious Practices in Pakistan
Walking with Nanak
Imagining Lahore: The City That Is, the City That Was

PRAISE FOR THE BOOK

'It is a journey that builds momentum gradually. Khalid changes gears smoothly . . .'—*The Hindu*

'Armed with reporter's technique, Khalid has engaged very well with his subjects'—*Sunday Indian*

'This is ethnography at its best and it does present you the inner lives; the consciousness of the minorities in intimate detail'—*Express Tribune*

'Khalid challenges preconceptions, tears apart generalizations, and makes a genuine attempt to get himself acquainted with the astronomical diversity of these groups of people'—*Dawn*

'Khalid's narration of events that he pieces together from interviews is masterful'—The *News on Sunday*

A
WHITE TRAIL

A JOURNEY INTO THE HEART OF PAKISTAN'S RELIGIOUS MINORITIES

HAROON KHALID

VINTAGE
An imprint of Penguin Random House

VINTAGE

USA | Canada | UK | Ireland | Australia
New Zealand | India | South Africa | China

Vintage is part of the Penguin Random House group of companies
whose addresses can be found at global.penguinrandomhouse.com

Published by Penguin Random House India Pvt. Ltd
4th Floor, Capital Tower 1, MG Road,
Gurugram 122 002, Haryana, India

Penguin
Random House
India

First published in Vintage by Penguin Random House India 2023

Copyright © Haroon Khalid 2013

All rights reserved

10 9 8 7 6 5 4 3 2 1

The views and opinions expressed in this book are the author's own and the facts
are as reported by him which have been verified to the extent possible, and the
publishers are not in any way liable for the same.

ISBN 9780143460770

Typeset in Cochin LT Std by Manipal Technologies Limited, Manipal
Printed at Replika Press Pvt. Ltd, India

www.penguin.co.in

CONTENTS

REFLECTIONS TEN YEARS ON

It has been ten years since *A White Trail: A Journey into the Heart of Pakistan's Religious Minorities* was first published. A lot has changed since and a lot hasn't. At the time that I was writing the book, Pakistan had begun, yet again, another love affair with democracy. Musharraf had recently been booted out, and incidents of terrorism were becoming more widespread. In the aftermath of 9/11, the juxtaposition of Islamic 'fundamentalism' and 'terrorism', and the looming threat of Islamic militancy within the country, the Pakistani State had begun projecting a softer image of itself—a more progressive, tolerant and liberal image, crafted in contrast to Islamic 'fundamentalism'. The seeds of that image were laid out in Musharraf's 'Enlightened Moderation', defined loosely as 'Moderate Islam'. These terms have slowly faded away from public memory and state discourse, but the concept, the need to project a softer, milder, tolerant image of Pakistan continues to be a priority.

Many of the recent actions of the Pakistani State vis-à-vis religious minorities—the opening of the Kartarpur Sahib Corridor, the renovation of several other Sikh gurdwaras, the erection of the statue of Maharaja Ranjit

Singh at the Lahore Fort, allotting funds for the upkeep of historical Hindu temples, announcing government holidays to commemorate non-Muslim festivals and others, need to be seen through this lens of the moderation that it wants to project. The projection of religious minorities, particularly Sikh and Hindu, to highlight the diversity of the country, plays a strategic role in crafting a tolerant image of the country. Traces of this changing attitude and how that impacts the daily lives of religious minorities in Pakistan are scattered all over the interviews that have been included in *A White Trail*. From the revival of Holi in Multan to the growth of the festival of Navratri in Bahawalnagar, to the exertion of a stronger identity by the youth of the Sikh community at Nankana Sahib—all of these stories tell the tale of a state increasingly incorporating the religious minorities into its national identity.

However, this isn't a seamless process. This new inclusive identity stands in direct conflict with the state's primordial identity created in opposition to a Hindu India. For seven decades and counting, this exclusivist identity has been concretized through different state institutions, education, media, bureaucracy, law and others. So even while the Pakistani State is attempting to challenge parts of this exclusivist identity, there are several instances of the state reverting to its primary identity, almost instinctively when it feels threatened or challenged. There have been several instances of political leaders using anti-Hindu language and rhetoric to appease a particular political base as Fayyaz Chohan, former information minister of Punjab did in 2019. At a time of heightened political tension with India, Chohan in a statement had called Hindus 'cow urine drinkers'.

Thus, while the state tries to craft a newer, tolerant image, the exclusivist structures that have for the past seven decades constructed an anti-Hindu, anti-Sikh narrative, primarily through the education system, survive unchallenged. This has created a contradictory state, which on one hand is trying to be more inclusive, while on the other hand, continues to undermine its efforts through other state structures. This tension often leads to violence with the religious minorities bearing the brunt of it. *A White Trail* documents many of these stories from the wars of 1965 and 1971, the destruction of the Babri Masjid in 1992 and several others. In the recent years, these acts of violence have manifested themselves in actions against a proposed Hindu temple in Islamabad and the repeated attacks on the statue of Maharaja Ranjit Singh.

* * *

On a rainy day of March 2011, I was on my way to Katas Raj, an ancient Hindu temple in the Salt Range of Punjab, when I received the news that the Federal Minister for Minorities Affairs, Shahbaz Bhatti, had been shot dead in Islamabad. This had come only three months after the assassination of the Governor of Punjab, Salman Taseer, by his own bodyguard, Mumtaz Qadri. Both of these assassinations were in relation to the support of these two leaders to a Christian woman accused of blasphemy, Aasia Bibi, who had been accorded capital punishment in 2010. Salman Taseer, Shahbaz Bhatti and a few other prominent political leaders had come out in support of Aasia Bibi while also criticizing the misuse of the blasphemy laws in Pakistan. They argued that the law was being used to target the vulnerable non-Muslim communities of the country. Salman Taseer and others even suggested making amendments to the law. For a brief moment in Pakistan's history, there was mainstream discussion on pushing back some of the institutional Islamization that had been experienced in the 1980s and 1990s. Those discussions came to a halt with these two assassinations.

Perhaps even more than the assassination of Salman Taseer, it was the reaction of the country that put an end to any debate about the blasphemy laws. A wide segment of society, including lawyers, judges, police officials and media personalities, celebrated the killer, and referred to Salman Taseer as a blasphemer. For many, the myth of a silent 'tolerant' majority was shattered. The hate-filled and acrimonious narrative state institutions had spewed over the past seven decades was exhibiting itself through popular sentiment. Mumtaz Qadri was subsequently hanged in 2016. Thousands and thousands of protestors came out in support of him. His funeral prayer was attended by a sea of people. A shrine was raised in his memory on the outskirts of Islamabad.

I remember I was having a conversation with a Sikh scholar a few days after the assassination of Salman Taseer. Having observed people literally showering rose petals on Qadri and a former high court chief justice coming out in support of him, he said that he thought that Qadri would eventually be freed and end up getting a ticket from a political party to contest for elections. Given the history of Pakistani state institutions buckling under right-wing pressure, and the outpouring of love for Mumtaz Qadri, his analysis didn't seem that far-fetched at that point. Of course, things didn't unfold the way he predicted, but from this incident and the protests after the death of Mumtaz Qadri, a new political party emerged, Tehreek-e-Labbaik, whose entire politics is based around protection of the blasphemy laws using the symbol of Mumtaz Qadri. In the first general election that it ran for in 2018, it emerged as the fifth-largest political party of the country, with many of its candidates coming a close second or third in several constituencies. Many of their political banners carried a photo of Qadri. In a few years of its existence Tehreek-e-Labbaik has already emerged as a formidable political force.

In 2018, after spending eight years in prison, most of them in solitary confinement and regular torture by jail officials and other inmates, Aasia Bibi was acquitted by the Supreme Court. Tehreek-e-Labbaik arranged another big protest, shutting down the twin cities of Rawalpindi and Islamabad. Aasia Bibi was quietly flown out to Canada, where she now resides with her family.

I had just begun conducting interviews with members of the religious minorities when in 2010 the case of Aasia Bibi burst on the national platform. Salman Taseer coming out in support of her, him being labelled a blasphemer, his assassination and the celebration of Mumtaz Qadri as a hero were all happening around the time I was conducting my interviews. Even then, we were aware of the gravity of this case and its far-reaching implications. The case was always present in the room with us as we were conducting interviews.

There was a sense of fear, paranoia almost, of not saying the wrong thing, something that could be construed as blasphemous. The assassination of Salman Taseer had blurred further the boundaries of what it was to be blasphemous. I was acutely aware of that when I was writing the book. It informed the way I conducted the interviews, the questions I asked, it informed the way religious minorities responded, informed what they shared and what they held back, forcing me to also take a note of things that were not said but expressed subtly. This tension, threat and fear is palatable in *A White Trail*.

Over the past ten years or so, the situation has only worsened. Any debate on amending the blasphemy laws is construed to be blasphemous. Politicians, police officials, lawyers and even members of the judiciary, who may be sympathetic to the plight of religious minorities often find themselves surrendering to fear. While *A White Trail* is not a deep historical and political analysis of the blasphemy laws, it is an ethnographic study of the everyday lived experiences of the diverse members of the religious minorities living under the shadow of this law and the violence generated through it. Though researched and written between 2010 and 2013, the structures that shape the interactions recorded in the book aren't very different today.

* * *

I am grateful to Penguin Random House, to Milee Ashwarya and Karthik Venkatesh, for giving *A White Trail* a second life. Karthik was also the editor of the first edition of this book. I am grateful for all the effort he has put into this work. Thank you Kaniskha Gupta, my agent, my friend, for all your support. Thank you to my wife, Anam Zakaria, for always helping me flesh out my ideas and thoughts, and always being my first reader, editor and critic. Thank you to our beautiful daughter, Lina Khalid Zakaria, for making our lives wonderful.

February 2023   Haroon Khalid
Toronto

INTRODUCTION

I started writing for newspapers and magazines in 2008. Initially, most of my articles were focused on history and archaeology. I would visit an obscure monument around Lahore and write about it. It was the beginning of a startling journey, a kind of engagement with history that one can never experience sitting in a classroom or by reading books. I started to focus particularly on Hindu and Sikh monuments and history because of a fascination with these two religions that years of negative state propaganda had given birth to. Pakistani historiography discards Hindu and Sikh narratives from its discourse and wherever they are mentioned, they are always mentioned negatively. This created in me a thirst to learn more about these religions and their histories, with which the history of Pakistan is inextricably intertwined. I was fascinated by my discoveries: a Hindu temple, lying in the middle of a congested locality in the heart of Lahore or a Sikh gurdwara associated with the founder of the religion, Guru Nanak, lying on the outskirts of a village, invisible to the undiscerning eye. Through my research, I began to explore different aspects of Pakistani heritage and culture that were not part of the mainstream narrative and my writings became a reflection of my field work.

I recall calling my editor one day, telling her that I had an idea for a series of articles. I wanted to visit the four religious minorities living in Lahore (Hindu, Sikh, Christian and Baha'i) and write articles about their lifestyles and practices. 'Haroon, I do not think we should do it. Especially not for a newspaper,' she replied. The Gojra incident, where a Christian-dominated village had been attacked by a fanatic Muslim mob, was fresh in everyone's mind. 'We should not be exposing minorities, especially at a time like this,' she told me. I disagreed with her rationale. The solution, in my opinion, was not to stop talking about them for fear of inviting a backlash. In fact, I believe that given the negative propaganda against them, it is imperative to talk about them, their histories, religions and their daily struggles, in the process humanizing them, instead of imagining them as abstract notions of communities. 'Maybe you should write this for a scholarly journal,' she advised. It was a dead end and the idea receded to the periphery.

About a year later when I was being interviewed by Sharmeen Obaid-Chinoy, president of the Citizens Archive of Pakistan (CAP) for a part-time position in Lahore, the idea resurfaced. Somehow our conversation was directed to the topic of a project on religious minorities in Lahore, something that both of us were keen on working on, and thus was born the Minority Project.

* * *

The CAP Minority Project officially began in September 2010. Over the course of the two years that the project ran, I collected over 200 oral history interviews (long and short) from the five religious communities living in and around Lahore (Hindus, Christians, Sikhs, Baha'is and Zoroastrians). Often this involved sitting with interviewees for hours, engrossed in their experiences, beliefs and traditions. A few of these interviews went up to twelve hours (spread over several sessions).

These long narratives explored the interviewees' lives and lifestyles during the pre-Partition, Partition and post-Partition years. The oral history questionnaires were divided into several sections, covering childhood years, school life, neighbourhoods, entertainment, job experiences and so forth. The normal procedure was to conduct one generic interview, and then to return with a personalized questionnaire based on the person's life experiences. The idea was to learn about the history of the individual, the community, and then build up a larger narrative about the history of the country. In addition, I would also focus on their religious beliefs, folk tales and places of worship.

Several challenges cropped up during the course of the project. Perhaps the biggest obstacle was the constant fear in the minds of the minorities, which would lead to self-imposed restrictions when responding to slightly 'controversial' questions. In order to overcome this, I would spend time before, after and during an interview, to create a relationship with the interviewee, establishing a level of trust so that they felt comfortable while answering questions. Another technique that I would follow was asking a series of 'warm-up' questions. This helped in disarming the interviewees of their initial inhibition, thereby gradually easing them into the interview process. However, at times, even these methods failed to completely put some people at ease. For such well-guarded people, it was important to read between the lines and look for truth amidst their sugarcoated answers.

We collected about fifty narratives in all, implementing the pattern of long structured interviews. Besides these, I also attended religious festivals where I conducted short interviews with the attendees. At these festivals, I would talk to people about the significance of particular events; what it meant to them, how it was celebrated and, in a few cases, the importance of the shrine where the festivals were being celebrated. Conducting an interview in the midst of festivities had its challenges. Firstly, as opposed to the controlled environment of the detailed interview sessions, background noise was a constant in these short interviews. Secondly, I would always be surrounded by an army of observers, which took its toll on the narration of oral history. Sometimes at a festival, I would also come across a ritual that I was earlier unaware of, and hence, unprepared to ask questions about. In such cases, I relied on improvisation.

* * *

A *White Trail* is a journey or a pilgrimage through the various religious shrines, rituals and festivals of non-Muslim Pakistan. The name, suggested by my wife, Anam, takes its inspiration from the white part of the Pakistani flag, which is said to represent the minorities of the country. It is a trail because it is a physical journey through the festivals and lives of the country's religious minorities.

The process of writing this book began in October 2010, when I attended the Hindu celebration of Navratri at Bahawalnagar. Fascinated, I came back and wrote about it for a magazine. This led to a series of articles that talked about several issues revolving around the discussion of religious minorities in the country, issues overlooked by mainstream media in their quest to focus on the victimization aspect. Through my experience with the religious communities, I realized that there is much more to the minority debate than just the aspect of victimization. It is this partial debate and a lack of research in this particular topic that inspired me to write this book, which discusses a whole range of issues and aspects regarding the religious minorities of Pakistan. The book, which uses both long and short interviews from the Minority Project, along with my own observations and research, is not merely a description of a particular event and its rituals, but along with description, it also delves deep into the history and mythology, and also attempts an anthropological and historical analysis. It picks up some of the themes and problems from the interviews and incorporates their insights into explaining the environment of the festival, in order to bring a coherent picture to the reader. Some of the interviews used for the book are those that took place off the record, in candid discussions, which while not necessarily taking place during the course of the festival, have been presented in that framework for the purpose of understanding.

To put it simply, *A White Trail* is a journey through the festivals of Pakistan's minority groups, weaving together the religious, historical and cultural significance of that particular event, and incorporating oral histories of the people present at the festival and also those who were interviewed elsewhere. The book is about why, how and who celebrates these festivals. Using the narrative that builds around the festival, I have attempted to present a larger picture of the socio-economic and political conditions of the religious minorities in the areas that I have covered. This is a book written for an average Pakistani and anyone else from any other part of the world, who has an interest in this multicultural country. I have made a conscious effort to maintain simple language and explain the basic tenets of all the religions through the course of these festivals, providing the unacquainted reader with a context. Finally, the book aims to freeze the religious minorities of these areas in this time warp, as they exist at this moment, and present it to the readers who years down the line might not be living in a similar Pakistan.

The Muslim population of the country at the moment is about 97 per cent. Out of the 3 per cent non-Muslims, a large chunk belongs to the Ahmadiyya community; former Muslims, but now declared non-Muslims according to the Constitution of the country. Of the remaining percentage, the majority are Hindus living in the 'faraway' 'peripheral' regions of southern Punjab, inner Sindh and Baluchistan. In 1947, when the country was created, the population of the non-Muslims was about 30 per cent (without including the Ahmadiyya community), a majority of whom have migrated or converted to Islam because of socio-political and economic reasons. Such a drastic decrease in the minority population highlights the urgency of the situation of minorities and the importance of recording and preserving their heritage and their voice for future generations.

Before concluding, I would like to answer a question that is often posed to me regarding this project. I'm frequently asked, 'So will you portray a negative image of the country?' This question comes from the generally accepted knowledge that the religious minorities of Pakistan are a persecuted group and therefore any work on them from within the country is likely to focus only on that persecuted aspect. If that is the case, then the Government of Pakistan is failing to do its job of protecting its own citizens, which is a rather shameful state of affairs. But that aside, I would like to answer this question here:

Firstly, if the minorities are being persecuted, which indeed they are, then there is a crying need to highlight those instances, with the process of rectifying it being a second step. The solution is definitely not to hide the dust under the carpet. However, I would want to explain here that this book is not a list of tortures that people of the religious minorities have to face. It seeks to present a human face to these abstractly defined groups. It looks at their histories, traditions, personalities and stories of resilience. The book is an attempt to expand the discussion of religious minorities beyond the narrowly defined agenda of religious persecution.

In a lot of instances, I heard stories where youngsters have been able to revive religious traditions. There are narratives of how, in this threatening environment, minorities have been able to expand the parameters of their space, a space which is being renegotiated all the time. The result is that that the minorities are asserting themselves more and more now. This goes against conventional wisdom. There are also stories about syncretism, where Muslims take part in Hindu and Sikh festivals. This book hopes to shatter a lot of stereotypes Pakistanis have about themselves and others have about us.

Haroon Khalid

DISCLAIMER

The research involved in this publication was made possible from interviews, pictures and other material obtained from the archives of The Citizens Archive of Pakistan (as part of its Minority Project, amongst other initiatives) and therefore such research was financially supported by The Citizens Archive of Pakistan (CAP). All such research referred to or relied upon in this publication is with permission of The Citizens Archive of Pakistan. However, The Citizens Archive of Pakistan takes no responsibility for the accuracy or completeness neither of the research nor for the facts stated therein, opinions expressed or conclusions reached in this publication, all of which are entirely borne by the author.

AUTHOR'S NOTE

Given the socio-political realities of Pakistan, I have changed the names of members of the religious minorities referred to in the book, in order to preserve their privacy and protect them from any backlash that the book might cause. Even though this is a non-fiction book, in some instances, I have taken the liberty to stray from strictly speaking, non-fiction, to create the essence of the story being narrated. However, where I have done that, I have taken care to maintain the spirit of the truth.

AUTHOR'S NOTE

HINDU

HOLI AT MULTAN

'I was preparing lunch while my mother and sister were sleeping in the other room,' says Parvati Devi, a forty-four-year-old classically trained professional singer from Multan, who is also a social activist. 'Pervaiz, an eight-year-old boy from the *mohalla* (community), rushed into the house, without knocking or ringing the bell. He was out of breath and his eyes looked as if they had seen a ghost.' 'They are coming,' he said. 'Who is?' 'They, the Muslims! They are looking for you. They have destroyed the Valmiki temple.'

Though gripped by fear, Devi's mind stayed alert. The temple is only a couple of streets away, she thought to herself. Without waiting for Pervaiz to complete his sentence, she rose from the stool, leaving the half-cooked roti burning on the *chulha* and went to her bedroom where her mother lay napping along with her sister and her nephew. Pervaiz followed her, still panting. 'I heard them saying they will burn the house down. They are carrying a blue canister.' He was finally able to deliver the complete message. 'Go back to your house and avoid running into them,' Devi advised Pervaiz, who nodded and ran out. She helped lift her mother from the bed, gripping her mother's walking stick with the

3

other hand. Her sister picked up the baby, who started to cry, unaware of the approaching danger, unaware of the fact that his fate had already been sealed as a Hindu boy born on the wrong side of the border; a minor geographical miscalculation on the part of nature.

'We didn't even have time to get our dupattas,' recalls Devi. 'We were out on the streets, three women, running away from the mob, which wanted to burn me alive. There were thousands of them, shouting *'Naraiye Takbir, Allah o Akbar.' 'Shaheed Babri Masjid ka badla, le kar rahenge* (We will avenge the martyrdom of Babri Mosque).'

* * *

Devi goes back into her house and returns with a platter full of berries, which she offers to the devotees gathered for the ritualistic burning of Holika. She picks out a little vermillion from a small cup placed on the plate and makes a vertical mark on the forehead of each one she hands out the berries to. 'This will protect them from evil,' she explains.

It is about midnight. The colourful festival of Holi will be celebrated in the morning. Within a congested settlement, this is the only spacious area where a community event can be organized. Graffiti in Urdu on one of the walls reads 'Diwali *Mubarak*'. Diwali was in October and this is March.

A group of women gather around a pyre made out of hay and little sticks, placed at the centre of the courtyard. The women are dressed in glittery shalwar kameez, bright in colours, their heads covered with dupattas, a sign of modesty that a religious event like this demands. They compliment each other on their choice of clothes and jewellery. Sugarcoated comments are returned with equally sweetened welcomes. Children gather around the pyre, curious to see what their mothers are up to. The only men around are old, those who have retired and spend their days at home. This is primarily an all-women's event and the men generally tend to leave it to them. There are about thirty people here at the moment.

Devi is the only woman standing on the side, not next to the pyre. She is wearing a simple pink and blue shalwar kameez as opposed to the elaborate clothes of the other women. The only visible jewellery is her nose pin. Her expression is that of self-assuredness, of someone who has overcome obstacles in life and is not afraid to confront any new ones. Despite her interaction with the other women, there is a detachment about her presence here. 'Only married women take part in this ceremony,' she says. Devi, the only earning member in her family, is still unmarried and plans to remain that way. 'I had a boyfriend a few years ago—a healthy, well-built man, with a huge moustache,' she says as she twirls her imagined moustache. 'But he couldn't handle my independence and I refuse to be a housewife.' It is clear now that her self-assuredness bordering on arrogance is actually a defence mechanism to protect herself from the gossip of the community. The idea of remaining single by choice, and that too, a woman, is still alien to them. The strong sexuality that she emanates can be construed as fuelling their imagination. She travels frequently to Islamabad and Lahore for her work at the NGO and makes powerful speeches for the rights of the minorities. Her posture, straight, almost bending backwards, illustrates that she demands respect in the community, but the bitterness in her eyes and downward arch of the lips reflects her alienation from the community that she has vowed to fight for.

A young girl carrying a platter of halwa distributes it to the people. Taking a handful in her fingers, the girl puts it on the palm of the attendants. Halwa and berries are offered as prasad to the devotees, an offering to God, consumed by mortals.

Singing devotional songs, the women start circling the symbolical Holika, the pyre. They carry a steel glass in one hand and pour a transparent liquid on to the hay. Carrying a thread in the other hand, they wrap it around the pyre as they walk around it. After seven rounds, they move away, shouting at their children to get away as well. Children gather around their mothers and those standing on the side take a step backwards. A young man, about thirty, squats next to the pyre, digging deep into it, with a lit stick. A small fire begins at the base, and the man steps back.

There is a blast and the pyre is completely on fire. The liquid that the women had been pouring was oil. The fire gains height almost unexpectedly, rising well above the roofs of the single-storey white houses around it. It touches the young banyan tree that arches above the courtyard, setting alight a few leaves. The temperature begins to rise and the children cover their faces with their hands, while a few younger ones start to cry. Some of the devotees, who have climbed on to the rooftops, are caught too close to the fire. A few women start screaming as the sounds of prayers rise. For a few moments, it feels as if the fire would consume the entire community, an angry Holika seeking revenge from those who have gathered to celebrate her defeat. But nothing happens as the fire dies as quickly as it had erupted.

The hay burns out completely, leaving only bright pink ash. Relieved, the attendees rejoice. 'Holika has been burnt. Holi has begun. Tomorrow, people will celebrate the victory of good over evil by throwing colours on each other,' says Devi. 'Evil has been burnt and now it's time to rejoice.'

* * *

According to folk legend, Holika was the evil sister of Hiranyakashipu, the tyrant who is believed to have ruled the city of Multan thousands of years ago. He was a true devotee of Lord Vishnu, one of the most important deities in the Hindu pantheon. Impressed by his devotion, the Lord gave him special powers. Gradually, the king became arrogant and began to think of himself as the Almighty. He forbade the worship of Lord Vishnu in the entire city, casting a sense of fear and panic amongst the residents. In order to teach Hiranyakashipu a lesson, Lord Vishnu himself took birth in his house in the shape of his son—Prahlad Bhagat.

When Prahlad Bhagat grew up, he revolted against his father, exhorting people of the city to stop worshipping Hiranyakashipu and turn towards the real God. His father made several attempts on his son's life but failed every time. As a last resort, he turned to his sister Holika. Holika had a magical shawl which protected its wearer from fire. She decided to enter into blazing flames with her nephew, believing that while the shawl would protect her, it would burn Prahlad to death. According to the legend, as she entered the fire with Prahlad, a gust of wind blew, taking the shawl off her and covering Prahlad instead. As it happened, Holika was burnt while Prahlad was saved. The burning of a pyre on the eve of Holi is a commemoration of this triumph, which marks the death of evil in the form of Holika. Eventually, Prahlad Bhagat was able to kill his father too and restore the moral balance of the world. His devotees built a temple in the memory of Prahlad at the spot where he supposedly killed his father—on a mound outside the city, which later became a popular spiritual site with mystics and saints. The temple stands even today, a worn-down building with several cracks in its walls. It has remained abandoned ever since Partition, occasionally becoming victim to the passion of fanatic mobs like the one in 1992.

Because of the association of the mound with the temple of Prahlad Bhagat, the area came to be considered holy, as a result of which Muslim mystics were also attracted towards it. One such mystic who came and settled next to the temple was Bahauddin Zakariya (1170–1267) whose shrine came to be situated next to the temple. The tide of fortune has now turned and the temple which was once the fount of spirituality at this particular spot now lies in obscurity under the shadow of this massive shrine, which has become the symbol of the Muslim city of Multan.

Thousands of devotees visit this shrine every day, oblivious to the religious syncretism of which this shrine is a product. There was a time when Hindu temples and Muslim shrines could share a wall and devotees visited both of them, an act almost unimaginable in a post-Partition Pakistan. The temple, even though in shambles now, is an anomaly next to the shrine, an unacceptable act of treason in 'Muslim' Pakistan, carved out of a 'Hindu' India on the basis of the 'Two-Nation Theory'. The fluidity of the religious traditions that once existed between these two shrines defies the rigidity of religiosity that became the basis of this new country and therefore an acceptance of this aspect of history would be challenging the notion of separatism and Pakistani nationhood. Thus, this part of history is not unconsciously ignored but deliberately eliminated to ensure the conformity of history to the dominant nationalistic discourse. The city of Multan continues to move forward, unaware of its ancient past and the mythical association that it has with the story of Hiranyakashipu and Prahlad Bhagat. The group of thirty-odd women, who took part in the burning of Holika, are now the only link that the city has with that story. These Hindus, who have now become a religious minority, strangers in their own home, lived here before Multan became a part of Pakistan. In a sense, they are the true descendants of this land, who are now sadly unwelcome in this Muslim country.

* * *

As the last of Holika burns, Devi heads back to her house, which is a street away. She will be entertaining a few Muslim friends there tomorrow, who are coming from Lahore, to witness the Holi festivities.

'We had no place to go when the mob was chasing us. We ran from one street to another, playing hide and seek with them. Finally, a friend's family took us in. We hid there and waited for the mob to return. They left when they couldn't find me. I didn't dare go back to my house for weeks. They wanted to burn me alive because I was the only Hindu they knew of,' she says emotionlessly, as she settles on the floor after serving tea. 'I used to regularly appear on television and radio. People knew me by my real name. I used to sing bhajans on religious occasions.' She still lives in the same house from where she had escaped about twenty years ago. Her life changed after that event. She took up a Muslim name, Shaila Bibi, and stopped appearing on radio and television altogether.

On 6 December 1992, a mob of Hindu fanatics climbed the historical Babri Mosque in Ayodhya, India, and tore it down. Their rationale was that the mosque had been built by the first Mughal Emperor Babar (1483–1530) on the site of a Hindu temple, birth site of the mythological Hindu king, Ram. The act of vandalism sent ripples throughout the world, and its repercussions bore heavily on Pakistan. Various rallies were organized all over the country in protest. The Babri Mosque was labelled as the 'Martyred (*shaheed*) mosque'. Pakistani historiography depicts Babar as an Islamic warrior who spread the light of religion in pagan India. On the other hand, the nationalistic discourse in India regards Babar as a foreign invader. In this re-interpretation of history after the creation of India–Pakistan, the religious minorities in these two countries struggle to find a place for themselves.

Post the Babri Masjid demolition, demagogue leaders and rabble rousers started calling for a tit-for-tat response. They wanted to reciprocate by attacking Hindu temples all over the country. In the next few days, several historical temples were attacked by mobs. Sitla Mandir at Shah Alami, Lahore, Jain Mandir at Anarkali, Lahore and Bhadra Kali Mandir at Thokar Niaz Baig, Lahore were a few prominent temples that were attacked. None of them were functional at that time as the majority of the Hindu community had migrated to India post-Partition. Most of these temples were occupied by migrant families who had been chased out of their land following the riots of Partition. Some of the temples were also being used as schools. However, in the days following the Babri Mosque incident, the residents of the houses and the students of the schools led the attacks on their own properties, motivated by religious passion and fervour. These temples had ceased to be temples since 1947, but their past became their crime. In the craziness that followed, a few people who had climbed to the top of the structures to raze them also lost their lives when the temple fell. They were recognized as martyrs in the name of religion—*shaheed*.

Functional temples like Krishna Mandir on the Ravi road and Valmiki Mandir at Neela Gumbad, both in Lahore, were also burned down. Hindu communities in Sindh and Quetta were attacked. Well-known Hindus living in the cities of Punjab had to hide for several months after the incident.

Bhagat Advit Bhatti, a priest at the Neela Gumbad Mandir, had to leave his house for six months with his entire family. There were rumours in the right-wing media that he had fled to India; however, these rumours proved to be false when he eventually resurfaced after the situation had settled down. Another Hindu from Lahore, Shami Lal, who continues using his Hindu name even though his family and friends have adopted dual names to dilute their religious identities, recalls how he shut down his business for several months after 1992. All his clients knew that he was a Hindu and he felt that his life was in danger. 'It has taken me many years to recover from the trauma of 1992. It was like Partition all over again.' Lal was a teenager when Partition riots spread in Lahore. Despite repeated warnings, his grandfather refused to leave his ancestral home. 'After the Babri mosque, there was a sense of fear. I was in Nowshera (in Khyber Pakhtunkhwa) when the Babri Mosque incident happened. Several Hindu temples were razed to the ground in front of my eyes and I couldn't do anything. They were thousands of people. Had they known I was a Hindu, they would have killed me as well.'

* * *

At noon the following morning, people start gathering to celebrate Holi in the courtyard where Holika had been burnt the night before. The gathering is much bigger this time. Young men and boys, dressed in old, faded clothes gather in groups. The women of the house step out with their children, this time free of the make-up and jewellery they were wearing last night. A *dhol-wala*, wearing a white shalwar kameez, accompanied by his assistant, stands on one of the roofs. Children run around collecting plastic bottles, buckets, water-guns, all of which will be valuable possessions later in the day.

Under normal circumstances, bhang, a traditional intoxicant would have been consumed, mixed in almond-milk, but preparing it requires tedious work. Boys instead resort to drinking alcohol, which is easier to obtain and consume. Banned all over the country, alcohol can be legally purchased by non-Muslims if they have a permit card, provided to them by the government for the purchase and consumption of alcohol. However, despite this categorization and limits on its sale, alcohol is readily available throughout the country and sold to people without permits. But permits do provide a benefit to the non-Muslims as alcohol is sold at a lower price on this licence. Using this economic advantage, some non-Muslim boys and men purchase alcohol in bulk and sell it to their Muslim clients at exorbitant prices. Most of the boys carry mixtures of vodka and water in plastic water bottles. Standing in corners, the boys drink with anxious expressions, gulping down the mixture to get rid of evidence as soon as possible. Their anxiety shows that they are doing something wrong. Despite being readily available, drinking remains a guilty pleasure in Muslim Pakistan.

This locality, which is situated next to the railway station, is one of several areas where the Hindu community of the city is located. Despite their low population (little more than a thousand), there isn't a centralized celebration. Different localities have their independent festivities. However, the people are related by familial bonds and so, several families and groups end up visiting different areas during the course of the day.

There are a total of about a hundred houses in this settlement, most of which are single- or double-room quarters, with only about ten to twelve belonging to Hindu families. There is one temple here which caters to the local population; it is a single room, where no more than twenty people can pray at a time. A bell at the entrance needs to be rung to herald the arrival of a devotee into the house of God. A statue of Lord Valmiki covered in a red cloth is placed on a wooden palanquin, at one end of the long room, accompanied by pictures of Kali Mata, Lord Krishna, Lord Vishnu, while a picture of Guru Nanak,[1] the founder of the Sikh religion, flanks them. Next to it lies the Shivalinga, a phallic structure, representing the potent force of the Hindu deity, Lord Shiva. Colourful frills and festoons hang from the room and there is a poster of Lord Valmiki reading the Ramayana next to a picture of Lord Krishna playing the flute, up on the wall.

'That temple of Prahlad Bhagat next to the shrine of Bahauddin Zakariya comes under the jurisdiction of the Awqaf department (a government institution that looks after all the historical Muslim shrines and mosques of the country). It is our demand that the temple be restored and given to the Hindus of the city who are its real owners,' says Devi. 'There were several historical temples in Multan from the pre-Partition days. All of them have become ruins now. The authorities would not let us use them, so the community found other spaces, converting them into makeshift temples to serve their needs,' she adds.

She recalls how in 2006 and 2008, the authorities at the shrine of the saint Bahauddin Zakariya extended the shrine into the premises of the historical Prahlad Temple by constructing a place for ablutions first and then a *langar hall* for devotees visiting the shrine of the Muslim saint. In normal circumstances, their actions would have gone unnoticed. The majority of the Hindu community of the city is uneducated and unaware of its political rights. Given the demonization of the community in Pakistani society—through education, media, cinema, etc.—most of them are too traumatized by the struggle of their daily existence to take up the cause of an abandoned temple. The mantle, however, was picked up a group of young, educated Muslim boys from the city. Twenty-five-year-old Usman Chaudary, president of the RAS (Organization for Religious and Sexual Minorities) Society filed a petition in the high court against the steps taken by the shrine and the court passed a stay order against any further construction on the premises of the temple. The RAS Society has petitioned that the temple be handed back to the Hindu community in the city. This was the beginning of a long-lasting relationship between the RAS Society and the Hindu community of Multan.

As recently as 2010, the community still shied away from its religious traditions and festivals, historical baggage it carried with itself after the massacre at the time of Partition. Festivals, including Holi, were not celebrated in the city, as members of the community were afraid of attracting attention. This was a prudent choice for them, as they lacked numerical strength. Engaging with the youth of the community, Usman worked hard to revive their religious traditions. Devi, who calls Usman her brother, helped him in this cause. The same year, Usman rallied a few people from the community and organized a token celebration of Holi in front of the Multan Press Club, to highlight the lack of facilities the community suffers from. The intended purpose was achieved and the plight of the community was recognized for the first time by a section within the local media. However, there were others who alleged that Usman was an Indian agent working against the interests of Pakistan. More than once, he along with his friends, has been physically attacked.

Despite these setbacks, Usman's actions along with Devi's has spurred a momentum of greater awareness among Hindu youth in the city. Encouraged by them, the youth now insist on celebrating their religious events abandoned after Partition by their elders. Holi, even though on a small scale, is now celebrated every year in Multan due to the efforts of liberal Muslims like Usman and passionate Hindus like Devi, and these events are regularly featured in the local media.

* * *

The dhol-wala starts playing, his sound resonating from the neighbouring buildings. There is an overhead bridge behind the settlement passing over the rail tracks. People stop on the bridge to observe the celebrations. In a few minutes, the entire area has been painted with the colours of Holi. Faces have become indistinguishable, covered in purple and silver, amongst other colours. The ground has become completely wet, with a mixture of water and coloured powder. Children run around with plastic bottles full of colour. The tops of the bottles show off carefully carved holes; each time a child squeezes the bottle, colour flows out, splashing itself everywhere. A woman in her forties, soaked in water, stands in the middle of the courtyard while the boys throw water at each other using the rubber pipe that she has dragged out from one of the neighbouring houses. She is drunk and is the only woman playing Holi at the centre, while the rest of the women are spectators, standing in the corner and watching boys drench each other. Laughing and playing with the boys, throwing water on each other, would be considered improper in the 'Muslim' environment that the community now lives in. This is Holi with a tinge of Muslim piety. Water and colour flow into the courtyard as the boys begin to dance to the beat of the dhol. The forty-year-old woman leaves her pipe and starts dancing with the boys.

Devi watches from the side, her head uncovered, unlike the other women. She has a red towel wrapped around her shoulders. Her status in the community and the authority her personality commands have ensured that she has been spared the onslaught of the colours. She is too important to be painted with the colours of Holi. A young boy takes a little red colour, dares to walk up to her and smears a little on her cheek. She smiles and reciprocates his gesture by smearing his face with some colour as well. A dot of red appears amongst the silver with which his face is already covered. His white shirt bears spots of red, pink, orange and purple.

Usman is not as lucky as Devi. As soon as he enters with another Muslim companion, both of them are dragged into the centre of the crowd, where they are attacked with colour and water. It takes a matter of seconds for them to be completely hidden behind the thick layers of colour. Drenched, Usman makes his way out of the dancing crowd to meet Devi. He takes a handful of colour and puts it on her cheek and she does the same to him. 'Holi Mubarak,' he wishes her. Their blissful smiles to each other conceal the struggles they both have undergone to make this event possible, something that has always been otherwise permitted by the Constitution of the country, yet not allowed because of social biases.

Amidst the dancing and the shouting, the elder boys ask the younger ones to move aside. After having cleared the area, a group of ten boys gather at the centre. There is a *matka* tied to a black wire running between two buildings across the courtyard. The boys put their arms around each other's shoulders and bend forward to join their heads. One of them asks everyone to put their right legs at the centre of the circle. They all comply. A loud shout comes from the middle, '*Bolo bolo bolo Durga Mata ki*' to which everyone in the crowd yells, '*Jai*'. There is another call, '*Bolo Sheranwali ki*', '*Jai*'.

The dhol continues playing but the dancing stops. All the attention is now on this group of boys, who attempt to break the matka. A man standing on the wall of one of the houses, looking down at the boys, takes over the water pipe and directs it towards them. His aim, it seems, is to make the task even more difficult for them. Women and children respond by throwing colours and water from the roofs. The boys stand resolutely.

Once the boys look stable, a group of four younger and lighter boys climb on their backs. Supporting each other, this group stands on the shoulders of the older boys. One of the boys on the top loses his balance and is about to slip as he grabs on to the shirt of another, ripping it apart. The other boy holds his arm and saves him from falling. Women standing at the base shout at them to be careful. Children jump in excitement. Colour and water rushes in from every corner. Three of the four boys make a second layer of human pyramid by putting their arms around each other's shoulders. A boy of about fourteen years, the youngest of the lot, covered in silver and purple, attempts to climb the second layer. The pyramid oscillates as the boys at the base tremble due to the weight at the top. Just as he is halfway up, one of the boys from the base pulls out, succumbing to the pressure. The human pyramid collapses; bodies blunt the fall of the boys from the top. The audience murmurs in dismay as their excitement has met with disappointment. The boy who pulled out complains that too much water is being thrown at them. He wipes the water off his face with the edge of his kameez. Once everyone has recovered from the fall, the group makes another effort. There is no other sport that requires greater team coordination.

The base is set strong and then the second layer is built upon it. The fourteen-year-old boy climbs to the top. He is holding a small stone with which he is meant to break the target. He grabs the matka, trying to maintain his balance as the pyramid below him oscillates. Pink-coloured water falls out of the vessel. The boy stands on the top, holding it, trying hard to even himself out. The pyramid loses its balance and falls again. This time the boy hangs on to the matka as people below him scatter. Attached to a wire, the weight of the boy manages to pull down the vessel. Just before touching the ground, the boy makes an attempt at breaking it but fails. He tries once more but fails again as he now reaches the ground holding the matka and the wire. One of the elder boys, disappointed that the sport has been spoilt, takes the rock from him and breaks the vessel. The pink that oozes out adds to the colour on the ground. Everyone cheers at the much-awaited breaking of the matka. The boys who were a part of the human pyramid resume dancing to the beat of the dhol and they are joined by children who had been witnessing the activities from the side. The drunken woman also joins them. The audiences on the rooftops dance along in celebration.

In the meantime, a man standing on the wall of one of the houses grabs the wire with a stick and ties another matka to it. The victory dance lasts only a few minutes before the group reorganizes itself to take over the new target. In the next hour, the boys take a shot at two other matkas, both of which result in many failed attempts. The tradition of the breaking of the matka comes from the legend of Lord Krishna. This is a commemorative re-enactment of baby Krishna stealing butter from the vessel.

The festivities at this settlement come to an end after the breaking of the three matkas. The media photographers leave and people return to their homes. But the boys are still in a mood to celebrate. They make their way to another settlement, where there is a larger Holi celebration. Crossing the railway track, they walk on the roads soaked in colour and water. People look at them with amazement, pointing and laughing at them. Leaving the sanctuary of their community, they are once again a minority now; their coloured bodies and torn clothes an unusual sight in the untainted surroundings. A few elderly, piety-inflicted men look at them as a nuisance rather than a colourful break from the routine or an interesting topic of discussion as they are for other onlookers. The boys don't seem to care; the adrenaline of the matka-breaking sport mixed with alcohol takes priority over social considerations.

On one of the main roads, they enter a settlement protected by a giant iron gate. There is a large cross on the gate, clearly stating that it is a Christian settlement. The religious distinctions between Hindus and Christians have become blurred in urban Punjab.[2]

This enclosed area is the Christian colony. It is next to the Water and Power Development Authority (WAPDA) office of the city. There are several residential quarters inside. The floor is made of concrete, covered with coloured water. At the moment it is purple, but soon it will become red as the game of Holi continues. Women stand outside their houses, resting their infants on their hips. The younger ones stand next to them, shirtless, their bodies painted with different colours. The older ones are resting on *charpais* that have been placed outside in the courtyard. In the middle of the courtyard, the boys and the men play Holi.

This is a bigger gathering than the one visited earlier. There are about two hundred people here. Buckets of water have been placed for anyone to wash themselves and to also refill their bottles and water-guns. The houses in the vicinity have ceased to be private spaces and instead have become a part of the extended domain, supplying water and pipes for the continuous celebration of Holi. Anyone can enter any house, use the washroom and clean themselves.

There are trays of dry colour on the other side, which are quickly depleting. These contain orange, red, blue and purple powder. Young boys and girls use this occasion to flirt with each other, which would not be an acceptable act in normal circumstances. A young boy picks up a bucket full of water and pours it on a girl of his age; everyone standing nearby laughs at his audacity. The girl rushes towards the dry colours to take her revenge as the boy runs away from her. She chases him before throwing the colour, which spreads in the air, becoming orange dust. Newly married couples hug each other in public, another act that is not socially permissible under normal circumstances. They apply colour paste on each other's faces as an act of love.

A group of boys gather at the centre of the courtyard to break a new series of matkas attached to a black wire connected to two opposite buildings. Those who are not part of the ceremony fill their buckets with water and colour, pouring them on these young warriors. Undeterred, honouring the gravity of the situation, they form the pyramid—the water and colour entering their ears and nose only add to their resolve. There are three matkas to be broken and the expectations of those who stare at them from the sides and the rooftops to be fulfilled; some trying to impress their girlfriends, others their young wives. The dhol continues to play as a boy from the centre shouts, '*Bolo bolo bolo Durga Mata ki.*'

NAVRATRI AT BAHAWALNAGAR

Fifteen years ago, it was just one tiny room, with cracks in the walls and paint peeling off. There was a portrait of Durga seated on a tiger in one corner of the room and pictures of Valmiki, Guru Nanak, Shiva and Krishna were placed around her. On holy days, families would visit the makeshift temple to seek the blessings of the deities. Next to the shrine, there was a vacant ground that was a part of the temple property, but it was being used as a garbage dumping area.

'There was no sense of ownership,' explains thirty-five-year-old Babar Raza, wearing a pink kurta and white shalwar. He has just returned home after an entire day of preparations for the final night of Navratri celebrations. His wife walks in carrying a black raw silk kurta that he has to wear that night, and hangs it on a nail on the wall. She leaves without saying anything. Amog Lila, a twenty-two-year-old priest, sits next to Raza. He is wearing a white kurta with a black dhoti. His forehead bears a vermillion mark and a yellow scarf, covered with Sanskrit text, is draped around his neck. He is one of the priests at the Durga Temple and part of the younger generation of the

Hindu community here who are responsible for religious revivalism in this area.

Sitting cross-legged, Raza taps his feet impatiently; he is eager to get back to the preparations. 'I was about twenty at that time and used to study in college. All my Muslim friends were very passionate about their religion.' Raza is talking about the late 1980s when the 'Islamization' process of General Zia-ul-Haq (1978–88) was in full force. Curriculums of subjects were changed to accommodate the puritanical religiosity of the military ruler. As a new generation of Pakistanis fed on this religiously inclined education, the country took a turn towards Islamization. 'I thought to myself that like the Muslims, we Hindus should also pay attention to our religion and practices. None of our elders knew anything about Hinduism at that time and that bothered me. I wanted to explore my roots and revive our religious traditions,' says Raza. As Raza's friends in college explored their 'Islamic roots', Raza was inspired to trace his 'Hindu roots'. Strangely, the Hinduization of Raza and other young people from the community was a byproduct of the Islamization of the Pakistani Muslim youth. 'I discussed the situation of the temple with my friends from the community and we decided that we should do something about its condition,' says Raza. He along with ten other boys spent the next few days clearing garbage from the premises. Once the temple property was clean, they went door to door asking for donations to renovate the shrine.

'A lot of people are sceptical when youngsters ask for money. "How can we trust you?" they would question us with raised eyebrows. There were only a few who were supportive.' Raza and his friends used the little money they collected for the renovation of the shrine. They bought an idol of Durga from Karachi and placed it at the temple where it continues to reside. However, once other members of the community saw the sincerity with which the boys were working, donations started flowing in. 'People started trusting us. We would get a lot of money,' recalls Raza, getting excited as he recalls those days.

Encouraged by the positive response of the people, Raza and his friends decided to organize the celebrations of Navratri—a festival dedicated to Durga—here at the temple. They called a band of musicians from Bahawalpur, an area with a considerable population of Hindus, about 165 km from here. The band performed all night and it was a successful programme. This was the first time after Partition that a Hindu religious festival had been celebrated on such a scale at the Akaliyan Mohalla, Bahawalnagar, a community dominated by over a hundred Hindu and Christian families. Prior to this festival, visits to the temple or celebrations of festivals remained a private affair, limited to prayers within the family. But now that was changing; the entire community was participating in the celebrations.

* * *

Akaliyan Mohalla literally means 'Community of the Minorities'. This is a pre-Partition settlement, though the name is post-Partition, reflecting the changing demographics of the city. Compared to central Punjab, southern Punjab has been historically tolerant towards other non-Muslim faiths, which is why a significant Hindu population continues to live here. One of the major reasons for this is that violence here during Partition never scaled the heights it did in the other regions; therefore the resentments between communities that seeped in after 1947 were not that serious. Bahawalnagar, a journey of about four hours by car from Lahore, is in southern Punjab. Built during the colonial era, Bahawalnagar became an important trading centre because of the railway station that was built here in the early half of the twentieth century. More than half a century after the departure of the British, the city still seems to be stuck in a time warp. It's a sleepy town, with wide roads and several government buildings from the British era standing tall. It is a Muslim-majority area, with a population of above two million, according to the last census conducted in 1998. The Hindu and Christian communities clustered in the Akaliyan Mohalla near the Bahawali Chowk make up a tiny proportion of the population of the city.

Akaliyan Mohalla is a well-kept area in comparison to the other areas of the city. The drainage system works effectively and the streets are clean. The houses are well built, some several storeys high. Most of the people living here are financially strong. Motorcycles are parked in front of a number of houses. A couple of the residents even own cars. The majority of the people belong to business or trading backgrounds. A distinguishing feature of the houses here is the use of colourful paints, instead of the conventional white, grey and the like. Here the houses are pink, purple, green, blue, cream and yellow. It seems that the use of colourful paints is a part of their religious duty. Muslim houses all over the country tend to be more sombrely painted.

At the time of a festival, the area is decorated according to the theme of the event. Since this is the festival of Navratri, the walls are covered with posters of the Devi. '*Jai Mata Sheranwali Navratre*,' reads one of them. Durga is also known as Sheranwali or the 'One with the Tiger.' This is because she rides a tiger. Another poster calls out to pilgrims for the annual pilgrimage to Hinglaj, where a Hindu temple honours an incarnation of Durga. Hinglaj is in Baluchistan, about 250 km from the coastal city of Karachi. Thousands of Hindu pilgrims go there every year in October, making it one of the largest Hindu festivals in the country. Next to the poster, a symbol of *Om*, cut out of red paper and bordered by silver glitter, is pasted on the wall. This is an important Hindu emblem, representing an eternal sound. On another wall, a Swastika has been pasted, using purple chart paper and silver glitter. The symbol is believed to evoke *shakti*, or cosmic energy. Throughout the community, small multicoloured paper flags, called *jhandiyan* in parlance, have been hung between the buildings. In some parts, colourful cloths have been tied across buildings, hanging over the streets. All these are the results of efforts made by the youngsters. The streets surrounding the community are narrow and allow for several entrances into the mohalla.

* * *

Raza gets up and changes his shirt as he continues speaking, 'Ever since then, we have made it a point to celebrate Navratri here. The festival has only gotten bigger over these years. Earlier it was only the people of the city who would participate, then of the neighbouring areas, and now there are pilgrims pouring in from as far as Karachi. This is one of the largest Hindu gatherings in the country.' His other family members are still getting ready for the event as Raza leaves the house, located near the Bahawali Chowk.

It's ten in the night and the date is 16 October 2010. The boys are busy preparing palanquins for *kunwaris* or the virgins, since morning. Women are busy helping the three kunwaris prepare for the occasion in different parts of the community. They are dressed up like brides on their wedding day. Wearing a red bridal dress, their hands are decorated with henna. Women apply make-up on them; thick layers of foundation, along with deep red lipstick and bright pink blush. This is a community affair, in which women from various households take part. These kunwari girls have been chosen specially for the occasion. They have to be young, not older than fourteen in this case. While they get dressed, a group of boys prepare the palanquins.

From Raza's house, one has to walk around a corner and then enter an alley in order to get into the community. The city outside is asleep. Only a few hours ago, the same place was bustling with activity. The small restaurants having spread out their charpais on the road were serving their clients, next to a square, box-like tin dhaba selling cheap cigarettes and cold drinks. A nearby CD shop had been playing Indian music all day, only stopping to the call of the Muslim prayer, the *azaan*. Only a motorcycle workshop near the music shop is still open, while the rest of them shut early, at about eight. There are a couple of people sleeping on charpais, a few feet away from Raza's house. These are the waiters of the small restaurants.

The world changes the minute one enters the alley. Here the night is just about beginning, everyone is wide awake. There are bright lights hanging above the streets. A dhol-wala stands near the edge playing loudly. A group of boys have gathered around him, dancing. Women peep through their balconies and over their rooftops. A vendor stands at the corner of the street, wrapping up business for the day. He has been here since morning, selling miniature idols

and *chunris* (scarves). All of these idols have been brought
from Karachi, where there are still a reasonable number
of Hindus living or from India through illegal channels.
The tradition of idol-making in Punjab died a natural death
during the massacres of the Partition. A man with an ice-
cream cart stands next to him. He has been lured in by
the sounds of the dhol and the lights. Throughout the day,
devotees have been buying chunris from the vendor's stall
and presenting it to the idol of Durga inside the temple.
One does this with the belief that Maa Durga (Mother
Durga) would grant them their wishes. Presenting the
chunri to the Devi is an important rite that the devotees
observe at this festival.

* * *

Standing at the pavement of one of the houses and facing the
stall is forty-two-year-old Charan Das. He leans forward
and smiles. Das wears a red kurta with a white shalwar. He
has a short beard and long hair. His feet are bare. There is a
thick bangle around his ankle and several around his wrist.
'I am on my way to take it off,' he says, lifting his foot to
signal towards the bangle. *'Mata* (Mother-deity) fulfilled my
wish. Nobody ever returns disappointed from her abode.'
he says. Das has been wearing the bangle for a year. He
also hasn't worn shoes in the meantime. Shiia Muslims in
Pakistan also indulge in similar offerings to God, promising
not to wear shoes or taking up bangles for a particular
gift. Despite separate categorization of religious identities
as distinct and often conflicting with each other, there are
several religious rationales and practices such as this that
transcend those boundaries. He lifts his feet up to show the

underside. There is a thick layer of mud on them. Cracks have hardened at his heels. There are no blisters any more. 'I will wear shoes tonight,' he says.

Das is a peon at the DIG of Police Office in Multan, about 200 km from here. Last year, he came to the shrine to present a chunri to the Devi and prayed for a job. He had been unemployed for a whole year. To prove his devotion to the goddess, he promised that he wouldn't wear shoes till the time of the next festival and would also wear a thick bangle around his ankle. If his wish was granted, he would cycle to the shrine. As soon as Das returned to Multan, he found a job.

'All sorts of miracles happen here,' he says, trying to explain the phenomenon once seated inside his house. 'Women are bestowed with children. Girls get married. Disabled people start walking again,' he points towards his cousin who is sitting next to him in a white shalwar kameez. Mithin Das, 18, lifts his shalwar up to his knee, revealing one of his disabled legs. It is as thin as his arm. 'He cycled with me. Mata gave him the power to do so,' declares Charan. It took them two days to get here. 'Mata gives you the strength,' says Mithin. 'On the way here, I kept on reciting, "*Jai Mata di, Jai Mata di.*" Sometimes we would chant it out aloud in a group and sometimes I would say it quietly under my breath. It keeps you focused,' he says.

Charan has come to the shrine with another wish this time. He is praying for his brother's job. However, at the moment, his own job seems to be in jeopardy. Hindu festivals are not officially recognized in Pakistan, so Hindus working at offices have to ask for special holidays. When Charan asked for a five-day leave, his boss rejected his application.

Nonetheless, Charan, having made a promise to the deity, took off. 'Mata takes care of everything,' he is confident.

* * *

The streets are teeming with pilgrims. There are more than 2000 pilgrims this year, according to Raza. Since the past five years, the festival of Navratri has emerged as the most popular event here. Pilgrims travel by foot, or cycle to present a chunri to the shrine. They believe that Mata will fulfill all their wishes if they observe this rite. A greater number come by buses and other modes of transportation. There are no separate arrangements made for sheltering the pilgrims. They end up sharing houses with the locals. Everyone is a distant relative of someone or the other, so the community becomes one huge family at the time of the festival. Charan is staying at his sister-in-law's cousin's house. The distinction between public and private space becomes unclear. During the night, the pilgrims can be seen roaming the streets. There are people everywhere.

Turning into the street of the temple, one comes across food being prepared for the pilgrims. Five cauldrons in a line are being used for cooking. Three men are looking after them. Behind them, on a charpai, three men are cutting vegetables. There are a few empty cauldrons placed next to them. 'All the preparations for food are done by us,' says Raza. 'The pilgrims give donations, which help us bear the expenses,' he says. A few years ago, they constructed a langar hall inside the compound of the shrine, which can accommodate several hundred people at one time. Most pilgrims eat there.

There was only one small room at the time that Raza and his friends started looking after the temple. Now it is a complex, with two other temples and a langar hall. The complex is protected by a wall and one has to enter through a gate. Cloths of different colours are used to decorate the entrance. They are tied to buildings across the street. Upon entering the complex, there is a peepal tree on the right; behind which is a shrine dedicated to Sri Valmiki, considered to be the original writer of the Hindu holy book, the Ramayana. This tree is held sacred by the community. A small boundary has been made around the tree and the shrine. One is required to take one's shoes off before entering this area.

The Sri Valmiki shrine rests in a single room, with a green dome on the top. The structure bears an uncanny similarity to small Muslim shrines dedicated to Sufi saints, dotting the length and breadth of the country. The peepal tree at the entrance is also found near several Sufi shrines, raised to special spiritual status because of its association with saints. The peepal tree remains sacred in all the religious traditions of South Asia. If not for an Om mark and a bell at the entrance, which one has to ring before entering, this structure could have been easily confused for a Muslim shrine. There is small table at one end of the room on which are pictures of several deities, including a picture of Lord Valmiki writing the Ramayana with a peacock feather. There is also a picture of Narasimha, tearing Hiranyakashipu apart. A picture of young Krishna, playing the flute standing in front of a cow, rests next to it. There is a small statue of Krishna in the same pose in front of the picture with a copy of the Ramayana, covered in a red cloth next to it, not very different from how the holy book of the Quran would be maintained. A small golden statue of Lord Shiva is placed next to the religious book.

There is another temple behind the shrine, bigger than this one. Its shiny tile work and fresh white paint on the inside are a testimony to the fact that this is a recent construction, a product of the religious revivalism that this community is experiencing currently. There is a big poster of Lord Shiva, the god of destruction, in the middle of the room, standing next to a river, with a trident in his hand and several Shiv-Lings behind him; his depiction similar to a superhero. There are pictures of other deities: one portraying Lord Brahma, Vishnu and Shiva in one picture, the three supreme gods of the Hindu trinity. There is a picture next to it, with a symbol of Om in the centre and writing on the top that says, '*Aum* sweet *Aum*.'

A few devotees are present at the temple. One of them is forty-five-year-old Deepak Rana. He is wearing a light green shalwar kameez and there is a red chunri, decorated with a golden thread, around his neck. He has a short moustache and there is a vertical vermillion mark on his forehead. He prostrates in front of Lord Shiva's picture. His three-year-old son mimics him. Standing up, he lifts his son and positions him on his shoulders. 'He is probably the youngest pilgrim here,' he says shaking his son playfully, who lets out a chuckle in response. Rana arrived in the city last night at about eight from a place called Haroonabad, 45 km from here.

'I was leading a group of forty people. This included children, the elderly, women, men, boys, and girls. We left at about six in the morning and walked all day. Here we presented a chunri to the Mata's shrine.' The shrine is across this building and can be seen through a window. A picture of baby Krishna has been pasted on the exterior wall. It is the desire of the devotee that his/her chunri be placed on the idol. However, that is not possible given the number of visitors. Instead, the chunri is entrusted to the priests, who later make use of it.

'Our trip almost got sabotaged. I contacted the police officials of my area telling them that we are taking out this procession and we would need police security,' he says. Processions towards the shrine are easily identifiable as most of them wear the chunris purchased for Mata over their heads or put them around their necks. Some even bring flags along. They have vermillion marks on their foreheads and they chant or sing songs about Mata on the way. Yesterday a group of twelve boys entered the community on bicycles saying, '*Ek do teen char, Mata teri jai jai kar,*' ringing their bells alongside. All of them were wearing bright orange T-shirts, which read '*Jai Mata Ki*' in gold. They chanted this slogan throughout their journey, which started from Bahawalpur. Before entering, the group of boys circled around the community to make their presence felt. They must have been a rather odd group when travelling because one doesn't expect to see Hindus parading their religiosity so openly. Onlookers probably went into a state of shock at the sight of this group challenging their notions of a uniform Muslim nationhood.

'We were told by the authorities to cancel our plan. They thought it was too dangerous given the present situation,' he says. The morning that they were supposed to leave, the authorities blocked all the leading ways out of the city. However, whereas Rana had informed them that they would leave at eight in the morning, they left at six instead. 'Mata does not let anything happen to her devotees,' he says, giving his son a jerk while he continues to swing above his shoulders. They both smile at each other.

* * *

Most of the groups reached here last night, which was the eighth night of Navratri. All of them visited the shrine first, chanting, singing and clapping as they walked in. When Rana and his group came, they entered with four people holding the chunri from each side. Rana and another man held the front two corners, whereas two women held the back ones. The rest of the group shouted, '*Jai Mata Ki.*'

The complex was crowded last night. Hundreds of women sat facing the stage, which had a 20-foot-tall figure of Durga Mata cut out of cardboard watching the proceedings. The image of the Devi which still stands is that of her riding a lion, holding ancient weapons in each of her several hands, including an arrow, a sword and a trident. On her head she is wearing a tiara, as the queen of the universe and she is decorated with jewellery, including gold earrings, nose pin, necklaces and bracelets. Her sari is pink and her blouse green. Unlike the goddess though, the women here wear shalwar kameez, modestly covering their heads, blending into Pakistani society, instead of standing out by wearing a sari. Frequently worn earlier, the sari, sometime after the years of Islamization, became associated with Hindu women and was no longer appreciated in a Muslim country. The proceedings last night included a welcome to the pilgrims by the administration and musical performances by several devotee musicians who have come to attend the festival. Others not interested in the show loitered around in the langar hall, also within this complex. The temple of the Devi is on the other side of the stage, so every time a pilgrim group arrived with their chunri offering, the women had to make way for them. The entire courtyard is covered with multicoloured *jhandiyan*, whereas a web of lights is cast over the buildings.

The temple of the goddess, recently renovated, is a single-storey white building. This was the original temple, while the rest of them were built after the renovations. The idol of the goddess rests within a colourful niche made out of cardboard. She was wearing a red dress yesterday, which was changed to a green one today. Every time her clothes are changed, all the attendees and male priests are sent out and the doors and windows closed. There are three plates at her feet, which can be used to perform the *aarti*. The devotees stand in front of her, holding both their hands in front of their chests and read a silent prayer. This is followed by the performance of the aarti.

The room is painted white from the inside and decorated with Hindu motifs made of chart paper. Next to the idol, a priest sits tending to the fire which is lit at all times. He has a chunri tied around his forehead and another around his neck. A woman sits next to him, collecting chunris from the arriving pilgrims. They attend to some devotees by tying a protection thread around their wrists or marking their foreheads with vermillion. Taking a roll of red thread, the priest cuts out a little piece. Holding it with both the hands, he places it on top of the fire, reciting a prayer under his breath. He then ties the thread around the wrist of the devotee, still reciting something. The thread is supposed to protect a devotee from all harm. This is also tied to devotees visiting Muslim Sufi shrines, a tradition which clearly overlaps between Hindu and Muslim pilgrims. After this, the woman takes some vermillion from a paste in a golden utensil placed next to her and applies it on the forehead of the devotee. The woman then asks for some money and the devotee always obliges. Taking the money, she places it under her knee, as she sits squatting on the floor.

* * *

The courtyard is empty at the moment and the stage deserted; the instruments of the musicians rest on it, to be used later in the night. A DJ sitting next to the stage has put on a devotional song dedicated to Kali Mata, an incarnation of Durga. The song extols people to refrain from sins otherwise the goddess would kill them. '*Kali Mata kat ∂alegii*,' (The black goddess will kill) is the chorus. A group of young boys in their early teens have flocked on to the stage. One of them, referred to as Mohammad Rafi (an iconic singer from the Indian film industry), is urged by his colleagues to dance to the bhajan. After some protest, he shows a few moves.

In the street next to the shrine, a group of boys are preparing the palanquin and this is where Raza is heading. 'Everything all right?' he asks the boys upon arrival. 'You have taken so long, Balram,' says one of the boys, wearing a cap, a black faded T-shirt and jeans. He is yet to get ready. They are already behind schedule. 'My real name is Balram,' Raza explains. 'I adopted the name Babar when I joined college. It would have gotten me into unnecessary friction with my colleagues,' he says. A lot of Hindus in Punjab do this, passing off as Muslims or Christians by taking up non-Hindu names. This is a survival technique in a hostile environment.

Wooden boards are used to make a palanquin, with a chair at the centre. The board is covered with chart paper, cloth and glitter paper. The space on the sides is covered with frills and festoons. Two logs have been joined at the base in order to lift up the palanquin. There is a bulb at the centre and its wire has been placed underneath the sheets, attached to a battery at the base. Only the front is uncovered, decorated with charts, making an arch. Hindu symbols are drawn inside, at the back of the palanquin.

At about eleven in the night, the kunwaris emerge, dressed up like brides. All the palanquins have been brought to one street. They would head in different directions from here, to meet inside the temple. The three girls take their seats inside the palanquins. Devotees throng to them, putting garlands on them. Some put money near their feet and ask for blessings. The girls have ceased to be girls which they were only a few minutes ago and have taken up the persona of the living goddess.

With a tiara on their heads, they sit with one hand resting on their thighs and the other raised, blessing people. They are wearing gold bangles, earrings and nose pins. Their hands are decorated with a *mehndi* design: a circle on the palm and bordered fingertips. Women come and perform aarti, while others adjust their clothes. A young man holding a coconut kneels on the ground, raising it high with both his hands, he smashes it on to the ground. The crowd shouts, '*Jai Mata Di.*' The coconut breaks and the ceremony begins. Breaking of the coconut before any important task is considered auspicious, explains Amog Lila, the priest from the Durga temple.

The boys pick up the palanquins and start the ceremony with a dhol-wala leading all of them. Groups of boys dance in front of it, while women move behind the palanquin. Devotees, who had earlier missed the opportunity to seek the blessings of the goddess, do so as the procession progresses. The goddesses look dead straight, unmoved by the attention they are getting. The women who had helped them get ready must have also taught them how to behave. The youngest out of the three girls is about ten years old and the oldest about fourteen.

Navratri, which literally means 'nine nights', is a celebration associated with the worship of nine different incarnations of the goddess. Walking on the side of the palanquin, Amog Lila explains the mythology of Navratri. 'The tradition comes from the Ramayana. When Sita was abducted by Ravana and taken to Lanka, she prayed for nine nights straight to the different incarnations of Durga Mata, while Ravana and Rama (Sita's husband) engaged in what seemed like an endless battle. On the tenth day, the goddess heard her plea and Ram was able to kill Ravana and thus won the war. The burning of Dussehra (on the tenth day) is a remembrance of that victory. Now, in remembrance of that event, every year we spend nine nights worshipping Durga. One of her incarnations is of an adolescent girl. The kunwari pooja is a worshipping of that incarnation,' he explains.

On one particular instance, the procession steps out of the community, where curious Muslim onlookers, surprised by the sudden burst of activity, stop everything and stare at it in curiosity, a sight so unusual and alien to them. Cars slow down, while the motorcycles and bicycles come to a complete halt, waiting for the procession to enter the community once again. At about midnight, the three processions enter the temple at the same time, while the community follows them.

The goddesses are seated on the stage under the overpowering figure of the Devi Mata on her lion. The dance continues for a little while, after which more people approach the goddesses with supplications. This is the last rite of the festival. 'We do not burn Dussehra here because of space issues. Maybe sometime in the future we will be able to revive that tradition as well,' says Raza, his voice pulsating with hope.

SHIVRATRI AT KILLA KATAS

Raindrops touch the surface of the turquoise pond resulting in tiny ripples. Small fish gather around underwater plants. A young child puts his finger into the water. The fish scatter. His friend is amused by the trick. 'Stay away from the water,' shouts Shakeel, as he notices the children playing at the steps of the pond from afar. Although they are standing away from the deep side of the water, he feels that he still needs to keep a vigilant eye on them. These are Hindu children who have come from Gujranawala and Shakeel is not too fond of them. There are a few Hindu adults nearby, busy preparing for the night, for which about 2000 pilgrims would pour in from different parts of the country, ready to celebrate Shivratri.

Wearing a brown shalwar kameez with a thick shawl wrapped around his body, Shakeel is heading towards the *haveli* of Hari Singh Nalwa, a general in the army of Maharaja Ranjit Singh (1780–1839), the erstwhile ruler of Punjab. The haveli is his favourite part of the complex. It's a giant structure, the tallest here, standing like a cube with a small dome at the top. The artwork has been recently renovated with depictions of Hindu deities on the walls, including that of Ganesh, an obese Hindu god who has the head of an elephant. Pictures of Krishna, standing cross-legged and playing the flute while he flirts with the maidens, have been painted intricately.

In the past five years, ever since he was employed here, Shakeel has perfected sentences in English, which he uses eloquently to impress his audience. 'Ganesh was the son of the Hindu god Shiva. Once Shiva went. Shiva's wife had a son while he was gone. Once she take a bath and ask Ganesh to stand at the gate, to guard. When Shiva come, Ganesh stop him. Angry, the Shiva cut his head off. When his mother saw, she cried terribly and Shiva realized that he is his son. He then take a head of a elephant and put it on Ganesh.' His English is not yet perfect, but he is confident of what he says. Experience has also taught him how to slip in personal information about himself, subtly mentioning his hardships and his will to study more, yet not being able to because of the lack of resources. This usually works in his favour and he ends up with a good tip by the time he finishes off the tour. He always starts his story with the pond.

The turquoise pond changes its colour at the shallower ends. It is round. A rock placed underneath the pond separates a small section of it from the larger body of water. This holds clear water, only 3 feet deep. Plants growing at the base can be seen from the surface. Ancient buildings stand at the edge of the deeper end, covering it from that side. Balconies and alleys open up towards the water. The structure, which is light brown in colour, shows signs of weathering, its perfect reflection visible in the water. The pond is clearly the lifeline of this complex. Numerous myths have developed around it. 'No one knows how deep it is,' Shakeel explains to the tourists. 'Several attempts have been made to check the length, but no one ever touch the base. There are poisonous lizards and snakes living inside,' he tells everyone. These are some of the ancient stories that have been passed on for generations. 'If you look at the pond from the top, you will see that it is in the shape of an eye. The Hindus believe that when Shiva's (the Hindu deity of destruction) wife Sati dead, he shed a tear, which fall at this place and this pond was created. Another tear fall in Ajmer Sharif, India, where there is another ancient pond, like this one.'

Shakeel, a twenty-five-year-old graduate, lives in Kalar Kahar, a few kilometres away from here. The Archaeology Department appointed him and a few other people as guides for the location when it was renovated. He mentions that he wants to do his Masters in Archaeology from Punjab University, Lahore. 'The truth is that this is an ancient area. Several million years ago, this place was under the sea. When it emerged, this pond was formed,' he says. He picks up a piece of rock from the ground and asks the tourists to look at it carefully. There is a fossil of a leaf on it. 'There are hundreds of such rocks here, all from that time when this area was underwater.' Later, he takes the tourists into a cave, across the road from the complex. It has a small entrance. Cone-shaped structures hang from the roof. These are mineral deposits called stalactites. Shakeel picks up another piece of rock from here, which has a fauna fossil, and hands it over to one of the female photographers in the group. 'This is my gift to you,' he says with a smile.

Next to the haveli, he points out a Buddhist stupa that has been partially excavated. 'This is from the third century BC, from the time of Taxila (an ancient city near Islamabad, with ruins dating back to the sixth century BCE),' says

Shakeel. This is a huge, round structure with untrimmed grass growing on it. This must have been a plinth of the stupa. More than half of the structure is still underground. Climbing a few steps, Shakeel leads the tourists to the ancient Hindu temples. According to him, the three tall, cone-shaped structures are from the time of the Mahabharata. 'When the Pandavas were exiled from their kingdom, they came and settled here and constructed these temples at that time,' he tells the curious crowd around him. His story is confirmed by a blue board put up by the authorities here, noting the date of the Mahabharata to be around 1500 BCE.

Across the road, Shakeel takes his group to the top of a mound that overlooks the temple complex. On the other side, one can see a vast plain, interspersed with a few houses and restaurants. Taking the tourists to the edge, he points to an ancient staircase leading up to the mound. 'These were used to get to the university,' he says, pointing to a newly constructed single-storey rectangular structure. 'This was the site of a world-famous ancient Hindu university. Al-Beruni, a Muslim scholar from the eleventh century studied Hindu religion at this university. Here he also calculated the radius of world, the first time anyone ever did. Muslim scholars were famous world over at that time,' says Shakeel, hurrying to finish off the tour in his professional tour guide manner.

As the night descends, the sky clears and it stops raining for a little while. The full moon illuminates the area otherwise engulfed in darkness. The wind is chilly. Millions of stars shine in the backdrop of the darkness, adding richness to the sky. A lone sound of someone playing the flute floats in from a distance, breaking the utter silence. Al-Beruni probably sat here for countless nights under this sky, gaping at the stars, astonished at their beauty. He would have made friends with them as he attended to their light out here, all alone. He used these stars to calculate the radius of the world. He was the very first one in the world to do so. Noticing that his group is lost in the beauty of the stars, Shakeel interrupts by announcing that he is leaving. Surprised, the female photographer takes out a thousand-rupee note from her bag and gives it to him. 'No, please! There is no need for this,' he objects. 'I insist,' she says. Shrugging his shoulders, he takes the note and puts it in his pocket, leaving the tourists under the open sky.

* * *

Al-Beruni came to India during the first half of the eleventh century, after the Muslim invader Shah Mahmood Ghaznvi attacked Punjab. Al-Beruni arrived at this temple, which was known as a seat of learning at that time. He spent several years here, learning and reading about the language, religion and culture of the Hindus. Experts say that these temples were constructed between the seventh and tenth centuries CE, when this area was under the influence of the Kashmiri kingdom. Al-Beruni compiled his observations in a book called *Al-Hind*, which is considered to be one of the best anthropological works of all time. It is the first study which introduced the Indian people and their religion to the Western world. In his book, he claims that the Hindus are believers of one God, like the Muslims, and are *'Ahl-e-Kitab'* or the 'Followers of the Book,' a term used in the Muslim holy book, the Quran, to refer to the Christians and the Jews. By referring to the Hindus as the followers of the book, Al-Beruni raises their status in the eyes of the Muslim readers and urges them to not view them as 'lowly pagans' but rather followers of the same god that they worship. The title also permits the Muslims to have food with the Hindus and intermarry. However, in contemporary Pakistan, where nationalism is premised upon hatred for Hindus, such a claim would not only be shunned but also taken offence to.

This complex—with a natural pond and fossils dating back to millions of years, ancient caves, an unexcavated Buddhist stupa, Hindu temples said to be thousands of years old and a university which attracted scholars from other parts of the world—is known as Katas Raj or Killa Katas. Situated near the small town of Kalar Kahar, this is a complex of immense historical significance. The presence of ancient structures here points to the fact that this has been a holy site for thousands of years. In his pursuit of spiritual enlightenment, the founder of the Sikh religion, Guru Nanak (1469–1539) also came here, as it was a popular destination for ascetics at that time.[1]

There are several small temples built around the pond, dedicated to different Hindu deities. Today, an iron fence protects the complex from its surroundings and only one entrance leads into it. However, there are other ways of entering the temple, especially if one is adamant, and one such way is by climbing the mound. Across the road, next to the mound where the university was situated, there is a newly constructed single-storey building. This was constructed a few years ago and now acts as the Archaeology Department office. Major renovation work of the temple was undertaken by the department in 2005. After the pond was cleaned and the buildings were painted and restored, blue boards were raised around the area, highlighting the significance of particular spots in the area.

Katas Raj was a popular religious site for the Hindus before Partition. Thousands of pilgrims used to descend here from faraway places on the occasion of Shivratri, a Hindu festival dedicated to the worship of Lord Shiva. This temple was abandoned as a result of Partition resulting in the buildings falling into disrepair and the pond being polluted. Over the years, a few cement factories opened in the surrounding area and started sucking the water out from here. There was no one to guard the shrine from the people of the neighbouring villages and cities, who would often visit and leave their mark on the temple walls. Several phone numbers and names are still engraved on them, a testimony of those years of neglect. A few Hindus would visit occasionally, pretending to be tourists exploring the ruins. However, given their small number, they were not able to exert enough pressure to rectify the damage done to their holy shrine.

Prem Gupta, a forty-year-old Hindu activist from Lahore, visited Katas Raj for the first time in 2003. 'There were boys jumping from the windows and alleys of temples into this sacred pond. They would leave juice boxes and chips wrappers in the water,' he recalls. For the Hindus, this pond, believed to be created from the tear of Lord Shiva, is holy. They believe that a dip in the pond would cleanse them of their sins.

Things changed for the shrine in 2005, when the veteran Indian politician L.K. Advani came here and expressed displeasure at the neglect of the authorities. In response, the Government of Pakistan started renovation work. In the subsequent year, the government invited Indian pilgrims to visit the shrine on the occasion of Shivratri. About 300 pilgrims came, which became national news. As a result, the shrine became popular. Several local tourists started coming here. Local Hindus, who did not know about it earlier, also started to visit. The Indian pilgrims would stay here for three days, during which the government would ensure security and shelter for them. They would reside at the building at the site of the ancient university where they would be given free food. The entire area would be cordoned off while the Indians visited and no one would be allowed to come into the complex. This continued until 2008. But after the Mumbai attacks in which the city was held hostage between 26 and 29 November 2008 and resulted in the death of several locals and foreigners, allegedly at the hands of Pakistani terrorists, the relationship between India and Pakistan which had been warming up, nosedived. Pilgrims didn't come to Katas for Shivratri in 2009.

For the local Hindus, this proved to be an opportunity. In 2010, a few Hindu organizations met and decided that they would celebrate the festival of Shivratri here that year. 'We wrote to the Archaeology Department, Evacuee Trust Property Board (ETPB, an organization that looks after the property of non-Muslim shrines. It is also referred to as Hindu Awqaf or Wakf), police, Ministry of Minorities, and so forth, asking for permission to celebrate the festival of Shivratri at Katas Raj,' says Prem Gupta, who is the head of the Hindu Sudhar Sabha, one of the organizations involved. The Hindus did not receive any response. Gupta, who also works at a local NGO and often travels to remote corners of the country, is familiar with the red tape of the bureaucracy. Along with other organizations, they decided to go ahead with the celebration. About 2000 Hindus came to Katas from various cities of Pakistan unannounced, including Lahore, Rahim Yar Khan, Peshawar and

Nowshera, and celebrated Shivratri. Encouraged by the success, the Hindus decided to organize the celebration again in 2011.

* * *

While Shakeel showed the visitors around Katas, Gupta stood at the gate of the complex, busy with the preparations. He has put up a banner at the entrance which reads, 'Welcome *Yatrees* (pilgrims)' in English, a language that the majority of his guests are unfamiliar with. There is a large picture of Lord Shiva on it. A snake is coiled around his neck. A third eye, which he can use to destroy the world, is visible on his forehead. The moon is in his hair and one hand is lifted up to bless the devotees. A few other workers are putting up a canopy inside the complex, where the pilgrims are expected to stay. Gupta knows that there is not enough space for everyone out here. Besides, it is too cold to sleep in the open.

The date is 2 March 2011. It has been raining all day, which has caused the temperature to drop by several degrees. A few Hindu families have already arrived and are helping Gupta with the preparations. The children are playing next to the pond. Some women are visiting the shrines while others have gone to the restaurant down the road. A few police officials stand at the gate with Gupta. The local guides have informed the police that Hindus are planning to celebrate the event here, for which they do not have official permission. These are only five officials, who watch closely as Gupta sets up the banner and the tent. They have been placed here to look after the security of the thousands of pilgrims who would descend here. The number of officials deployed is an indication of the scant importance that Hindu pilgrims are accorded.

A group of college girls arrive accompanied by a professor. They have come from the National College of Arts (NCA, established in Lahore in 1857, is considered to be the most prestigious art college in the country). They are stopped at the gate by the police officials. 'Muslims are not allowed inside today,' says one of them to the professor. Gupta standing nearby gives him a smile and gets back to instructing the workers. The professor stays for a little while, looking at the ongoing preparations. Then, without resistance, he takes his students to the caves, after which they would return to Lahore. Another group of boys tries to enter the complex and are also stopped by police officials. 'Let them go,' says Gupta, as he walks away talking over the phone. These are Hindu boys. Gupta's eighteen-year-old son, Vinod, hands the boys a tag. It reads 'Maha Shivratri' with a picture of Lord Shiva, similar to the banner placed at the entrance. 'Let in anyone carrying this identification pass,' Gupta instructs the police officers.

A tall sturdy man with hazel eyes, Prem Gupta is based in Lahore, where he lives with his family near the famous Muslim shrine, Bibi Pak Daman. He visits the shrines often, which is associated with the Shiia sect of Islam, but is also visited by Sunni Muslims, all part of the religious syncretism that was once part of this land but is now vanishing. He resides there with his father, mother, wife, children, brothers, nephew, nieces and uncles. In a neighbourhood dominated by Muslims, theirs are the only Hindu houses. Unlike the majority of the Hindus living in Lahore, they have refused to take up dual names. His father still calls himself Shami Lal. His eldest son, Vinod, is a second-year student at the Forman Christian College, Lahore, one of the oldest colleges set up by Christian missionaries, under the 5 per cent reserved for minorities. His entire family has come for the festival.

'There is some terrible news,' Gupta comes back from his phone call. 'Shahbaz Bhatti has been murdered this morning in Islamabad, outside his residence. I have just been told,' he says. Bhatti, a Roman Catholic, was the federal minister for minorities when he was assassinated. A vocal critic of oppression against minorities, Bhatti recently had focused on the blasphemy laws, which are used to target minorities in Pakistan. A couple of months ago, the Governor of Punjab Salman Taseer was gunned down by his bodyguard in Islamabad for criticizing the law. It is being assumed that Bhatti has also been killed for his views. 'Everyone is scared,' Gupta adds. 'They were on the way when the news came. What is happening in this country?' Gupta does not stop the preparations; he heads to the restaurant to recover from the trauma.

* * *

Down the road, there is a small building, the only restaurant in the area. A few pilgrims, who have arrived, are gathering here. The waiters are busy serving tea and garam roti. The owner, sitting behind his table, is watching the news, covering the assassination of the minister earlier in the day. The restaurant is full. Just a few years ago, this place would have refused to serve these people, ironically following a tradition that upper-caste Hindus used to practise against Muslims in the pre-Partition days. But now things have changed and untouchability, at least here, has receded to the background. The restaurant has the only washroom the pilgrims can use. It would close at eleven in the night, after which the pilgrims would once again have to camp out in the open. *Teandas* are available for dinner, but none of the pilgrims are having it. They are saving themselves for the langar in the night.

Hindu pilgrims from Peshawar have arrived in two large buses. This group is headed by forty-two-year-old Haroon Sarab Diyal. President of the All Pakistan Hindu Rights Movement (another organization responsible for arranging this pilgrimage), Diyal is one of the most famous Hindu activists in the country. His statements regarding minority issues often appear in the national newspapers. There are about a hundred people with him: women, children, men and the elderly.

'There are more buses on the way,' he tells Gupta, upon arrival. These are two from Nowshera (Khyber Pakhtunkhwa). Gupta tells him that the buses from Rahim Yaar Khan and Bahawalpur are also on their way. Contrary to the stereotype of being a religiously oppressive area, since Partition, the province of Khyber Pakhtunkhwa (KPK) has been home to a large proportion of religious minorities who have lived there rather peacefully. These are primarily Hindus, who form the largest minority. Thousands of them are part of the mainstream society, visible often in the economic and political fabric, which is hardly the case in Punjab, which is much more monolithic. Hindu festivals are celebrated with much pomp in these areas; more so than in Lahore. 'If you want to see the lights of Diwali, go to Peshawar. You will find nothing in Lahore,' Gupta often jokes. The primary reason for that is that, unlike Punjab, the riots were less intense due to the influence of the Indian National Congress there. A lot of Hindus and Sikhs continued living in their ancestral lands even after the creation of Pakistan.

Diyal is not happy with the arrangements at the temple. There is no electricity and it is dark by now. A tube light in the courtyard of the Archaeology Department is the only light in the surroundings. The tents have been set up, but hardly anyone is resting here. A few old men, too tired to stand in the rain, have laid out their bedding on the ground and are lying down inside the complex. Diyal has brought a generator with him, fearing the worst. He asks a few boys to set it up. They plan to light a bulb at the temple on their own.

'The authorities have not paid the bill of this temple for the past three months. Electricity has been cut off, therefore,' says an angry Diyal. There is a pole next to the temple of Shiva, with a transformer resting on it, of no use at the moment. 'Ever since the Indians have stopped coming, they have become negligent again. The temple is falling into disrepair,' he says.

The boys have still not been able to set up the generator. One can hear the sound of its engine trying to start in the background. 'What's the problem? Does it have petrol?' asks a frustrated Diyal. 'It does. I don't know why it is not starting. There seems to be some problem with the engine. We will try again.'

Diyal has been upset ever since he heard the news about Bhatti's murder. In fact, he is the one who called Gupta. Being an activist, he has met the former minister several times. 'I had told him about this pilgrimage. He had assured me he would take care of everything,' says Diyal. His tone has changed now. There is a deep sadness in his voice which has replaced the fury. 'But then this happened.

I cannot even call his secretary,' he adds. Besides activism, Diyal teaches comparative religion at Peshawar University. He holds a master's degree in Islamic studies. 'I believe that being a minority living in a Muslim state, it is imperative for us to learn about Islam. I urge all other members of the minority communities to do so,' he says. A lot of educated non-Muslims feel the same. The trend has gained momentum more so recently after archaic Islamic laws are used to persecute the members of religious minorities. The educated lot feel that if the members of the communities are better aware of Islam and its laws, they would be able to avoid the persecution that interpretation of Islamic laws brings with itself, sometimes.

* * *

The numbers of pilgrims has now increased manifold. All the buses have arrived and are parked on the road. There are about a thousand people. The restaurant has closed. But for a few, most of the devotees have gathered at the courtyard of the Archaeology Department office. A senior police official, Deputy Superintendent of Police (DSP), has arrived. His official jeep stands in the courtyard amongst the people. Gupta argues with him to open the hall of the department, so that at least the women, children and the elderly can rest. It is still drizzling. The DSP argues back, saying that the Hindus had been told not to come here. He cites the security conditions of the country as his reason. He remains adamant that he cannot open the hall as he does not have jurisdiction over it.

After a little while, Gupta is finally able to convince the DSP, who opens one of the halls of the building and allows a few pilgrims to rest inside. On Gupta's instructions, only the women, old people and children are allowed inside, while a couple of young boys stand at the entrance stopping anyone else from going in. Young boys, looking for an opportunity to flirt with the girls inside, make random excuses to go into the hall. In front of the hall, on a small lawn, a group of boys set up a sound system. Bhajans blare out of them, while the boys dance in front. Next to the ground, in the courtyard, men start making arrangements for langar. Lentils would be cooked for dinner along with tea. Across the road, in the temple, the generator has failed to work. The innovative young technicians have taken a wire from the Archaeology office and lit one bulb in the complex. A few exhausted old men rest here, hiding under their blankets.

Standing next to a cauldron, Gupta is overseeing the food preparations. He is wearing a badge that his son was distributing to the pilgrims in order to be allowed access into the temple. All the pilgrims are wearing one. The celebration of Shivratri, which literally means the 'the night of Shiva', includes the worship of Shiva throughout the night, as well as a symbolic marriage between him and his counterpart Parvati. 'After langar, women would take the mehndi of Shiva to the temple, as sisters and sisters-in-law do so for the grooms,' Gupta explains. Mehndi is an important part of Pakistani marriages, during which the women apply henna on the hands of the groom and the bride. In this case, this would only be a symbolic gesture. However, there would also be real marriages during the Shivratri celebration. 'This is an auspicious night so we have organized four other marriages here. These are girls from Khyber Pakhtunkhwa and FATA, who suffered during the foods of 2010. Some of these girls cannot afford a proper marriage. A few lost their families during the catastrophe. The marriages have been organized by the contributions of the *Sangat* (the Hindu community present),' says Gupta.

Dinner is served at eleven in the night. Two white plastic sheets are spread on the floor as pilgrims squat on them while other young volunteers serve them. The children are put to sleep after dinner, while women set out to prepare for the breakfast. For some pilgrims this meal would mark the start of their fast that they would then break at noon tomorrow, in lieu of the Shivratri festival.

Following the dinner, a musical band gathers in the courtyard, playing popular Indian songs on a trumpet, bass drum, crashes and other drums. They have also come from Peshawar. Boys, who were earlier dancing to the bhajan, gather around the band. Women go into the hall and bring out the mehndi that would be taken to the shrine. These are small decorated plates, containing oil lamps and lumps of henna. Another group of women take out a shawl and hold it up high, with four women holding the four corners. In a conventional wedding, the groom would walk under this, but since this is the wedding procession of Lord Shiva, there is no one standing underneath it. The group gathers in a procession, with the boys and the men dancing in front as the women follow. Leaving the department's courtyard, the procession steps out on to the road. It is deserted at this time of the night. The buses of the pilgrims stand in one corner, next to the ancient staircase leading up to the university. The procession comes to halt for a little while as the group decides to stop and dance. The boys drag in other men who had been watching from the corner. A few women also join them.

Inside the temple complex, the procession moves towards the shrine of Lord Shiva, situated next to the pool.

The floor is made out of marble and is wet at the moment. Leading, the men enter first, taking their shoes off at the steps. The floor is cold but, motivated by religious fervour, they are able to withstand it.

It is a small, light brown building, with a small dome at the top. There is a wooden door covered with floral decorations. At the centre of the room there is a phallic-like structure, called the Shiv ling. This structure represents the potent force of Lord Shiv. It is a small room, which can only accommodate about ten people. Leading the group is Diyal. Elderly women, holding aarti and mehndi are allowed to enter. They place the mehndi plates at the base of the deity and perform the aarti. The band stands next to the threshold and continues to play, enhancing the festivities. There is a rush of people at the entrance, climbing over each other's shoulders to get a view of the proceedings inside.

A couple of men bring a container of milk. Holding the container with the help of another man, Diyal pours it on to the Shiv ling. This is an offering to the god by the devotees. Following this, all the devotees pray. This marks the conclusion of the ceremony. The women head back to the hall, whereas the men sleep wherever they find a place.

* * *

At about nine in the morning, the officials of the Archaeology Department, unaware of the situation, come to work. They find their offices invaded and the temples full of sleeping pilgrims. Across the road, the pilgrims are preparing for the festivities of the day. Traders are setting up their stalls by spreading out their wares on the roadside. These include small idols, pictures of deities, CDs of bhajan recordings, toys for children, *bindiyas* and *mangalsutras*. Unwilling to wait for everyone to wake up and vacate the hall, which the pilgrims were going to do in a couple of hours anyway, junior officials from the department enter the hall and start picking up their luggage and throwing it out into the courtyard. This causes a panic as the women shout and fight back. The officials refuse to listen to anyone. Another group picks up the utensils and other material used to prepare the langar, including rice, and throw it on the road.

Both Gupta and Diyal rush to the scene. Women sit at the foot of the hall beating their chests and wailing. Others try to rescue their bags from the officials. Some are picking up their clothes from the floor. Diyal asks the boys to pick up the utensils and other eatables from the road and put them inside the temple. Gupta tries to argue with the officials to allow them to vacate peacefully, Diyal makes a few frenzied calls to his friends in the media. He wants to use the threat of the media to placate the officials.

* * *

It has been an hour since the officials threw out the devotees and there is still no sign of the media. The pilgrims who were not able to explore the temple yesterday are wandering around. A few are having their photographs taken next to the pool. It is too cold to take a bath so they enjoy its scenic beauty instead. A few take some water from the pond in their hands and pour it on their heads. This is a substitute to performing a ritual ablution or *ashnan*. Children are playing with the toys that they have bought from the stalls.

Diyal tries to call his friends in the media again but no one responds. The officials have cleaned the hall and are at work there now. Unlike the previous day, it is a sunny day, perfect for the pilgrims to enjoy themselves in the open.

BAISAKHI AT RAM THAMMAN

Boisterous Punjabi music emerges out of the loudspeakers set in the middle of the well. A small door allows people to come in. A pole, situated in the middle of the loudspeakers, supports the canopy at the top. About a dozen eunuchs, or *Khwaja Saras* in local parlance, young and old, walk into the arena, while Muneer Ahmad, a daredevil and the real attraction of the show, takes a cigarette break. The eunuchs have made-up faces and blow-dried hair, and are wearing colourful shalwar kameez. With the skin-tight shirts that show off their plunging necklines and lacy red and black bras, their sexually provocative dance moves seem to specially cater to the teenage boys, the dominant crowd at the well. In between, they blow a flying kiss or wink at someone, resulting in the admirer throwing a note of five or ten rupees as a token of appreciation. Catching it midway, or seductively sweeping it off the floor, they slide it into their bras. They repeat this performance several times in the three days that the festival is celebrated here.

After about fifteen minutes their chubby contractor leads them out so that the well is empty for its main act. In comes Ahmad, a svelte-looking man in his forties, wearing his hair like Waheed Murad, the iconic Pakistani film actor from the 1970s; silky hair, jet-black, tilted towards one side, falling daintily on his forehead. He has a thick, short beard, and is wearing a grayish, baggy shalwar kameez. He enters through the small door in a stoop. All the buttons of his shirt are open, the collar thrown back, displaying his manhood, asserting that he is ready for the challenge. A lit cigarette dangles from his mouth. His habit of smoking *hashish* has aged him. Ahmad picks up his mountain motorbike resting on the wall of the well. Both—his and the bike's weight—are crucial for this acrobatic balance of the centripetal and centrifugal forces. The bike does not start immediately. A man who looks like a junkie, wearing an old black T-shirt and long faded blue shorts, with a shaven head and an unkempt beard, offers to push. He was standing there throughout the performance of the eunuchs, collecting money thrown in the air, which the eunuchs would miss. At first Ahmad rebukes him, gesturing for him to go away. But the man is persistent. After one failed attempt, Ahmad does not bother to stop him again.

With his push the bike starts, its engine roaring, a loud echo reverberating from the surroundings and grey smoke swirling in the air. Ahmad uses the slight slope at the base of the well to get his bike on the wooden surface, and within no time he is taking rounds of the *Maut ka kuan*. The entire structure oscillates with his movement. He takes his hands off from the handle, but the bike continues to revolve uniformly. He completes his circles within seconds. A man from the crowd extends a ten-rupee note. Ahmad reaches out to grab it, but fails. His bike descends a little, so he puts his hands back on the handle and regains control. He tries again but fails again. He struggles to catch the note a third time and succeeds. Clutching it in his fist, he puts it in his mouth and extends both of his hands to the sides, while his bike performs a victory lap. He then throws his collection mid-air. The junkie grabs at it below. Another man extends a ten-rupee note, which Ahmad manages to catch in his first attempt. The wheel of the bike misses the edge of the wall by inches, making this an extremely dangerous stunt. The Maut ka kuan or the 'Well of Death' derives its name from this dangerous act that Ahmad just demonstrated. This is a round structure, joined together by planks of wood, and covered with a blue canopy. There is a circular platform on the outer-wall of the well, where the audience can stand and peek in.

* * *

This is the celebration of Baisakhi in a small village called Ram Thamman, on the outskirts of Kasur. Challenging the monolithic perception of the country, the people of this village, primarily Muslims, have continued the tradition, which some would argue is an 'un-Islamic practice'. The shrine and this festival serve to dispute stereotypes about rural Pakistan being plagued by intolerance and backwardness.

Baba Ram Thamman, as the name suggests, was a Hindu saint. According to the *Encyclopedia of Sikh Literature*, he was an older cousin of the founder of the Sikh religion, Baba Guru Nanak. He belonged to the neighbouring village of Khalu Khara; however, during his lifetime he settled at this spot, where his *samadhi* (final resting place) was eventually built. It was a common tradition for *Bhagati* or *Sufis* (hermits) to sit on the outskirts of a city or village for meditation. It is reported that Baba Guru Nanak also visited him here more than once. According to the *Encyclopedia*, after his death, a shrine was built to commemorate the spot, which eventually expanded into a 22-acre complex, comprising several buildings and structures.

Khalu Khara is now an abandoned station lying a few kilometres away on the road that connects Ferozepur Road to Raiwind, which is at a distance of 20 km. In the pre-Partition days, this station used to come to life in April, at the time of Baisakhi. Special trains used to come here carrying pilgrims from Amritsar, Ferozepur and other parts of Punjab. Groups of devotees used to set off on foot from different locations, carrying flags and chunris to present to the shrine, like the pilgrims visiting the Durga shrine at Bahawalnagar. In his famous work *Heer*, Waris Shah, the Sufi poet from the eighteenth century, describes the arrival of Heer's *baarat* as, '*Jevein log nigahein te raatan thaman dhol marde te rang lawande ne,*' comparing the festivities of the baarat with the festivities at Ram Thamman (during the Baisakhi celebration). The pilgrims also included Muslims, along with Sikhs and Hindus. According to police intelligence reports in the archives of the Punjab Secretariat at Lahore, about 35,000 people attended this festival in the year 1946. This was also the last time Baisakhi was celebrated on such a scale at Ram Thamman.

Partition in 1947 divided Punjab and resulted in the migration of Hindus and Sikhs from the area. Nonetheless, this festival was kept alive by the Muslims who used to come here in the pre-Partition days, although on a smaller scale. To this day, Baisakhi is celebrated at Ram Thamman in the month of April, attracting thousands of people. Ghulam Hussain, an eighty-five-year-old, has played a critical role in ensuring that the tradition is carried on and the shrine is not desecrated. Standing inside the main room, he narrates the story of the festival and this temple. The date is 14 April 2011.

His grandfather, a Muslim, was a *sadhu* (hermit) here. They originally belonged to a village from the neighbouring Ferozepur District (now part of India). 'After Partition, our family settled here,' he says. As the family was associated with the shrine, they understood its religious significance. 'We locked up the main room, which contains the samadhi of Baba Ram Thamman, and moved into a building adjacent to it, where there is a temple dedicated to the Hindu deities, Kali and Shiva.' They watched as other migrants from Ferozepur and Amritsar took over parts of the complex, strengthening their resolve to ensure that no one infringed upon the main shrine.

* * *

A walk around the village reveals several historical buildings from different eras. Some of the architectural features are from the nineteenth century, which is also known as the Sikh period. Facades of havelis stand tall in the middle of single-storey buildings. The bricks are smaller than the ones preferred by the British. This means that the structures were raised before their arrival, which in Punjab was in the middle of the nineteenth century. However, the buildings behind the facades have been razed and the houses divided. Occasionally, one comes across remains of walls, portals and facades made out of the thin brick, surrounded by the newly made thick brick structures. This complex was not constructed at one particular time, but expanded over several years.

A tall façade that must have been an entrance to a haveli soars high behind the shrine. The arch at the entrance is in three tiers and there are remnants of floral frescoes underneath, now fading away. Inside, the haveli has been divided into numerous compartments by migrant families. Some of the bricks taken from the razed structures have been used to construct the floor. Placed together without any cement, they move every time one steps on it. There is only one room here which was part of the original structure. This is within the building of the façade. From the courtyard, a steep staircase leads into this room. The ceiling is a dome, now gray in colour. Faded lines of red and blue can be seen on the roof. These are the last remaining marks of the elaborate frescoes that beautified this haveli and others like it. The walls have now been whitewashed. There is a huge trunk on one side of the room, covered with a white cloth. There are several other smaller trunks on the top. A single bed, neatly made, lies next to it.

'We plan to whitewash the ceiling soon,' says Aslam, a forty-three-year-old farmer, who lives in this house with his family. This room belongs to his eldest daughter, who is being married off in a month. The trunks contain her dowry. She was studying in this room a little while ago but was asked to leave because of the visitors; her tenth-grade English grammar book is still on the bed. Modestly covered, she stands in the courtyard with the rest of the women who are surprised at the invasion of their home by strangers, curiously staring at faded lines on the walls, fascinated by what seems most ordinary to the ladies. Aslam's daughter has stared at these lines for hours from her bed, but never has she been this interested. She giggles along with her sister and mother, covering their lips with their dupattas.

The family's prized possession of buffaloes are tied behind them, next to a trough. Aslam's youngest son stands next to his father as he shows his guests around. 'This entire room was filled with such designs. Most of them were plants, but there were some animals too. No human figure, though. With time, they faded. Last year, we whitewashed the walls and now we will do the same with the ceiling,' he says. There is an ominous crack across the roof but for now Aslam is not bothered.

'This was one big courtyard when our family moved here,' he says descending the stairs. His family shifted here from a village in Ferozepur district. With so many boundary walls, it looks more like a maze than a courtyard. 'There are seven houses within this one haveli,' he adds. The walls are weak; bricks placed next to each other without any cement. Hollow gaps have been left between the walls for people to move around from one area to the other. Towards the other end of the courtyard, there is another small entrance: a single arch with a strong wooden gate. Bricks have been adjusted in front of it to block it permanently.

* * *

Only the main shrine and the adjacent temple have survived this onslaught of migrants. Had it not been for Hussain and his family's care and dedication, this would have also been taken over by the refugees and converted into a household, like the hundreds of temples and gurdwaras all over Pakistani Punjab. The shrine remains locked all year round and is only opened up a few days before Baisakhi. Being a devotee, Hussain himself sweeps the floor and changes the *chadar* at the samadhi. 'Sometimes we open the lock when some visitors come to visit the shrine. Sikhs and Hindus come occasionally to pay their tributes to the Baba. I also offer a prayer along with them whenever I open the door,' he says.

There is a small canopy at one end of the room, decorated with colourful paper and frills. A little lump lies in the centre of the canopy. It has been made out of white marble like the rest of the floor. This is the samadhi of Baba Ram Thamman, covered with an orange cloth. After the cremation of the body, ash is collected from the pyre and buried in the ground in a container. A small lump like this one is made to mark the spot. This is called a samadhi. It is done for important people in the Hindu and Sikh tradition. A picture of an old man wearing a turban and sitting on a chair while resting one hand on his stick is engraved on the floor next to the samadhi. He is offering a rosary with the other hand. This is probably in memory of a generous devotee who donated money for the construction of the shrine. There is a bell at the threshold of the room. Hussain is wearing a beige shalwar kameez and has tied a red cloth with golden embroidery on his head, similar in texture to what the Hindu pilgrims at Bahawalnagar wore. His son, Abid Hussain, fifty-seven, stands next to him. He looks after the shrine now.

The samadhi is a single-storey white structure. It is a cone-like construction emerging from the middle of the houses. The temple of Kali Mata, a ferocious Hindu deity, now home to Hussain and his family, is similar. There is a courtyard next to the temple, with a few rooms at one end. There is a big tank in front of the building, about eight acres in size. Giant steps disappear into the water, going all the way to its base. Only a few steps are visible. The water is toxic green in colour, with bubbles bursting in the middle. Plastic bags, rotten fruit, broken toys, used newspapers and other material float on the surface. A dark green shell of a turtle emerges from the water. A few boys rush to the pool, carrying branches of trees and sticks. They poke its shell, giggling merrily. The turtle sticks its neck out from under the water and looks at its oppressors before disappearing completely. The boys run back, carrying plastic toys in their hands. On the other end of the tank is a cluster of newly built houses, raised only in the past few years in what used to be known as the far end of the village.

There is a small building with two half-sunk arches at the base of the temple. A cluster of plastic bags surround it. Similar constructions are visible at other ends of the tank. These were used to fill fresh water into the tank and drain stale water through a drainage system that drew water from River Sutlej, a few kilometres from here. The drainage system is now blocked and hence the water has not been drained for several years.

'This used to be clean water. So clean that we would drink from it,' recalls Hussain. 'Women used to wash clothes on these steps, while the children used to bathe in the pool. We would jump from the roof of the temple into the water,' he says, pointing to the roof of the Kali Mata temple. 'There was a separate enclosure for women to bathe. But now look at its condition. The people living around it have blocked the drainage. They think the pool is a garbage tank. This water has not been removed since the past several years. There are so many problems because of that. This tank has become a breeding ground for diseases. The people living around it have all kinds of skin diseases and breathing problems. Dengue and malaria are widespread as well. These very people who have polluted the tank now suffer because of it,' he finishes off with an air of frustration.

There are stalls around the water tank. Tents have been raised to ward off the heat, while there are several tables selling different items. Next to the pool, a vendor is selling plastic toys. Another one is selling cheap jewellery for girls. One of them, sitting on the table amidst his items, puts the leftovers of his lunch in a plastic bag and aims for the pool. Bouncing off the first step, it plunges into the water.

A few women have made space for their glass bangle stalls on the ground, under the shadow of the temple. They have done this by laying out a mat on the floor. In the night, after the festivities end, they will pack up their things and sleep at the same place. Most of the vendors have come from other cities and villages. They descend upon this village every year. According to the locals, more than a thousand people come here during these three days (it begins on 13 April, which corresponds with the first of Baisakhi according to the local calendar). The third and last day is reserved for women only. No male is allowed to visit the stalls or the rides for the entire day.

Stalls greet the visitor at the entrance of the village. They are spread out over an area of nearly 2 km. There is only one road that heads towards the shrine, which is covered with tents and stalls on both sides. Vendors are busy selling stickers depicting truck art and catchy one-liners, like *Haran de rasta le, Ma ki dua jannat ki hawa, Jalne wale tera mun kala* and *Tera intezar karte hain*. Another stall has posters of Bollywood actors and Pakistani cricketers.

On one side of this long street is a thick wall which is the boundary of the Ram Thamman complex. The other, temporarily covered with tents, has open fields behind it.

Various babas, calling themselves 'Master of the Universe' and 'Curers of all diseases', sit on the pavements. Their colourful handkerchiefs have been tied to a rope as a mark of their spirituality. Saffron, green and the occasional black are important Sufi and Bhagati spiritual colours. The Babas offer rings containing stones with magical properties to the sufferers. Lockets reading Ya-Ali or the more secular ones of 'Love' and 'Friendship' hang from wires in front of them as they sit cross-legged, waiting for their next customer. Stalls offer eatables, including jalebi, kababs, falooda, hareesa and fish, the last three being the speciality of the nearby Kasur city. The eatables are prepared in front of the customer and served on tables and chairs placed in front of the stall. Small carts carry recycled bottles of fizzy drinks like Pepsi, Mirinda and Sprite. The attached loudspeakers scream out catchy phrases in Punjabi which praise the homemade drinks, or play 1990s music from Indian movies. Further up the road is the entertainment section. This includes the jumping pad, swings, a small Ferris wheel, a pirate ship and more. At the end of the road, where the accompanying building gives way to the open field, is the Maut ka kuan.

Even though this is still the second day and women will get their chance on the third, several of them explore the stalls. A few are squatting in front of the bangle vendor next to the shrine, trying bangles in different colours. At another nearby stall, which sells cheap cosmetic items like talcum powder and lipsticks, a few are haggling with the vendor. He is requesting them to take the money back that one of them has forced into his hand for the products which she now clutches in a plastic bag. She refuses and walks away. The vendor keeps on shouting that he has been robbed but she moves away, least bothered. Giving up, he puts the money into his top pocket and goes back to fanning himself with a worn-out book.

* * *

A bangle vendor, carrying a wooden plank on his shoulder which showcases his items, appears from an alley next to the shrine. He is a short, thin man, wearing a pink shalwar kameez. Stopping next to the female bangle vendor, he rests his wooden plank next to the wall of the shrine and sits resting on both of his feet, squatting next to her. He wipes his sweat using a scarf that he had placed on his shoulder to act as a cushion between his bones and the wooden plank. His name is Abdul Razzak and the female vendor is his wife. Another female bangle vendor sitting across from them is her sister-in-law, who is feeding Razzak's two children, a boy and a girl.

Razzak is forty years old and has been coming to this festival for the past twenty-five years, ever since he started selling bangles. He originally belongs to the city of Pak Pattan, about 150 km away from here. He also travels to other shrines and festivals around the country but has a particular association with the shrine of Ram Thamman for he is the third generation from his family who has been coming to sell bangles here. Visiting this festival for him is therefore not just an economic opportunity but a spiritual and a traditional obligation.

'In the earlier days we used to come and stay here for an entire week,' he says, 'but now the world moves too fast. The festival doesn't last that long and we are on a train back the fourth day from our arrival.' Razzak recalls the stories his grandfather and father used to share about the festival here. They would tell him about the number of people who used to visit and the different activities that used to take place. Famous wrestlers would come to take part in wrestling competitions. Popular folk theatre companies would dance and sing for days, tapping on popular folk stories like Heer-Ranjha, Sohni-Mahiwal and Raja Rasalu. The festivities of today are different.

Hussain has seen those days as a child, when he used to come with his father to visit his grandfather at the time of the festival. 'There used to be a sea of people. I remember my father used to warn me that in case I get lost I should not look for him but we would instead choose a meeting point where we would all gather in the evening,' he says.

A local resident of the village, who has seen the festivities from the pre-Partition days, is seventy-six-year-old Munawar Bibi. She lives in a house next to the shrine with her children and grandchildren. She is wearing a brown shalwar kameez and has covered her head with a white dupatta. 'We would stock food, water and other supplies and then lock ourselves inside our houses for three days when the festival would begin. There used to be so many people that one would hardly find any place to walk on the streets,' she recalls, sitting on a charpai inside her house. 'This is nothing compared to what it used to be,' she says. However, even today the festival is famous in the surrounding regions. Several Muslims come here to pay their respects to the shrine all year around. They bring chadars which they then present to the samadhi of Baba Ram Thamman.

* * *

The sound of sticks clicking against each other accompanied by the beat of the dhol floats in from a house a few metres away from the shrine. A group of old men are sitting on charpais next to the house, whereas young children have climbed on to the roof to watch the scene unfold in the courtyard. The door is open for anyone to walk in. The house is one long single-storey building with several rooms. A wooden ladder rests on the building, which the children are using to get to the top. There is an open courtyard in front of the building and a couple of buffaloes are tied at one end. The attention is focused upon the clicking sound that is coming from a group of eight boys standing in a circle in the middle of the courtyard. Holding little sticks in both their hands, they tap them to create a rhythm.

For now they are following a simple routine; two taps on your own sticks, two to the person on the right, two to the person on the left, and then again two with your own. A dhol-wala giving them the background beat is standing next to them. One of the boys signals that the sound is too loud and that he should play with his hands instead. He obliges. There is an audience of about fifty people, including men, women and children, gathered around them. Soon their performance increases in fervour as the tempo rises. The boys start moving in an anti-clockwise direction, while tapping the sticks with each other. The routine also changes, becoming more complicated.

A green chadar, containing Quranic verses written with a golden thread, has been spread on a charpai at one end of the courtyard. There are a few notes spread over it. Impressed by the passionate performance of the group, several attendees throw some money on it. This chadar has been brought by the group as a gift to the saint, whereas the money given by the audience is a gift for the performers. There is no mandatory remuneration for such a performance, as all contributions are voluntary. The wooden stick, an essential part of their dance, is called *dandiya*.

'I have been playing dandiya at various religious festivals since the past fifteen years,' says twenty-two-year-old Ghulam Ali, one of the members of the group. The various shrines that they have played at include Bulleh Shah's, Data Darbar's and Baba Fareed Shakar Ganj's, all of which are famous Muslim shrines. 'There is no invitation for such festivals. People come out of their devotion. This is a famous shrine. We have always wanted to see it, so this year we decided to come,' he says.

Known as Dandiya Raas, this is a traditional folk dance, in which pairs dance with two small sticks that they tap with each other, while a dhol or some other percussion plays in the background. It is considered to be a symbolic reenactment of Krishna flirting around with the *gopis* (maidens). Dandiya Raas is performed during Holi, Navratri and other cultural festivals. This group has no gopis, just Krishnas, and that too Muslim Krishnas.

One of the reasons why this festival has survived as opposed to other 'non-Muslim' festivals is because of its nature. Baisakhi essentially is a celebration of the beginning of the harvest season. This occasion, which is one of the most important days in the life of a farmer, has been given religious significance by the Sikh and the Hindu traditions. The festival marks the beginning of the month of Baisakh. Historically, farmers used to celebrate this event after which the harvest would begin. On the outskirts of the village, several families are busy cutting wheat. This festival is a celebration of the farmer, irrespective of religion. There are a few other Muslim villages and cities in Pakistan where this festival is still celebrated, despite it being considered a 'non-Muslim' celebration. These are Jaman in Lahore District and the shrine of Sakhi Sarwar in Dera Ghazi Khan. In Ram Thamman, this celebration is conjoined with the festival of the shrine, giving it a religious tone. Given that Muslims are visiting a non-Muslim shrine and paying their tributes to it makes this festival at Ram Thamman a unique case.

* * *

Encouraged by the way this celebration has been kept alive by Muslims over all these years, the Hindu/Christian community has also taken an interest in these celebrations.[1] In 2011, the priest of the Neela Gumbad Mandir, Bhagat Advit Bhatti, brought a delegation of 300 people from Lahore and neighbouring regions to perform religious rites at this shrine. They arrived on the night of 12 April and stayed out in the open, next to the shrine. Before sunrise, they gathered at the temple of Kali Mata and performed the necessary prayers, after which they performed an ablution (*ashnan*).

This is the first year after Partition that Hindus have performed a prayer here. The door of the temple was opened by Hussain for them. After the conclusion of the rites, the Hindu community distributed food to the poor people at the village and left, not staying back for the festivities, which began that day. Even though the Muslims have allowed them to offer prayers here and also revere the shrine, the interaction between the two is far from ideal. The Hindus stayed out in the open and no Muslim participated in their prayers. A few Muslims from the village feel that having food from the donation of the Hindu community is unacceptable. Similarly, the Hindus did not stay back for the festivities, which would have provided an opportunity to intermingle. However, it is likely that if this tradition continues, then the shrine of Ram Thamman would serve to bring the two communities closer. For now, the Hindus perform the religious rites, while the Muslims take part in the festivities.

* * *

Even though this is the first time that Hindus have led a prayer here, and attempted to reclaim their temple, Advit has visited this shrine several times. 'I used to come here with my aunt as a child on the occasion of Baisakhi and even otherwise,' he says. The version of the story that his aunt has narrated to him about its history is different from what is written in the *Encyclopedia of Sikh Literature*. She told him that the pool was first dug by the monkey deity, Hanuman. Hanuman was a follower of Ram and played a central role in the battle between Ram and Ravana. He is depicted as a mighty warrior, the Indian version of Hercules. Advit's aunt told him that Hanuman created this ancient pool, digging with a shovel only two and a half times.

This is a mythological claim that cannot be verified historically, but on the other hand, it is particularly important because it underscores the importance of this shrine and its pool to the Hindu community. Such myths have developed with ancient Hindu temples and pilgrimages, like Katas Raj and Hinglaj. It is therefore interesting to note that the myth of Hanuman was associated with a shrine whose history, according to the literature, only goes back about five centuries. Conventionally, such folklore is linked to much older sites. Raising more doubts is the story of Hussain, who says that Baisakhi is being celebrated here since 1200 years. He must have heard these tales from his forefathers, all of whom were related to the shrine. Also given that this was such a big event, history books are glaringly quiet about the relationship between the festival of Baisakhi and this shrine; why is Baisakhi celebrated at Ram Thamman?

All of these factors point towards the direction that there is some aspect of the history of this shrine which was missed by historians of that time. It is likely that this was an ancient temple, though on a smaller scale at the time that Baba Ram Thamman came and settled here. Later, when Guru Nanak visited his cousin, its significance increased manifold and this became an important shrine.

* * *

Because of its association with the Hindu religion, the festival has been criticized by the orthodox section of the village. In recent years, they have tried using the force of the authorities to curb the celebrations here. One of the tactics that they use is to remove the loudspeakers from the stalls and Maut ka kuan, which are an important way of attracting crowds. However, the popularity and the support of the festival is such that it has managed to thrive. For the majority of the people, this is a cultural event that they have been celebrating all their lives. 'I know that this is not our festival,' says Ahmad the stuntman. 'But this festival provides space for the local community to forget about their worries and celebrate. In a time where security threats have sapped the life out of larger religious festivals, these small village events are the only real festivals that are left. There is nothing un-Islamic about celebrating and having fun now, is there?'

SHRI VALMIKI'S BIRTHDAY AT LAHORE

For Bishna Ram, Asghar Khokhar and Pandit Bhagat Advit Bhatti, the Valmiki temple at the Neela Gumbad Mandir is like a community centre. They get together here every evening at about seven to take part in a ritual prayer. On most of the days, they are the only ones present. Advit, at fifty-eight, is the youngest in this fraternity of elderly men, the rest of whom are above eighty. Together, they constitute the administrative body of the temple. Ram is the treasurer while Advit is the general secretary. Advit is also the priest or the pandit, who has inherited the post from his father. The temple serves a small community of Balmiki Hindus in Lahore, numbering only a few hundred, most of whom are Christians on record.

* * *

Set inside the historical market of Anarkali, which is named after the legendary lover of the Mughal Emperor Jahangir, Valmiki Mandir has stood here for many generations.

Facing the temple is a narrow alley, once known as Valmiki Street. In a symbiotic relationship between a place of worship and the establishment of a residential area around it, this street was populated by Valmikis who were the guardians of this temple. But then when Partition forced out the community, the name of the street was also changed. A small blue door leads inside this temple, which can be easily overlooked amidst all the shops. This area over the years has become the largest tyre market in the city, hard economic realities eating away historical and cultural spaces that existed here before this market was established. The Pak Tea House, just a few shops away, once famed for its gatherings of the leading intelligentsia of the city, is now on its way to becoming yet another tyre shop.

Hoisted on the entrance gate, a triangle-shaped orange flag with a golden border greets the visitor. This flag is an essential feature of all Valmiki temples. There are no guards or intelligence officials stopping non-related people from going inside, as one would find at Christian churches and Sikh gurdwaras. The temple is unassuming with a small courtyard, where all the religious festivals are organized. The entire area is only about 20–50 square yards. On one side of the courtyard is a small building where Advit's brother and his family reside. They look after the temple. Across the courtyard, on the opposite side, the temple is a modest building divided into two rooms.

There is a bell at the entrance to both of these rooms, which the devotees ring to announce their entrance into the abode of gods. One of the rooms has pictures of deities from the Hindu pantheon, including a few statues of Ganesh, Krishna and Radha. Durga Mata, Kali Mata, Parvati, Krishna, Ram and Sita's portraits hang on the walls, covered with garlands. The other room has a statue of Valmiki, in an orange cloth and adorned with flowers. Lamps are lit under the deities in both of the rooms. Shri Valmiki sits inside a small palanquin amongst walls that have been decorated with all kinds of colourful frills and cloth. Next to the enclosure is a small cradle meant to be used during the Krishna Janmashtami, as Krishna's symbolic cradle.

* * *

'The idol of Valmiki was designed by students of the Punjab University in the pre-Partition days. It was a testimony to fine craftsmanship and the statue was embellished with expensive jewellery,' says eighty-six-year-old Bishna Ram, who is also known as Yousuf Ali. 'There was a beautiful statue of Krishna, made out of white marble, in the next room. They were both smashed and destroyed in front of my eyes by a mob protesting the desecration of the Babri Mosque in India. The entire temple was burned down and they took away everything the temple owned, even our bicycles, utensils and cauldrons. The mob even stole the iron bars that came out of the ceiling. I can't describe all the things these eyes have seen,' says Ram, as he struggles to hold back his tears. 'This new idol is nothing compared to the original one.' He was twenty-five when Partition happened. From his house in Lahore, he saw the burning of the Hindu-dominated market of Shah Alami, still one of the largest wholesale markets in the city. 'The Hindus had their shops in the front, while they lived at the back. Using the gutters, the Muslims entered that area and burnt everything. I remember it was night when we heard screams coming from that side. We got to the roof and saw that the entire community was in flames. I could see people on fire, screaming.' Overcome by grief, Ram breaks down and starts crying. 'I remember our friends and relatives telling us that we should move to India; that Lahore was no longer safe for us. But you know we are Valmikis. We would have remained Valmikis in India as well—untouchables!'

Thrusting back his slouched shoulders, Asghar Khokhar recalls the days when no one could have made him fall off his feet. His strength had earned him the title of *Haathi Pehlwan* or the Elephant Wrestler. Now eighty-two, Khokhar struggles to stand on his two feet. Originally known as Khem Chand, sometime after the Partition he started using Asghar, a well-known Muslim name. 'We were a couple of Valmiki wrestlers. We once went to a famous wrestling arena near Kashmiri Gate. Looking at our skin colour, the Muslim wrestlers realized that we were Valmikis and refused to fight with us. We decided that day to make our own arena. Here at the temple, at the courtyard, we had a wrestling arena where Valmiki wrestlers used to practise. It was removed when the temple was renovated after the destruction of 1992. Before Partition, we Valmikis and the Muslims were untouchables for the Hindus. After Partition, with the Hindus gone, we became untouchables for the Muslims.' Khokhar recalls when sometime after the creation of Pakistan he went to a small city called Renala Khurd with a wedding procession. On the way when they stopped, he and a couple of other guests went to a tea stall and had a cup of tea. 'Somehow the owner of the shop, who was a Muslim, found out that we were Valmikis. He made us pay for the cups we had used as he said he would never use those cups again.'

But the pandit, who is a generation younger than both Ram and Khokhar, feels that attitudes are changing for good. 'When I was a child, I used to go to a curd shop daily in the morning to buy some milk in old Anarkali. In the earlier days, the shopkeeper, who was a Muslim and knew my family and my religion, would make sure that he wouldn't touch my utensil. I would place it on the counter and he would pour milk from the top making sure that even his utensil didn't touch mine. But then over the years, his attitude became lax and sometimes his utensil would touch mine. In the end, he would just hold the utensil and pour the milk inside. It is funny, however, that our hands would sometimes touch when I would give him money, which he would immediately put into his pocket,' the pandit chuckles.

All of these individuals have been associated with this particular temple for several years. Before them, their forefathers would come here daily. On 7 December 1992, when the temple was attacked by a mob in retaliation for an attack on a mosque hundreds of kilometres away from here, all of them got here earlier than usual. 'No one had asked us. It was instinctive,' says the pandit. And while they were here discussing the ramifications the event was likely to have, they heard the chants of thousands of people headed towards them. 'They poured in through the gate, thousands of them, carrying weapons, including guns. They didn't say anything to us but started attacking the building. Quietly we got up and left the temple. My bicycle was parked in the courtyard. While I was walking away with it, a man stopped me. Without a word, I gave him my bicycle. I saw another group take away our cauldron that we would use to cook food for religious festivals. They didn't even spare our shoes. We later found out that the temple had been knocked down and then burned. For days the fire raged as it also spread to the neighbouring buildings, into the shops and the houses of the people who had instigated the attacks.' 'We knew who the attackers were,' adds Ram. 'We used to interact with them daily. The pandit still keeps an acquaintance with them. They were our neighbours.'

A few kilometres from here, in between the Shah Alami and Lohari gates of the walled city of Lahore, there is a single cone-shaped temple standing in the middle of a residential area. This is the Sitla Mandir, a historical temple spread over several acres and visited by thousands of people when it was functional in the pre-Partition days. Ram remembers visiting it as a child. 'Different temples and deities have specialities. There was a pool facing the temple and it was believed that people with all sorts of diseases would be cured after taking a dip in it. Mothers used to bring their children there every Thursday. Many Muslims also used to visit the temple.' The pool has now been encroached upon and replaced by a community park. Other residential structures associated with the temple have been taken over by migrants coming from the other side of the border fleeing Partition riots. Of the main temple, just this cone-shaped structure survives as the only remaining link with its pre-Pakistan past. The rest of the structure has been divided into several apartments, one of which is occupied by an Islamic seminary by the name of Madrassa Noor-ul-Quran. The family of the *maulvi* in charge of the seminary moved in here after Partition and subsequently leased out the rest of the temple as they became the owner of the property by default.

In December 1992, it was ironically the maulvi who instigated the people of his community to attack the structure which had been home to his family since 1947. Thousands of people gathered around the structure and a bulldozer was brought in to destroy the adjoining structures, all of which were homes to people. One boy overcome by religious fervour climbed to the summit of the structure, which was several feet from the ground and started hammering it. Succumbing to the pressure from below and above, the top of the cone fell and the boy also fell with the structure and died. Posthumously, he was given the title of 'Shaheed'. Today, the remnant of that structure still stands, as a witness to the hostilities of 1992. A small plate which reads *Ya Allah* rests in a niche in that structure. It was placed here after it was brutalized during the riots.

Following the destruction of Neela Gumbad Mandir, Pandit Advit Bhatti, a reasonably well-known person from the community, disappeared for a few months and waited for things to cool down. During the six months that he was gone, there were rumours in the right-wing media that the pandit had fled to India with his family. In that state of hibernation that the community found itself in after the rising tension, it also collected funds to renovate the temple. Within a year or so after the attack, a brand-new construction came up and the temple was made functional once again.

* * *

On religious festivals like Holi, Diwali and Shri Valmiki's birthday, the Neela Gumbad Mandir becomes an island of religious syncretism in Lahore. One of the walls in the portico depicts a painting of Lord Valmiki teaching his two pupils, Luv and Kush, next to River Parsuni—an image from Hindu mythology. Facing this wall there is a small wooden cross hanging on the wall, a symbol associated with the Christian religion. Many Muslims around the area, who occasionally interact with the members of this community, refer to them as Christians. This has its roots in the bloody Partition of Punjab, after which social prejudice and stigma attached with being a Hindu increased immensely. Government school textbooks are filled with references labelling the Hindus as mischievous and conniving, and they are blamed for the bloodshed during the Partition. Over the years, this state propaganda has resulted in the Hindu becoming a taboo in this Muslim puritanical society. In order to avoid the social prejudice associated with their religion, a lot of Hindus have now taken up Christian and Muslim names to avoid being noticed in society. A few have even converted to Christianity or Islam. However, for all practical purposes, this marriage of convenience is more out of prudence than actual conviction.

'Bishna Ram would draw attention. Yousuf Ali gels in,' explains Ram. From his family, Khokhar is the last remaining Valmiki Hindu. His son converted to Christianity and now his grandson is a Christian as well. Occasionally, they visit the temple to stay in touch with their roots. There are several other such families, now Christians or Muslims whose ancestors were Valmikis. These families visit the temple on religious occasions retaining a few of their religious traditions.

* * *

The word Balmiki is a mispronunciation of the word 'Valmiki'. Balmiki is a sect which is centred on the sage Valmiki. His followers are referred to as Valmikis or Balmikis. Lord Valmiki was a shudra and hence, Balmikis belong to the shudra caste. However, Lord Valmiki rebelled against the hierarchal structure of his time and became a philosopher and a poet. He wrote the first-ever version of the Ramayana, which is now referred to as Valmiki's Ramayana. This was written several centuries before the Ramayana of Tulsidas. According to the legend, Valmiki's ashram was on the bank of River Parsuni, which is the old name of River Ravi, flowing next to the city of Lahore. Sita gave birth to the twin sons of Ram, Luv and Kush, while she was here after she had been banished by Ram. Lahore and Kasur are said to be named after Luv and Kush. There is a temple near the Alamgiri gate of Lahore Fort, called the temple of Luv. It is believed that the original temple was built by Luv himself, whereas the current structure goes back to the Mughal era.

A high-caste woman living at the ashram of a sage, who belonged to a low caste, was another challenge to societal norms. Valmiki challenged the concept of divinely sanctioned division of labour that the caste hierarchy of Hinduism represented, when he decided to write the Ramayana, after which he sanctified his status as a true sage, despite being a shudra, by narrating how a kshatriya woman stayed in his ashram and that too the perfect woman, the wife of Ram. For ordinary shudras, whose daily existence is marred by caste discrimination, one can imagine the pride the image of Valmiki is likely to conjure—a philosopher-critic of the caste-based hierarchy. In their pantheon, Lord Valmiki has been accorded the highest status. His birthday, celebrated on 22 October 2011 (the date changes every year on the basis of the Hindu religious calendar), is the most important religious occasion in the year for them, irrespective of their religious identities, for according to societal norms, an untouchable remains an untouchable no matter what religion he ascribes to. Lord Valmiki is the ultimate deity of the untouchables.

* * *

The temple takes up an air of celebration two days in advance. More devotees start attending the evening prayers, and as a result, the prayers also become more elaborate. On a regular day, the pandit, leading the prayers, would read from the holy scripture. This is followed by a communal prayer and then aarti, which would conclude the prayer. But a couple of days before the celebration, musicians from the community gather at the time of the prayer, practising till late in the night.

On 21 October, one day before the big event, forty-five-year-old Azad Chaudary comes to the temple with his son and daughter. Sitting in the portico, they practise as the pandit conducts the prayer inside. Chaudary plays the tabla, while his son, twelve-year-old Yashwa, plays the harmonium and sings. They are singing a bhajan, sung by Mohammed Rafi, the famous Bollywood singer. Wearing a green shalwar kameez, fourteen-year-old Teresa watches her father and brother perform. She will practise later in the night. As the prayers conclude, a few people come and sit around them, while others spread out to other corners of the temple to socialize. Chaudary was originally a Balmiki, but he became a Christian when he was twenty-two. Both of his children were born Christian. However, despite the conversion, Chaudary returns to the temple to express his devotion to the sage during the Valmiki festival.

Sitting next to them is thirty-five-year-old Musharraf Ali, a Muslim. At the end of the song, he compliments Yashwa for his skills. 'For a boy of your age, you have a lot of talent,' he tells him. Yashwa mutters a shy thank you. Ali is a professional flute player. A black bag, which carries his several flutes, is placed next to him. Like Chaudary, he also does not come to the temple regularly, but this after all is the festival of Valmiki. Ali was born a Muslim, but his father was a Balmiki. Taking part in this celebration helps connect him to his roots.

* * *

On the day of the festival, a few policemen stand at the main gate. Another one looks at the courtyard from the roof of the temple. Advit has requested the authorities to provide them with security. There is a stage in the courtyard which is flooded with lights. Two large speakers flank it on both sides while a young boy sits behind a mixer on the corner of the stage, busy fiddling with the equalizers. There is a red carpet in front of the stage, and a few dozen chairs behind it. Older men are seated on them, whereas the children are expected to sit on the carpet when the function begins. The crowd includes Muslims and Christians, most of whom have Balmiki roots, and Balmikis.

There is a group of people busy preparing langar, sitting next to Advit's brother's house. Originally vegetarians, a lot of Balmikis/Christians also consume chicken and meat now, having assimilated into a meat-eating environment. However the pandit makes sure that at least on holy days, like this one, only vegetarian food is served. Fresh puri is being prepared in a huge cauldron, burning on a fire. A child tends to the dough, which he hands over to the man cooking the puri. Another man next to them is making channa in the other cauldron.

At about seven in the evening, the communal prayer begins. Advit is reading and explaining from the holy book. He does so in a poetic manner, partially singing. Within his reading he says, '*Bolo Shri Valmiki Maharaj ki,*' to which the devotees respond in a huge prolonged cry '*Jai*'. The pandit repeats his call once again, invoking a similar response. He resumes the reading before replicating this act a number of times. The prayers are taking place at the shrine of Valmiki. The room is teeming with people, with the women sitting on one side and the men on the other. Advit is seated next to the idol of Valmiki. While reading, he is tending to a burning fire in front of him with oil. There is a platter next to it containing *halwa* to be used as *prasad* after the prayer.

There are more people outside than inside the shrine. Women, wearing several layers of make-up and jewellery, sit in the portico. There is hardly any space to walk through them. Shoes are spread out at the base of the verandah. Journalists, photographers and videographers are interviewing and shooting different scenes from the temple focusing particularly on young dressed-up girls, who pose stylishly in front of them. There is an increased interest in minority issues and their festivals in the Pakistani media since the past few years, ever since its liberalization during the era of General Pervez Musharraf (2001–08). However, for the most part, this interest in minorities is a result of the 'exotic' image that minorities hold in the minds of young Muslim professionals, who are otherwise subjected to history imbibed in dogmatic Muslim nationalism. Representation of minorities in the media remains paternalistic; that of an outsider group that needs to be protected and represented in a way that they know best.

Hindus celebrating Pakistan's Independence Day on 14 August becomes national news or Pakistani Sikhs holding a community prayer in their gurdwaras before a major India–Pakistan cricket match, praying for the victory of Pakistan, makes headlines. The inherent bias towards religious minorities and the fact that they are perceived as not belonging to the mainstream society but an 'exotic' group means that coverage of their festivals is merely to add colour to the dull political background of newspapers and channels. This lies at the core of all media representation of religious minorities. 'Hindus celebrate Shri Valmiki's birthday at the Neela Gumbad Mandir' would be front-page news tomorrow with a picture of the pandit or a few girls. This would be the only news about the festival.

* * *

Only in recent years has the Balmiki community been able to revive its traditions and practices that it was forced to repudiate after the creation of Pakistan. In the early years, the community remained docile, fearful of inviting a backlash. The wars of 1965 and 1971 between India and Pakistan, and the Babri Mosque incident in 1992 aggravated the situation. During those times, local Hindus became associated with India and had to bear the brunt of public fury. A lot of prominent Hindus from Lahore went into hiding during the wars, afraid of a hostile reaction.

The situation improved for the community following the 'Enlightened Moderation' years of General Pervez Musharraf, during which minorities were supported and their festivals regularly reported in the newly liberalized media of the country. Emboldened by the positive approach of the government, the community started inviting more people. Explaining the phenomenon, Pandit Advit says, 'Earlier we used to hold prayers inside the shrine on occasions like Holi or Diwali. However, since the past few years, we have come out of the rooms and started holding functions in the courtyard.' It is indeed ironical that this particular religious group owes more to a dictatorship than democratic regimes for its religious freedom.

Seated at the back of the crowd inside the shrine are Yashwa and his father Chaudary. As the pandit concludes his prayer, the pair starts singing the bhajan that they were practising yesterday. A few of the attendants who know the lyrics sing along, while others clap. A passionate devotee starts ringing the bell at the entrance of the shrine. The sound is loud enough to engulf all others. Irritated, Chaudary tries to signal him to stop, but the devotee is too lost in the bhajan to notice.

Just a little while after the prayer, food is served by young members of the community, who are seen running all over the courtyard, carrying paper plates filled with halwa puri and channa, making sure everyone has a serving. The real function would begin soon after.

Once all the attendees have eaten, they gather facing the stage. Ram goes and sits on it, checking to see if the microphone is connected. He is the host for the evening, who will invite performers during the proceedings. He does not want the show to continue till late in the night, as that would attract a lot of attention from the surrounding areas. At the moment, the sound would get lost in the bustling activities that are taking place outside the temple walls, where there are hundreds of cars and thousands of people carrying on with business as usual unaware of this 'Hindu' celebration within the precincts of this temple. In fact, most of them are unaware of the existence of any such temple. Children are invited on to the stage to recite poems that they have written themselves. After the conclusion of the third poem, the children want to recite a fourth one but Ram takes the microphone away. He then invites Chaudary and his son. Ram puts an end to their performance, too, after a while, by stopping them from performing their fourth song. Chaudary requests him for one more, but Ram is adamant. An angry Chaudary picks up his instrument and leaves the stage.

The final performance of the night, which is also the best, is of thirty-year-old Zohaib, a sarangi player. The sarangi is an ancient stringed instrument, much like the sitar, and is played with a stick just like the violin. Zohaib is the sixth generation of his family who has mastered the art of playing this instrument. In the old days when music was not commercialized, musicians and singers subscribed to particular *gharanas* or families, who specialized in a genre of music or instruments. There were gharanas for classical music, gharanas for tabla players, sarangi players, etc. Zohaib belongs to the gharana of sarangi players. Gharanas were a close-knit group, which trained future musicians and singers but kept the art within the family so that they did not lose their speciality. Zohaib, a Muslim, has been invited to the function by Mehboob. He has played with Mehboob on other occasions as well.

Accompanied by the tabla and Mehboob on the flute, Zohaib mesmerizes the audience. His playing primarily involves improvisation, changing beat, rhythm and even melody, according to the variations of the accompanying musicians. The battle, called *jugalbandi* between the tabla, sarangi and the flute, becomes a contest of sharpness and reaction. A slight improvisation is immediately identified by the other musician, who then takes the lead, carrying forward the entire melody into a new realm, which the other instruments are induced into following. In such situations, an outstanding musician like Zohaib, trained for six generations, does not allow other musicians to experiment outside the parameters set by him, which he playfully redefines over and over again. At the height of the festivities, following his performance around midnight, Ram announces that the function is over and that people should go back home. The mood is high and everyone wants the show to go on, but Ram insists that he cannot allow that to happen. The temple administration is concerned that if the show goes on until much later, then the only voice resonating from the surroundings would be from this temple, and that's the sort of attention this community is not ready to attract towards itself as it stands right now.

SHRI KRISHNA JANMASHTAMI AT LAHORE

It is the holy month of Ramadan—a month of fasting that begins with sunrise and ends at sunset. Elaborate *iftar* (breaking of the fast) parties are arranged all over the country throughout the month. This is an iftar feast arranged at Neela Gumbad Valmiki Mandir. A Muslim maulvi, with his trimmed beard, ankle-length shalwar and a green prayer cap on his head, invites all the Muslims present at the temple to break their fast at the sound of the *maghrib* prayer. Dates, a favourite of the Prophet, are passed around at the breaking of the azaan.

A red carpet has been spread at the centre of the courtyard. The food, which includes dates, pakora, dhein phale and Rooh Afza milk, all popular iftar items, is placed here. A professional DJ, hired for the evening celebrations, sits in a corner. He has just turned off his music prior to the azaan, so as not to offend the Muslims present here as well as those living and working in the surrounding areas, where they form the majority of the population. It was these 'neighbours' who, in 1992, led the attack on this temple, just like the 'neighbours' and 'friends' who attacked members of 'other' religious communities in the frenzy of 1947.

There are a dozen chairs placed around the temple for senior and important guests. The rest sit on the carpet, the portico or any other place where they can find a seat. The pandit and his family, which includes his wife, his two sons, a daughter, and a daughter-in-law, all serve the fasting Muslims, while other non-Muslims wait. A Christian child, about twelve, picks up a steel glass from the sheet and helps himself to a glass of milk. The pandit, otherwise a composed host, comes rushing to him, snatching the glass away. 'These are for the Muslim brothers,' he shouts. There are about a hundred people in the temple at the moment, most of whom are Hindus and Christians, with only a handful of Muslims. There will be a langar later in the night for other communities. This will be the customary halwa puri and channa served on paper plates.

The date is 22 August 2011 and the occasion is a Hindu religious festival called Krishna Janmashtami. Shri Krishna is one of the most important deities of the Hindu pantheon, considered to be an incarnation of Lord Vishnu, one of the supreme gods of the Hindu trinity, which includes Shiva and Brahma. Krishna was born to Vasudev and Devaki after the death of their first seven children. Devaki's brother, Kamsa, was the king at that time. When he heard the prophecy that a boy would dethrone him, he killed all seven of his sister's male children. Krishna was the eighth child and was able to survive as he was sent away at the time of his birth.

Along with regular Hindu/Christian attendees, the pandit has also invited his Muslim 'friends'. As the festival has fallen in the holy month of Ramadan, he has arranged for a small iftar party. There is also a Christian representative

from a church and a Sikh representative. The message that
the pandit wants to give out is loud and clear. Hindus,
Muslims, Christians and Sikhs come together to celebrate
the birthday of Krishna.

* * *

'Living as a minority in Pakistan is tough,' says forty-five-
year-old Shazia Waleed, a Hindu convert to Islam, who is
now employed at an international non-profit organization
that works with minorities. She used to come to the temple
on special occasions with her father, a prominent Hindu
businessman from Lahore who continued living here
despite Partition. Her parents were murdered in 1981,
when a Muslim fanatic took it upon himself to 'purge' this
'holy land' of Hindu 'infidels'. Shazia, who was originally
Sandhya Gupta, converted to Islam to marry a Muslim man
in 1989, as the laws of the country demanded. According to
Islamic laws, a Muslim man is allowed to marry a Jew or
a Christian as they are regarded as followers of the book.
However in practice, this is hardly the case. Christian
girls are converted to Islam before a Muslim man can
marry them. It is never the other way around. According
to Al-Beruni's definition, even Hindus are followers of the
book and therefore a Muslim man is allowed to marry a
Hindu woman according to the religious laws. However, in
Pakistan, not many people endorse his point of view and
marrying Hindus therefore remains un-Islamic. Shazia
had no option but to convert. According to Shazia, despite
her conversion, she has always remained an outsider for
'original' Muslims. This phenomenon of 'original' Muslims
as opposed to those who have converted can also be seen in

the way castes have shaped up in post-Partition Pakistan. Untouchable Hindus who converted in 1947 are referred to as Deendars or Musalis to distinguish them, and are still treated as untouchables by the high-caste Muslims of the area. Converts from the higher castes became Sheikhs. However, importantly, the caste titles remain, to distinguish those who have converted recently from those who were 'original' Muslims.

'In my childhood, we used to celebrate festivals at our home, where we would invite our Muslim friends. Sometimes we would visit the temple in the morning to offer prayers,' says Shazia. However, after the death of her parents and her subsequent conversion, she stopped visiting the temple. 'One constantly needs to give the reassurance that one also belongs to the same society. This is done by using words like *Inshallah*, *Mashallah* or just calling up people on Eid or other occasions,' she adds. On every Muslim occasion, like Eid and Eid Milad-un-Nabi, the pandit arranges a special prayer in the temple and calls his Muslim 'friends'. He does so for Christian functions as well. On Hindu festivals, which are now regularly covered by the press, he asks his non-Hindu friends, primarily Muslims, to attend as well. The iftar ceremony at the temple, before the celebration of Krishna Janmashtami, is part of the reassurance that Shazia was talking about. The pandit particularly wants to assert his Pakistani nationalism, something that he feels strongly about after he became a victim of this Pakistani nationalism. During the riots following the destruction of the Babri Mosque, right-wing newspapers alleged that the pandit was an Indian agent and had fled to India, primarily due to his religious affiliations. Shazia recalls that her father had to go into hiding during the wars of 1965 and 1971 because of the backlash his religious identity was likely to bring at the time of heightened nationalism.

Now, in a post 9/11 world in which the Muslims believe that they have been pitted against the rest of the world, there are repeated incidents of churches and Christian organizations being attacked in Pakistan in retaliation for what a few fanatic Christians did in Europe or the US. The Two-Nation Theory and 'Pakistan for the Muslims of India' phenomena comes back often to haunt the non-Muslims of the country. As the country derives its national identity from a religious affiliation, the people of Pakistan end up believing that like Pakistan is for Muslims, there are other countries earmarked for the people of other religious groups as well. In a world view where no other ideology or identity is permitted to exist, India becomes a Hindu country and Europe and the US become Christian.

To an average Pakistani, the vague idea of a unified Muslim nationalism, which includes all the Muslims of the world, irrespective of national boundaries, still survives. So the struggle of Palestinians against Israel does not remain a nationalistic struggle but becomes a religious one, in which the Pakistani Muslims stand with their Palestinian Muslim 'brothers'. The same logic applies to the struggle of Kashmiris in India. Ascribing to this particular world view, a lot of people end up believing that similar to them, the Christians and Hindus of Pakistan also hold similar affinities with Christians and Hindus beyond Pakistan. In this environment, the non-Muslims of the country need to exhibit their loyalty towards Pakistan and their sympathies for the Muslim faith when they feel that the Muslims of the country are offended by the actions of Hindus or Christians outside the country. By bitter experience, they have learnt that without the reiteration of their loyalty, they would be regarded as 'unpatriotic' Pakistanis primarily due to their religious beliefs. So when a magazine in Denmark decides to publish a caricature of the Prophet, the Church of Pakistan becomes the first one to protest, with banners condemning the cartoons placed in all churches, because they know that they might otherwise be attacked for the actions of Christians in Denmark. During the hype leading up to cricket matches between India and Pakistan, mainstream news channels and papers cover stories of how Hindus and Sikhs of Pakistan are praying for the victory of Team Pakistan, astonishing the 'true' Pakistanis, who can only be Muslims. The pandit inviting his Muslim, Christian and Sikh friends for the Krishna Janmashtami, an event which would be covered by the local press, is a particular message that the pandit feels is important to give in this passionate environment of religious insecurities.

* * *

Sitting around the courtyard, the non-Muslims wait for the iftar party to finish. The women are dressed in colourful, elaborately decorated shalwar kameez. Their faces are covered with layers of foundation, which becomes particularly prominent under the blinding light of a camera flash. They wear gold jewellery around their necks and in their ears and noses. The majority of them have covered their heads, an act of modesty in the presence of men.

The men, besides Bhagat Advit Bhatti, are wearing dress pants or shalwar kameez. The pandit is wearing a kurta pajama, with the kurta just ending above his knees. Conventionally, kurtas end at the knee in Pakistan. The pajama is also tighter than how it is usually worn by Pakistani men. On regular days, one would spot Advit wearing a black, blue or a white shirt, but on special occasions, he prefers orange or purple. Krishna, his one-year-old grandson, is dressed up in a Gujarati-style orange kurta pajama, wearing several necklaces, bangles and a tiara on his head. Like the pandit, he is also dark-complexioned.

Krishna is inseparable from his twenty-year-old mother, who is married to the pandit's son. Every visitor is paying special attention to Krishna tonight, as he is playing the symbolic role of Krishna, the deity whose birthday is being celebrated. Susheela, one of the few better-off Hindus in the city, is serving Krishna candy, which he chews constantly. After a little while, she tries to pick him up, but he starts to cry and hugs his mother tightly. Both the women let out a hearty laugh. There is a cradle on the porch, which is usually inside the temple of Valmiki. This is the symbolic cradle of Krishna. His mother tries putting him there, but he refuses to leave her. 'Hold on to the child,' her mother-in-law recommends as she passes by. Krishna's mother obliges but is not happy with the situation. The pandit's wife, her mother-in-law, goes inside the temple and brings out a portrait of Lord Krishna, eating butter from a vessel, and places it on the cradle. There is an actual pot of butter next to the cradle, a favourite of the baby deity.

The prayers, which includes a traditional reading by the pandit from the holy books, followed by bhajans, start about an hour after the breaking of the fast. The Muslim and Christian guests are also invited to attend, along with members of the media.

In the humid month of August, this tiny room becomes suffocating. The pandit's wife goes around the room, putting a vertical line of vermillion on the foreheads of the attendees. Everyone sweats profusely as the pandit leads the prayers, chanting from the religious books. Not all the attendees can be catered to in this small room, so the elders and men stay outside. Musicians sit next to the pandit, under the pictures of the idols. After the prayers, they will play the bhajan.

Everyone is facing the wall, which holds several pictures of the deities; Hanuman, the monkey deity carrying an entire mountain in his hand while flying back to Lanka, Saraswati, the female deity of knowledge, music, the arts and science, clad in a white sari standing with her sitar, Laxmi, the spouse of Lord Vishnu, resting on a lotus flower, and a picture of Guru Nanak. Placed under them is a picture of Durga, sitting on a tiger. Nearby, a picture of a young, dark-blue Krishna playing the flute covered with garlands is the focus of attention tonight.

At the conclusion of the reading, the pandit places his book on the shelf on the adjacent wall and picks up the aarti, rotating it in a clockwise direction. The musicians start singing the bhajan. His wife takes some vermillion and puts it on the portrait of Lord Krishna. Baby Krishna starts crying at the sudden burst of noise in the room and his mother takes him out. The pandit hands over the platter to his wife and stands in a corner, clapping his hands and singing along, while his wife performs the aarti. The pandit asks other people to come forward and perform the aarti as well. Everyone obliges. At the end, his wife takes a bit of prasad and places it near the lips of Krishna in his portrait, as if she were feeding him. Stuck to the frame, the oily halwa slowly glides downwards, eventually falling to the base. She then offers prasad to everyone else.

The devotees are escorted into the courtyard after the prayers, which lasts about thirty minutes. The pandit brings out a cake, meant to be the birthday cake of Lord Krishna and places it on a side table. He asks his Muslim, Sikh and Christian friends to cut the cake with him. Holding one knife, all of them cut the cake, as the media photographers flash away. They pose for a little while, holding the knife at the request of a photographer who wants a better shot. Cutting a small piece of the cake, the pandit looks around for his grandson. He is in his mother's lap, sitting nearby. The pandit tries to feed him the cake but he turns away, still irritated by the loud sounds from a little while ago. Next, he offers it to his non-Hindu friends, deliberately slowing down for the media photographers to get the right shots, shots which will highlight the religious tolerance of the occasion. After the posing, his wife takes the knife from him and starts cutting the cake into several pieces. Children gather around the table in anticipation. Her son brings her paper plates. She puts small pieces on them and hands the plates over to each child. The cake is finished before the elders get a chance to taste it.

The DJ, who has been waiting patiently, firstly for the azaan and then for the bhajan, turns on the music. Sounds of the latest remixed Indian songs spread through the area. Heads pop out of small windows from accompanying buildings. Undeterred by the gaze, the pandit's wife lifts one of the tiny hands of baby Krishna and starts dancing to the music. Her daughter-in-law also starts to groove. But baby Krishna is more interesting in chewing his toffee. He tries to pull his hand away from his grandmother, but in vain.

He screeches as loudly as he can, forcing his grandmother to concede to his wishes. Leaving him, she continues to dance to the music. Other children join her, as women and girls around her clap and raise the momentum of the evening. Men, seated on the chairs, look with interest. She drags her daughter into the dancing circle. Susheela also joins the revelry. Taking out a handful of candies from a bag that she is carrying in one hand, she throws them in the air; within seconds, they scatter all over the floor and children scramble to pick up as many as their little hands can hold. The pandit's wife makes an attempt to pick up her grandchild again but he is still not in a good mood. He clings to his mother who is trying to get him to dance to the beat of the music but to no avail. His grandmother turns away, making an angry face.

A little girl comes to baby Krishna and gives him a toffee that she has picked up from the floor. The baby holds it and tries to remove the wrapper. His mother comes to his aid and hands him the open candy. He chews on it. The pandit's wife takes out a handful of butter from the vessel placed next to the cradle and tries feeding it to Krishna. The baby turns his head away, more interested in the chocolate toffee that he holds in his hand—baby Krishna's eating interests have evolved over the centuries. He prefers chocolate toffees to butter. The era of stealing butter as a prized treat is clearly over.

* * *

Whereas, for the most part of its history, the temple has been allowed to function without interference from the authorities, recently it has landed itself in a controversy.

'Ever since the celebrations at this temple have increased in fervour, the authorities want to take over the administration of the shrine,' says Bhagat Advit Bhatti.

The administration and the festivals at Krishna Mandir, the only other functional Hindu temple in the city, is managed by the Awqaf Department (non-Muslim), on behalf of the government. The Awqaf Department was created during the tenure of General Ayub Khan in 1959, to control, administer and collect revenues from shrines all over the country. This temple was ignored for a long time because nothing was happening here until recently. Now that the celebrations have been revived, they want to control it like they control other shrines.

The pandit, on the other hand, feels that they are the rightful heirs of the temple and believes that they should be responsible for the administration here. His family, as well as others, has been affiliated with the governing of the temple for generations. The pandit says that he is now being 'harassed' and 'threatened' by the authorities to give away control of the temple, a fight that he is determined to win.

'There is vast property connected with the temple, which has belonged to us for generations,' he explains. 'These are shops and residential houses around the temple. After the creation of Pakistan, our elders were approached by officials to contribute financially to the newly formed government (and reinforce their loyalty). My father, who was in charge of the temple at that time, explained that they had nothing but the property of the temple, which was owned by the community collectively. With no other option, they told the authorities that they can have control over the shops outside of the temple and collect revenue from there, as a contribution of the Valmikis to the Jinnah fund (which was the name of the fund for which money was being asked),' explains Bhagat Advit. Ever since then, the control of that property has remained with the authorities. Even though the Jinnah fund no longer exists, the authorities still collect the revenues from the shops and the houses, now several thousands of rupees given the prime location of the property, while the Hindu community continues to live in poverty.

The pandit explains that there is a growing awareness in the community of being wronged and there is a growing realization that the revenues from the property should come to them, but he also knows that the delicate balance they have established in this hostile atmosphere for such a long time has the potential to be ruptured if they fight for their rights. 'We don't even know how much money they collect from our properties. But now, they want to wrest the control of this temple also from us. That is something I am not willing to concede. I will fight back as much as I can.'

CHRISTIAN

A Pilgrimage to Maryabad

Shahbaz Masih, eighteen, tucks away a couple of T-shirts in his worn-out backpack along with a small scarf for his head to protect him from the heat on the way. He has been to Maryamabad twice before but this time he wants it to be an experience. This time, he wants to perform his penitence, which he believes will result in his salvation. Three weeks ago, when he floated the idea to his family, they were glad he had finally decided to undertake this difficult journey. He was born a Christian and was baptized at the Saint James Church, Okara when he was fourteen. Every Christian-born child has to go through this rite, which marks an initiation into formal Christianity. Now that he has decided to undertake this journey of more than 150 km on a cycle, his family and peers feel that he will finally be initiated into adulthood. He has seen his cousins and friends do it for years and feels that the time has come for him to complete this rite of passage.

He visits a local tailor, and places an order for a few orange T-shirts on the backs of which would be embroidered 'I love Mother Mary' in gold thread. His entire group will wear this same shirt. On 7 September 2011, he, along with twenty-five other friends, leave for Maryamabad. They plan to cover the journey in two days and two nights. On the way, the boys stop occasionally under the shade of the roadside trees. Several cars slow down to look at this group all dressed in a uniform heading on a pilgrimage that most people in the country are unaware of. They will spend the night in Lahore, about 120 km from Okara and head to Maryamabad the next day. The festival begins on 9 September and will continue till the 11th.

* * *

A hundred kilometres away, Shahzad is also preparing for the same pilgrimage. He is a rickshaw driver in Faisalabad. With the help of a Christian friend who works at a local printing press, he has prepared a flex poster that he is putting up at the back of his blue rickshaw. It has a picture of Mother Mary holding baby Christ in her hands and looking at him lovingly. Shahzad is to be accompanied by five other people: two nephews, aged twelve and fourteen, and three cousins. He borrows a video camera from another friend, who works at a movie shop. Shahzad plans to record his experiences this year. This is not his first pilgrimage, so he knows that he also needs to carry blankets and sheets along. They will place them on the floor, around the church, wherever they find a place. Food will not be an issue, as there will be devotees distributing free food at the shrine. Besides, there will be many stalls.

* * *

The Maryabad (a vernacular version of Maryamabad) *yatra* (pilgrimage) has, in the past twenty years, become one of the largest Catholic festivals in the country. About an hour's journey from Sheikhupura, the neighbouring city of Lahore, this small village has been christened Maryamabad, where Maryam (Mother Mary) abides.

'A little before Partition, a couple of Christian men saw Mother Mary appear on that mound, situated next to the church,' says thirty-six-year-old Father Mushtaq, a priest from Narowal who has been appointed here by the Catholic Church to look after the administration of the festival. He is seated in his office inside the shrine. 'In the eighties, there was another report of a few children seeing the Mother at that particular spot again. There have been numerous other reports of saints sighted here. Every year on the second day, when the Bishop Sahib comes from Lahore to attend the ceremony, people are welcomed on the stage to report miracles that they have experienced here. Mothers bring their sick children and children their sick parents, and all are cured. There is a small spring just behind the mound. That water is considered holy and consumed by people for salvation,' he adds.

* * *

Thousands of people descend upon this small village every year in September and pay tribute to Mother Mary. They live in makeshift tents in and around the church, or out in the open. The Catholic Church looks after the arrangements. The government assists them with security.

The mound of Mother Mary, made out of stone, is the main religious attraction here. The entire complex is surrounded by high walls, covered by iron spikes and manned by police officials. There is only one entrance into this shrine and that is manned by a police official with a metal detector. These security arrangements are very different from what one is likely to expect at a Hindu temple or their religious festivals, where there is either no security at all or just a few police officials at the gate, reluctantly making inquiries from the attending pilgrims. Here, however, there is a sense of urgency as if the shrine is under some kind of immediate threat.

This is primarily because unlike the Hindus, the Christian community has a formidable presence in the Punjab. This means that the political parties and leaders also have to cater to their interests, unlike the Hindus, who are a smaller community in the Punjab and can therefore be ignored. The Christians are represented through powerful establishments like the churches and various other organizations, including schools, colleges and hospitals, which have been set up by Christian missionaries. Given the stake that Christians have in the politics and economics of the country, they cannot be as easily ignored as the Hindus are. Even though according to the census of 1998, the Hindu minority is the largest minority in the country, with Christians in the second place, most of the Hindus are scattered in Sindh, Baluchistan and Khyber Pakhtunkhwa, with only a few in Punjab. The Christians, on the other hand, have an overwhelming majority in the Punjab (among the minorities) and are visible in the social fabric, something that the Hindus are not. There are Christian communities in all the major cities and villages of the country, serving as an important vote bank. This perception of a visible Christian presence is also supplemented by huge colonial-era churches, still functional, and several schools, colleges and hospitals still run by Christian missionaries and set up before the creation of this Muslim state.

Hundreds of people stand in a long queue, waiting to get to the top of this mound, which is about 20 feet high. There is a statue of Mother Mary at the summit, her head covered in a white shawl holding baby Christ. Mother Mary was reported to have been sighted at this particular spot. There are several colourful shawls wrapped around her neck presented by devotees. A few light candles at the base of the statue. Holding both hands together they recite a silent prayer, before making way for the next person in the queue. A security guard struggles to keep the devotees in a uniform line. Eager to pay their respects, they gather in a horde around the statue. The guard, without touching the women, tries to escort them away. 'Sister, please move on,' he says in frustration.

A number of pilgrims who want to pay their tribute to the Mother but do not want to wait for hours in the line, stand at the base of this mound and pray from there. Smoke arises from the numerous candles that have been lit by them on the stones of the mound. Red rose petals are spread all over. Using lit candles, people light incense, which they then stick in between the rocks.

Both Masih and Shahzad seek the blessings of the Mother upon their arrival. Exhausted by his long journey, Masih prays from the base. Shahzad instead stands in the line to get to the top. Masih picks up an unlit candle from the mound and lights it with a lit one. Putting it in place, he holds his hands and prays for his studies. He will be appearing for his matriculation examination in March the following year. He hopes his penitence will secure him good results and then, a good job.

A lot of pilgrims purposefully make the journey difficult, by either walking or cycling to the shrine. Some even decide to travel without shoes, to make the journey much more spiritually rewarding. It is believed that God will forgive their sins and fulfil their wishes if they do so. Devotees pour in from different corners of the country for this festival. The festival and the rituals are similar in many ways to the pilgrimage to the shrine of Durga during the festival of Navratri. In a similar vein, the devotees intend to make their journey arduous, walking in groups, chanting slogans in honour of the Mother and also wearing uniform clothes for identification. Writings on the clothes of the Christian pilgrims are dedicated to the Mother of God, often referred to as Mata, exactly how Goddess Durga is referred to by Hindu pilgrims, who also wear similar kinds of shirts and uniforms before undertaking the pilgrimage.

People walk from cities as far as Lahore (a distance of about 70 km), Gujranwala (100 km away), Sialkot (150 km away), Faisalabad (150 km away) and Sheikupura (20 km away). They do this in groups. One would assume that given the physical difficulties that entail the completion of this task, most of the pilgrims would be boys and young men. But while the majority of them are youngsters, there are also a considerable number of older men, children and women. Travelling from Lahore to Maryabad, as soon as one crosses the city of Sheikupura, several processions can be spotted on the way. Some are as big as fifty people, while others are as small as five people. Pilgrims are seen resting on the sides of the road, under the shade of trees. While some are asleep, others watch fellow devotees pass them by. Groups are seen sitting and sipping tea at roadside cafes and restaurants. To distinguish themselves, these groups wear shirts with Christian symbols or hold posters, crosses and other paraphernalia. Buses rented specially for this trip are decorated with posters of Mother Mary, Christ and the cross. They stop on the way as other pilgrims jump on the already crowded buses for a ride to the festival.

A few kilometres away from the shrine, a procession rests under a tree. A young boy, no older than fifteen, holds a big wooden cross, taller than him, resting it on his right shoulder. He is wearing a black T-shirt. A cross, attached to a silver chain, hangs from his neck. Another boy, about twelve years old, holds a poster which is nearly as high as him. The poster depicts Mary with a radiating heart at the centre of her chest. There is a knife which passes through it and a garland of pink roses around it. With one hand she points towards her heart and with the other, she holds flowers. This group of about thirty people is a combination of children, women, young and old.

* * *

Vendors start appearing about a kilometre before the shrine, selling religious paraphernalia. Small shawls to be wrapped around Mother Mary's statue are bought from here. These are blue, white, red, yellow and pink in colour and decorated with a golden border. The shawls are hung on a stick shaped like a cross. Just like Durga Mata is offered chunris bought from in and around the shrine, Mother Mary is offered these shawls as a gift from the visiting devotees.

Christianity as a mainstream religion spread throughout South Asia during the British colonial era. A lot of converts formerly belonged to one of the several religions practised here, of which Hinduism was and remains the most dominant. Inspired by the egalitarian principles of Christianity and looking for an escape from the caste hierarchy of Hinduism, in which the untouchables are on the lowest rung, a lot of them took up the new religion. However, despite conversion, a sudden rupture from former religious beliefs, practices and traditions is impossible and therefore, like Islam before it, Christianity when adopted was also given a Hindu interpretation, of which the pilgrimage to Maryabad is just one example. Mother Mary takes the place of Mata Durga and the shawl replaces the chunri. The devotees believe that by undertaking this difficult journey to the shrine of Mother they would be offering their penance, similar to how Hindu devotees believe that by travelling to the shrine of Durga Mata all their wishes would come true. This shrine of Maryabad is a unique Christian temple which celebrates the amalgamation of Hindu religious traditions with a Christian flavour. It is also for this particular reason that educated Christians look down upon this shrine and the rituals around it, terming it as corruption of original Christianity.

Even though a lot of untouchable Hindus initially converted to avoid the stigma associated with their caste, it nonetheless continued to haunt them even after conversion. For the high-caste Muslims, these low-caste Christians remained untouchables, referred derogatorily to as *chuhras*. Islamic teachings allow Muslims to eat and intermingle with Christians, but in practice, a lot of Muslims continue treating these converts as low-caste, untouchable Hindus. Even in prominent cities like Lahore, several Muslims refuse to eat with Christians and consider utensils used by them to be impure. Ironically, it was the Muslims who were treated as untouchables by high caste-Hindus in the old days. In upholding this concept of untouchability, the Muslims of Pakistan are practising an Islam tainted with the flavour of the worst of Hinduism.

So even though this attitude of impurity originally started with low-caste Hindu converts to Christianity, it soon started dominating the nature of interaction with all Christians, even those who belonged to the former higher-castes of Hinduism. This came about when religious identities became a symbol of untouchability in a post-Partition environment, as opposed to castes earlier. In a Pakistan for Muslims, there was no basis for discrimination based on castes because of the propaganda against it during the Pakistan movement and instead religious identities became the focus. Untouchability not only stuck with low-caste Hindu converts but was also extended to former higher-caste Hindu converts to Christianity. The term 'Christian', instead of remaining a religious distinction, is now referred to as something akin to a caste. The derogatory word 'chuhra' is used to refer to not only a low-caste Christian but any Christian, irrespective of caste and socio-economic status. It is interesting to note that Europeans of Christian origin are not given this title. A lot of low-end hotels and restaurants not only in rural areas but even in metropolitan cities like Lahore have separate utensils for Christians. A common practice is for Christians to announce their 'caste' before eating at a small restaurant so that the owner takes the necessary precautions to avoid embarrassment later.

One of the most brutal cases of religious discrimination to come to light in recent years is the case of Aasia Bibi, a forty-year-old Christian woman, who belongs to a small village called Itanwali, near the historical city of Nankana Sahib, associated with the birth of the founder of the Sikh religion, Guru Nanak. This case received international coverage after the former Governor of Punjab, Salman Taseer, came out in support of this woman and was later killed for his pains. Only a few months later, Federal Minister for Minorities Shahbaz Bhatti, a Catholic Christian himself, was also assassinated, allegedly for the same reason.

The issue began when Aasia Bibi was working in the fields along with her Muslim colleagues on a hot summer day. Feeling thirsty, she approached the water pot but found that there was no water in it. She instead had water from a 'Muslim' vessel placed next to the 'Christian' vessel which she had earlier found empty. Having made impure the 'Muslim' vessel, her colleagues got into an argument with her, which is said to have provoked Aasia Bibi to use derogatory remarks against the Prophet of Islam, blasphemy according to the laws of Pakistan and punishable by death. Later when Taseer and Bhatti came to her rescue and asked for her acquittal on the basis of Presidential pardon, they were also labelled as blasphemers by the conservative elements of the society, as they were supporting a blasphemer, eventually resulting in their assassination. Conservative sections of society want to uphold the capital punishment for Aasia Bibi while the liberal section has been silenced after the death of two of their proponents. The irony is that in upholding the case of blasphemy against Aasia Bibi, the conservatives are using the basis of purity and impurity, a concept that they have borrowed from the Hindu caste structure. The cause of Pakistan was meant to be a departure from these abhorrent Hindu traditions, something that the Muslim conservatives repeat often, but in practice they are perpetuating a concept very Hindu in its origin but now given the garb of Islamic fundamentalism.

Colonel Chaudary, a high-caste Christian who resides in Lahore, served in the Pakistani army for thirty years and retired as a colonel about a decade ago. He recalls that once there were a few Muslim labourers employed in his house while he was still in the army, working on some structural renovation. When offered food by the Colonel's cook, they refused to have it because of the impurity associated with eating at a Christian's house.

Similarly, Dr Yousuf John, a politician and a social worker based in Lahore, recalls that when he was in school, he was instructed by his teachers and fellow students to not put his mouth to the only tap in the school to drink water, as was the practice, but instead use his hands to drink the water. This was because it was believed if he touched the tap with his lips like all the other Muslim students do, the water would become impure for the rest of the students. Even though the concept enraged John, he had no option but to concede. 'I was the only Christian student in the school, you see. They would have beaten me up had I objected. Even today when I go to a restaurant or a hotel and they tell me that they don't serve Christians I walk out instead of arguing with them. Issues get bigger if you argue back. Look at the issue of Aasia Bibi. The blasphemy law is a like a sword of Damocles over our necks. Right now, if you walk out of this house and just jokingly announce that Dr Yousuf John has committed blasphemy, my entire mohalla will come to kill me, without thinking twice about it. When it comes to matters of religion, they would not think about the good times we have shared together or the sort of person I am. All senses would be shut,' says John.

* * *

There are beggars on the road, counting on the generosity of the arriving pilgrims. A man wearing a cap displays crosses in black threads, hung on another cross-shaped stand. Crosses on necklaces are popular with Catholic Christians. One can distinguish a Catholic from a Protestant by these. Protestants refrain from wearing such symbols. Behind him, an old man sells plum and phalsa juice on a cart. Several arriving visitors throng to him. Near him, another one sells bangles and paranthas.

Twin minarets, about a hundred feet high, greet the visitors from far away. There is a wooden pillar, about 5 feet high, on each of them. It is covered with shawls bought from vendors around the shrine. Iron bars are attached to the minaret, which serve as a ladder to the top. Only one person can use them at a given time. So each pilgrim makes his/her way to the top, ties the shawl and comes back while the next one waits.

Two men stand on top of the minarets helping other devotees climb the last steps and then help them tie the shawls. There is a large gathering of people at the base, watching young boys undertake this adventure. Word spreads that a woman is undertaking the task. A young girl, wearing a black shalwar kameez, has made her way half way up the minaret. The crowd at the foot of the mound increases. The two volunteers standing at the top of the minarets look down at her. As she edges towards the top, one of them extends a hand which she takes and is pulled up with a jerk. The crowd at the base rejoices at her accomplishment. Not being allowed to bask in her moment of glory for very long, she hurriedly ties the pink shawl around the wooden pillar and starts to come down. After having safely descended, she does not wait for people to congratulate her and instead disappears into the crowd as quickly as she had come into the limelight.

The church is across the road. The minarets are on the edge of a huge, vacant ground. There are a few houses on the other side, part of Maryabad village, with a population of a few thousand people, mostly Christians.

Thousands of tents have been set up at the empty ground. This is a temporary city of tents, which has come into existence in a matter of hours, and will disappear just as quickly. Temporary restaurants have been set up, cooking and serving all sorts of traditional eatables with tables and chairs placed in front of them for the clients.

Young boys have been employed by the owners to urge passersby to try the food from their tent. There are others who have decorated sweetmeats in front of them. They fan it constantly to make sure that flies do not rest on them. A vendor pours out a liquid from a dirty yellow bag into a big black cauldron. He is preparing the traditional sweet, jalebi. A young kid stands and watches the procedure, as the man moves the cloth in a circle, forming round shapes on the boiling oil. Finished, he yells at the boy to run away, scaring him with his Peshawari *chappal* that he has placed next to him. The boy backs off a little bit, but stops again to look at the treat. Under the minarets, the Bible Organization has set up its stalls. Two nuns, dressed in white gowns and headscarves, are standing behind the counter. They are wearing a cross around their necks. Copies of the Bible in Urdu, English and Punjabi have been laid on the tables. Next to them, another Christian organization is selling cassettes of devotional music. There are pictures of Mother Mary on the cover. Some portray the artists as well. There is a cassette with a picture of Noor Jehan, the legendary Pakistani singer in a green sari. There is a cross on the top and the title reads

'Jesus, the beautiful name' in Urdu. Nearby is a cassette with the title, 'I love you Jesus'. A picture of Christ with long brown hair and a beard and blue eyes is depicted underneath it. Next to this stall is another vendor, selling posters of Mother Mary and Christ. They are a popular feature of Christian, especially Catholic, houses. Many posters depict Jesus with his heart radiating eternal love. There is another picture of Christ shepherding his flock of sheep. Yet another poster shows scenes from the Sermon on the Mount.

Outside the camped city, sitting under the sun of the roadside village, is a man offering permanent tattoos for a mere twenty-five rupees. There is a board next to him, giving his customers the option to choose from several different designs, including a peacock, a lion, a bird and several fonts of names. The peacock and the lion, being slightly more complicated, cost forty rupees each. The tattoo artist sits on a small mat. His studio consists of a little table placed in front of him. His gadget, a gun with which he makes the tattoo, is placed on it. The table is decorated with colourful paints and bright pictures, akin to truck art, a characteristic form of art practised in Pakistan. Next to him another vendor sitting on a floor mat has laid out a number of cards in front of him. There is a caged parrot next to him. For twenty rupees he offers to foretell the future. This is done by releasing the parrot from the cage, which then picks out a card on behalf of the customer. The card contains one's 'hidden' destiny.

At the edge of the ground, a dhol-wala starts to play. A boy wearing a white T-shirt jumps into the middle of the circle that has formed around the dhol-wala and starts to dance provocatively. No one seems to mind his dance moves, as the circle is exclusively male. He pulls in a friend, who hesitates for a little while but then starts to respond to the provocative dance moves. In a strictly segregated society, such display of sexual innuendo to members of the same sex does not necessarily mean a sexual preference.

A group of pilgrims has just arrived. They walk in a line towards the entrance of the shrine, clapping their hands on the top of their heads singing 'Hallelujah'. This is a group of young men in their early twenties. All of them are wearing backpacks. Continuing to sing, they stand in the long queue of more than a hundred people who are all waiting to enter the shrine. A few of the devotees already standing in the queue start singing along with them. A police official, who is frisking everyone at the entrance, looks at them briefly before resuming his work. There is a separate line for women. After passing through this security check, pilgrims have to pass through a metal detector before they are finally allowed inside the shrine.

* * *

Masih's group has made their camp next to the church. They will stay here for three days after which they will return on bicycles. Before sleeping for a little while after lighting the candle, Masih tends to the blisters that have developed on his feet after hours of cycling. All of them had decided to cycle without shoes and instead wore two sets of socks. After applying Vaseline on his feet, he offers it to the others but they refuse, amused at the idea of tending to their blisters. Ignoring their jibes, Masih places his bag underneath his head and lies on the floor. He takes off the scarf from his head and puts it on his face, drifting into deep slumber amidst the festivities.

* * *

'The pilgrimage started in the initial years of Pakistan. In the early days, people used to come from the neighbouring villages, which eventually became districts. Gradually the popularity of the shrine spread to every nook and corner of the country and now there are people pouring in from as far as Karachi and Quetta. 2011 marks the sixty-second year of its celebration,' says Father Mushtaq. 'There will be a mound wherever there is a Christian parish (community). Mounds signify proximity with God. These devotees light candles, which signify the presence of our Lord, Jesus Christ. We believe that he exists wherever there is light.'

Whereas there are hundreds if not thousands of mounds dedicated to Mother Mary all across the country, this one at Maryabad has become particularly significant due to the story of Mother Mary being sighted here. The mound has become all the more sacred because of that image. In a region where Hindus have dedicated temples to the presence of deities in particular localities, Muslim Sufi shrines have sprung up around the grave of a saint and Sikh gurdwaras have been raised to commemorate a historical incident from the life of a guru, Christianity is devoid of any such physical connection with the saints or deity. This shrine whose popularity is based on the physical presence of Mother Mary provides an authentication to Christians, which it seems all religious traditions of South Asia demand. Because of its association with the colonial past, Christianity is increasingly viewed as a foreign import. Challenging that perception, this shrine localizes the religion, like Islam was prior to it. It is perhaps because of this authentication that this shrine has become such a major centre of pilgrimage over the years, providing historical and geographic sanction to the Christian community, which they lacked compared to the other religious traditions.

Leaning back in his chair, Father Mushtaq shuts the windows of his office to minimize the sound of loud devotional songs that wafts in from the outside. Wearing a white robe, which signifies that he is a member of the priesthood, he is sitting across the table where he has laid down the plan for the event. Tomorrow (10 September) is the most important day as that is when the bishop arrives. The day after that, pilgrims will leave. A Punjabi devotional song plays on repeat, as Father Mushtaq tries to explain the religious aspect of the festival. The tune comes from the popular folk song *Jugni*, sung recently by Arif Lohar and Meesha Shafi on the music show, Coke Studio.

'There was a time when famous singers like Madam Noor Jahan and Arif Lohar used to sing and record Christian gospels,' Father changes the topic realizing that it would be difficult to explain theology in such noise. 'These recordings are still available. This particular *Jugni* is not sung by Arif Lohar, however,' he jokes. 'The trend of popular singers and musicians singing devotional Christian songs is now on the ebb,' he adds. Before the years of Islamization unleashed by the Islamist military dictator Zia-ul-Haq during the 1980s, it was common enough for popular artists to sing Christian devotional music, which obviously has a huge market. However, now that the society has become so polarized given the Islamization of the young educated lot of the country, it is no longer safe for a mainstream artist to sing for non-Muslim communities. Such syncretism is likely to create doubts about their Muslim identity, which has become increasingly insecure in a post 9/11 world. Father Mushtaq knows that he is talking about a time which is no longer imaginable, an era which has receded to the periphery and only alive in the oral histories of the people who were present in the 1960s and 1970s, believed to be the secular years of the country.

His office is a small room in a single-storey building next to the mound. A stage has been set up near it, but it is empty at the moment. Two large speakers blasting music flank it. Other rooms in the building have been occupied by the rest of the members of the clergy. There is a security guard outside the building, making sure that no one enters without permission.

Thousands of pilgrims are inside the complex at the moment, with a greater number of people outside. There is a small courtyard in front of the stage, occupied by pilgrims. A few of them have laid out their blankets next to the walls of the church, the shadow of the building providing them shade. Lying on the floor, some of them rest while others socialize. A couple of the older ones are offering prayers on a rosary. This is considered an auspicious time to perform the rosary in the name of Mother Mary. Others are reading the Bible, or simply observing their surroundings. Having bought cheap toys from the stalls outside, children are busy playing with them. Youngsters, most of whom have made this journey by foot or cycle, stick to the group they have travelled with. In their clusters, they interact with other pilgrims — attempting specifically to flirt with young girls who have come with their families. There is a tube well behind the church, where a few boys are bathing.

The church is near the stage. It is a modest building made of red bricks and supported by white pillars. There are three entrances to the church—one towards the side of the offices, another opening from the side of the stage and the third one facing the tube well. Several slippers and shoes are gathered at the entrances. Usually churches do not require visitors to take off their shoes; however, a few people have done so, perhaps following a tradition borrowed from South Asian culture. A Muslim, Hindu or Sikh devotee is expected to take off his/her shoes while entering a shrine. But Christians, on the other hand, are usually not supposed to take off their shoes. However, here it seems that, inspired by the South Asian traditions, a few Christians have taken up the practice. A few other attendees have entered without abiding by this custom. The altar is at one end of the building behind which there are pictures and statues of Mother Mary, Jesus Christ and other saints. Unlike the Protestants, Catholics have several statues inside their churches. The Catholics also hold Mother Mary in high regard. On the other hand, the Protestants, while revering her, do not give her the same sort of religious significance. The temperature inside the church is cooler than the courtyard outside. The floor is made of chips. Several attendees sleep on it with their faces covered, resting their heads on their hands or clothes. A middle-aged woman, standing at the altar with her head covered, turns around after her prayer. Annoyed by so many people walking into the church with their shoes on, she yells at them to take them off. A few oblige, while others ignore her. Clearly irritated, she walks away, screaming about the lack of respect youngsters have nowadays.

* * *

Nasreen, fifty-four, is cutting vegetables in one of the many tents that have been raised behind the church. This is an open place with no construction. Recently a wall has been raised around this space to make it part of the complex and to also make it secure at a time when religious minorities have come under threat because of a rise in Islamic fundamentalism in Pakistani society. Police officials are spread all around this boundary to add to the security. Earlier it was an open area, allowing people to come in from here as well. With a mud track in the middle, this empty space is divided into two parts, one where there are tents and other where there are hundreds of eucalyptus trees planted in line next to each other. These are lucrative trees to plant, as they sell at high prices because of their demand in the paper and construction industry. The trees and the grass make this spot an ideal resting place for the pilgrims. Some have spread out a shawl, which would serve as bedding for the night.

Next to Nasreen, a few men and women are sitting on the floor, either cutting vegetables or taking a nap. One can smell food being cooked in the other part of the tent. Nasreen, a resident of Shahdara in Lahore, was not planning to come to the pilgrimage this year. She is a housewife and has three sons. Although she is a regular pilgrim, this year she had decided to skip it because of her poor health.

'Mother Mary had other plans for me,' she says. 'In the morning today, my sons left the house with a group of boys to walk to the shrine. After a few hours, I received a call from my nephew, who was also travelling with them, informing me that my youngest son was missing. Somehow, he got separated from the group and then got lost. I felt as if someone had pulled away the ground from beneath my feet. In that instant, without even changing or washing my face, I left home and embarked on a bus for Maryabad. On the way I kept on praying to Mother Mary on the rosary,' says an exhausted Nasreen. 'When I got here, my son was already at the church.' Pausing to flash a smile of conviction, she adds, 'It was a miracle of Mother Mary.'

Offering prayers on the beads of a rosary is significant in the Catholic doctrine. There are set prayers, which are recited on the rosary in praise of Mother Mary. Over the centuries, several popes have encouraged this practice. The rosary is seen as a symbol of the Catholic faith. Most of the members of the clergy are sporting one, either tucked in their belts or hung around their necks like a necklace. Some hold it in their hands. During the festival of Mother Mary, therefore, a lot of devotees spend extra time on their rosaries. This tradition is not popular with the Protestants.

Inspired by Nasreen's story, Aman, who had hitherto been lying on a quilt nearby, sits up eager to share his miracle. 'Two years ago, the administration caught me smoking inside the compound after which they locked me in a room. For two days, they did not serve me any food or water. I felt like I was dying. Just when I had given up hope, Mother Mary appeared. There was a halo around her head and her entire body radiated with light. She was covered in a white shawl. She came to me and placed a hand on my head. She told me to stop worrying and that everything would be all right. Just then someone opened the door and I was set free. It was a miracle.' Aman says he is thirty-five, but looks older. His unshaven beard is greying, but he has dyed his thick moustache black. He is balding and speaks slowly, as if intoxicated. There are dark circles underneath his eyes and it looks as if he is a hash addict. Maybe the authorities caught him smoking hash. There will be more stories of miracles shared tomorrow when the bishop arrives.

A couple of cauldrons are being cooked in the other section. A man, only wearing a shalwar, stands near one of the cauldrons mixing the ingredients with a long handle. 'That is *haleem* (a traditional dish, a mixture of several lentils and cooked for several hours over slow fire). It is being cooked since last night. It is almost ready now,' says a man standing next to him as he monitors its progress. His cotton shalwar kameez is sweaty.

His name is Sabar Elahi, a sixty-two-year-old entrepreneur from Shahdara, Lahore. He runs a hotel on the main road, right after the Ravi Bridge crossing. 'I have already given away thirty-five cauldrons of food this year in the name of Mother Mary, which has cost me somewhere around 1,00,000 rupees,' he says. Elahi has been coming here for the past thirty years, always bringing food with him to be distributed to the people. Nihari (another traditional dish made out of chicken and meat) is being cooked in the other cauldron. The cook making the haleem moves over to that cauldron as Elahi takes an inspection round, his hands held behind his back in a show of authority. Nasreen walks in holding a silver utensil in one hand. She is done with her cutting, volunteering for the service of the community. Elahi takes it from her and hands it over to another man, who comes running in from one side of the tent, where he was sitting in a shalwar and a vest amidst a group of devotees.

'In the morning, we gave halwa puri. Tomorrow we will make *bhog*,' he says. 'Giving in the name of religion adds blessings to your work. My work has prospered since I have started giving free food here.'

Palm Sunday at Sacred Heart Cathedral, Lahore

It is 7 a.m. on a Sunday morning. The date is 1 April 2012. Mall Road, one of the busiest boulevards in the city, is deserted. A few motorcycles race through, driven by boys wearing white cricket kits and carrying bats and wickets. All the grounds around the city will be occupied today, some even hosting more than one cricket match at a time—a usual Sunday feature.

A drive along the road is a journey through the colonial era. The Lahore High Court, combining European and Eastern architectural techniques, stands close to the Panorama Market. Facing it, the Lahore Cathedral built in the late nineteenth century is a model of the Gothic architectural tradition. A headless statue of the Hindu God Shiva sits alone in the garden of the Lahore Museum, waiting for visitors who will soon throng the building. Waiters of the accompanying restaurants clean tables and remove garbage. Two female students sit on the footpath next to the church, making sketches of the historic structure. One of them is wearing a headscarf, while the other isn't. These are students of the National College of Arts (NCA), situated next to the museum, another institution established during the colonial era. Facing it is the University of Punjab (old campus), the most prestigious university of its time. A black statue of Alfred Woolner, the vice-chancellor of the university in the pre-Partition days, stands outside the university perched on a platform, defying the iconoclastic streak of the country which emerged post 1947. It is one of the few statues of pre-Partition Lahore that has survived.

The Sacred Heart Cathedral, head of the Roman Catholic Church, Lahore diocese, is off the main road, near the Regale Chowk. A diocese is an area under the supervision of a bishop. Masjid Shuhad, a small white structure with an open courtyard, stands at this junction. Despite its small size, the mosque is teeming with pilgrims on Friday with mats spread on the accompanying road to cater to the hundreds of men who come here from several neighbouring offices. Today, the mosque is empty; a young boy, wearing a white shalwar kameez and a Muslim-skull cap, sweeps the marble floor of the mosque. In a tea stall next to it, chairs and the tables have been set up on the footpath, where a police official sits on one of the chairs ordering tea from a teenage waiter, who rushes back into the shop. Two day-labourers who appear intimidated by the sight of the police official sip their teas at an adjoining table.

A motorcycle turns from the mosque heading towards the hotel. It is a young Christian family, creatively balanced on a single bike: the father driving with his wife sitting behind him, her legs clamped together on the left side of the bike in a sign of modesty, holding an infant and the other two children, a boy and girl sitting in the front, on the petrol tank. Another bike soon follows it, with just a young couple on it. The girl hugs the boy tightly, a public display of affection that only Christians dare to exhibit in these heightened days of Islamization. A family crosses the road on foot: an old man, in his sixties, wearing a white shalwar kameez, followed by his wife and four teenage daughters, all wearing glittery clothes and lots of make-up. His youngest child, his only son of about eleven years, clings to his father's finger. Along with the young cricketers, these Christian families are the only travellers on this Sunday morning heading towards the church for the celebration of Palm Sunday.

* * *

Sacred Heart Cathedral is surrounded by a huge barbwired wall. The massive gates have protruding spikes on them. There are several entrances, all of which, except for one, are closed today. There are two security men at the gate, dressed in a navy blue uniform. They monitor the visitors entering the complex closely, waving at those they recognize from earlier gatherings, stopping those who don't look Christian enough. Checking their names on the identity card, they can tell if a person is a Christian or not. Unknown Muslims are not allowed inside the church as a security precaution. There is a long passage from the gate to the church. At the far end, another security guard directs the visitors to take their bikes and cars behind the building, which is the bishop's house. A few oblige readily, while others argue. This space would be used for the Palm Sunday procession. The bishop's house is a double-storey building with several rooms for different official purposes. A small mound hosting a statue of Mother Mary on the top stands next to the building. An ancient banyan tree, with its rope-like branches hanging towards the ground, stands next to the mound. The tree has acquired spiritual significance in all the major religions of South Asia, including Sufi Islam, Hinduism and Buddhism. There is an open ground next to the tree, which can accommodate hundreds of people at one time. Facing the ground, adjacent to the bishop's house, is the residency of the sisters of the church.

The church is next to the sisters' hostel. It is a huge structure. The building was consecrated in 1907. Its architectural tradition follows that of the Roman Byzantine Empire, with several spike-like towers pointing towards the sky. There is a bell on one of them to signal the time of prayer. Earlier used to gather people, the bell now plays a symbolic role. There is a dome on the top with white crosses around it. A small water fountain is situated at the entrance, but it has not seen water for years. Next to the church, separated by a wall, is the Sacred Heart Cathedral School. This is one of the leading schools in the city, run by the church.

* * *

Modern education in Pakistan was established during the colonial era, particularly by Christian missionaries. Most of these institutes were set up and maintained by them. St Anthony's, St Andrew's, the Convent of Jesus and Mary, all run by Christian missionaries, were the leading schools of their times. This is also true for colleges, several of which were set up by the church. One of the leading colleges in the city of Lahore, Forman Christian College (FC College) was one of the first English-medium institutes to be set up here, during the latter half of the nineteenth century. However, during the socialist stint of Zulfiqar Ali Bhutto in the 1970s, almost all of these schools and colleges were nationalized, including FC College. Prior to that, these missionary-run institutes were the hallmark of quality education in the country, producing the leading politicians, scientists and sports personalities of their time. However, after the state took over, they became victims of bureaucratic inefficiency and over the years lost their edge. To fill the vacuum, several private-run schools and colleges sprung up during the 1980s and continue to do so, providing quality education but at exorbitant prices. Before them, quality education through missionary schools and colleges was much cheaper, therefore allowing for economically weaker students to also obtain high-standard education. These missionary institutions allowed for various economic classes to intermingle within the premises, a utopia that looks all the more remote now in an increasingly economically segregated Pakistan.

In the recent years however, particularly during the era of General Pervez Musharraf, a number of these government-run schools were de-nationalized and are now once again attempting to stand on their feet. FC College is one such story. A highly-respected college till the 1970s, it saw a major downfall after nationalization. However, now that it has been de-nationalized again and is being run by Christian missionaries, it is once again attempting to reclaim its erstwhile fame. Forty-four-year-old Peeda James, head of the Protestant Education Board in Pakistan, has played a pivotal role in negotiating with the government during the process of de-nationalization. 'It is a difficult process,' she recalls. 'Most of the time, the teachers inducted by the government would physically attack us. They had gotten too used to loitering around, not coming to school and not teaching. However, back under the control of the missionaries, we expected them to work which would bother them. A lot of times they would also brainwash the students, telling them we want to teach them about Christianity and take them away from Islamic teachings and students would then join the protesting teachers. De-nationalization has really been a tough job but it is far from over. Roughly speaking, we have only gotten 40 per cent of our schools and colleges back and our demand is that we should get back all of them. This will take some time.'

Besides the impact on quality education, the nationalization of missionary and Church-run schools have also had other effects on the fabric of Pakistani society. Several European nuns used to teach in the schools and Christian and Hindu boys and girls would also study at these schools along with Muslim students. This was a truly multi-religious environment, thereby fostering a society with greater religious tolerance. The loss of these schools and colleges has not only meant the loss of quality educational institutions, but also of that multi-religious tolerant society. The elite schools which followed the missionary schools remain dominated by Muslim teachers and students who are a product of the Islamization that Pakistani society went through during the 1980s under General Zia-ul-Haq. Since most of these students and teachers live in a religiously isolated atmosphere with minimum interaction with other religious communities, their understanding of the religions of non-Muslims is shaped by stereotypes and generalizations. This religious reductionism condones acts of violence against religious minorities as non-Muslims, for the majority of the population in this isolated environment remain an abstract group instead of people they are likely to know, like they once did in that multi-religious environment.

Fifty-three-year-old Dr Anthony Joseph is a professor at FC College and a Catholic. He is the head of the education department and teaches a course on the philosophy of education. He feels that the time when intellectual debate about religion was possible no longer exists. 'I cannot talk about religion and particularly Islam with my Muslim colleagues. They are just no longer willing to listen. This is also the attitude of the students, particularly Muslims. I feel that the Christian or Hindu students generally tend to be more tolerant when talking about their religion. But there is another factor there. Muslims can easily accuse one of blasphemy if they don't like something you say. The Christians might take offence at your religious views but there is no threat of blasphemy with them—at least till now. Because of this, I am very guarded in my classes. You never know, one of these days a fanatic Muslim kid might accuse me of blasphemy. I remember during one of my classes, I once asked the students to think philosophically about the concept of heaven and hell, instead of them being real spaces. Now I wasn't challenging anyone's religion. I mean, after all, Christianity has notions of heaven and hell as well. However, this one student, a young boy with a short beard, took offence and started arguing with me in the class that I was challenging the teachings of Islam. I tried arguing with him for a little while but that seemed to heat him up even more. After the class was over, I called him over and explained to him that I was not teaching anything against Islam, which calmed him down. To be honest, I was afraid.'

Dr Joseph has every reason to be afraid. In recent years, the most absurd cases of blasphemy have been registered with the police. Sometime ago, a salesman visited a dentist who for some reason threw the business card of the salesman into the dustbin. It so turned out that Muhammad, the name of the Prophet of Islam, was part of the salesman's name; reason enough for the dentist to be accused of blasphemy. In another case, a factory owner was beaten to death by his factory workers after being accused of blasphemy. At the end of the year, the factory owner had taken off his calendar which had verses from the Quran and thrown it away. In yet another case of absurdity, a school principal in Lahore was accused of blasphemy when in an exam multiple-choice question, he asked the students to choose the personality who was their role model: the options included the name of the principal of the school along with the Prophet of Islam.

* * *

Several wooden benches are laid on both sides of the room, leaving enough space to walk through the middle. There is a small fountain near the entrance made out of white stone. The devotees are encouraged to ritualistically cleanse themselves there before sitting, but like the fountain outside, there is no water there either.

Big churches, like the Roman Cathedral or the Cathedral Church of Resurrection on the Mall, have more than one service for religious occasions like Easter and Christmas. There is one in English while the other is in Urdu. This is a legacy from the colonial era, when there were separate services for the English-speaking Europeans and vernacular-speaking natives. The first service of the day was attended by the leading colonial dignitaries of that era, along with high-class natives, who used English as their first language. These grand churches at that time were a symbol of power, splendid architectural structures rising amidst mediocre residential and official buildings. The clergy, all European at that time, also held sway over public perception because of their association with the colonial administrators. In a post-colonial country, whereas the grand structures remain, the symbolism behind them, the show of strength of the state, has diminished and these structures have become mere architectural remnants of what were once powerful political institutions.

The service begins. Almost half the hall is empty, reflecting the changing demographics of the city, as English remains an alien language to the majority of the people. Punjab was colonized almost a century after the colonization of Bengal by the British, as a result of which, the English language is not as institutionalized here. There are a few foreigners attending the service, some Filipino families, who are nowadays popular maidservants with the rich Pakistanis. There are also a few Africans and a handful of Europeans. Five of the front rows are taken up by nuns—Pakistanis and members of the clergy. Most of them are wearing white shalwar kameez, with their heads covered, while only a few wear long skirts with scarves covering their heads as opposed to dupattas. They hold sheets of paper containing the lyrics of the gospels being sung at intervals as part of the service of the church. All the songs are in English and the tunes Western and they are sung without music. During the colonial era, they used to be performed along with grand instruments, but now as the service in English has receded into oblivion so have the musicians and the instruments.

Most of the visitors are not familiar with the gospels and struggle to hum along.

Rays of light enter the hall from the windows above, looking like divine radiance as the sunrays brighten up the entire room. The architecture of the church is designed in such a way as to give this particular impression. At the altar standing under the benevolent gaze of St Francis Xavier on one side and St Francis of Assisi on the other, the priest conducts the prayer from behind the pulpit, reading out pieces from the Bible. St Francis Xavier was a Spanish monk from the sixteenth century who is said to have travelled all the way to Goa, India (which was a Portuguese colony at that time) and then to Indonesia and Japan for proselytizing. St Francis of Assisi, an Italian from the twelfth century, is considered to be the patron saint of animals. In a display of Catholic ritualistic tradition, the priest is wearing a white gown with a red drape over it. A couple of boys, training to be priests, standing behind him, listen attentively, wearing clothes similar to those of the priest. Next to them is the chair of the bishop; a finely crafted wooden seat, vacant at the moment. During the time when the service in English was the most important service of the day, the bishop used to conduct it himself, but not any more. He will come for the service in Urdu when thousands of devotees will come to the church, manifold greater in number than the hundred-odd people at the moment who are, as far as the bishop is concerned, politically irrelevant.

A Filipino family arrives during the middle of the sermon. Making their way to the front of the altar, they kneel one by one while the priest continues to read, following which they take their seats on the benches flanking the altar. Another family, who wants to leave, comes and kneels in front of the altar before leaving. Kneeling to the altar is a unique practice confined to the Catholic sect and a number of times during the prayer, the priest encourages the attendees to kneel down.

* * *

Despite being a sceptic, Dr Anthony Joseph makes it a point to visit the church regularly. He attends the weekly Sunday mass along with other religious festivals during the religious calendar. 'One doesn't go to a church purely for religious matters. It also allows people to interact and socialize. It is a community affair.' Today, he is accompanied by his children, a girl and a boy. His wife passed away a year ago, but Dr Joseph has not allowed that loss to diminish his spirit. He is a jolly person, always smiling. 'If one looks at the hall from the top, it will look like a cross. There is long sitting area in front of the altar. Then there are seating arrangements flanking it on both sides. Finally, there is some space behind the altar where people can sit,' he explains.

He points to a number of paintings that have been hung on the wall at standard intervals. These depict scenes of Christ carrying his crucifix through the streets of Jerusalem to the spot of his crucifixion. One picture depicts him wearing a crown of thorns, causing bleeding in his head. Good Friday, celebrated on the Friday following Palm Sunday, is a commemoration of the day when Jesus Christ was crucified. 'A procession would pass around them on Good Friday,' explains Dr Joseph.

* * *

Palm Sunday heralds the arrival of Easter week. It is followed by Good Friday and then Easter Sunday, which will take place on the following Sunday. Easter Sunday commemorates the resurrection of Christ on the third day after his crucifixion. Palm Sunday marks the triumphant entry of Christ, seated on a donkey, into the city of Jerusalem. According to the legend, the people of the city treated him as a king by laying out their cloaks and palm tree branches and leaves on the pathway, as a show of respect. Some others welcomed him by waving palm tree branches. Traditionally people wave palm leaves and sing songs about Jesus Christ on this day. This will happen in between the English and Urdu service.

A considerable number of people have gathered outside the church for the next service. A few walk in from the side door of the entrance. A worker of the church, wearing regular clothes, asks them to wait outside till the end of this service. As they leave, he locks the door from the inside and stands next to it. Over the remaining period of the service, people knock at the door but he doesn't respond for as long as this service continues. In the meantime, other workers walk around the aisles holding a green basket, which they hand over to the first person sitting on the bench. Putting some money into it with a closed fist, so that one knows how much money is donated, he/she hands it over to the next one, all of whom contribute. Soon, the basket is full up of ten- and twenty-rupee notes. A few red hundred-rupee notes can also be seen. While the service edges towards a conclusion, the workers get busy spreading out carpets and blankets around the aisles; this is for the massive number of people who will attend the Urdu service.

The priest moves from the pulpit to a table at the centre of the altar. Raising both his hands, he reads out a prayer from the Bible. The audience follows him. His voice echoes throughout the hall as he speaks into the microphone placed in front of him. He is reading out portions which deal with the Last Supper of Christ, where he mentioned that the food at the supper is his body and the wine his blood, both of which he is sacrificing for the salvation of his followers. While reciting these verses, the priest picks up a small cracker from one of the golden vessels in front of him and raises it in the air for everyone to see. The cracker is meant to be the symbolic body of Christ. He then pours a glass of wine into another vessel, which he declares to be the symbolic blood of Christ. After dipping the cracker into the wine, he puts it in his mouth, with the belief that this would be the reason for his salvation. He calls out to a couple of nuns from the front row and asks them to give the cracker and wine to the devotees. They come on stage, while the devotees collect in two lines facing them. To each devotee they hand a cracker dipped in wine, who accepts it with both of his/her hands and consumes it. This act marks the end of the service.

The gates of the church are then opened. There is a huge crowd of people at the exit, blocking the way for the ones wanting to leave. A few start shoving as they try to enter against the flow. The hall will fill up soon and they want the best seats. Amidst the struggle, the previous attendees manage to get out. A few will stay for the palm procession, while others will leave.

* * *

Outside, in front of the bishop's house, the bishop, Sebastian Shaw, and Father Andrew Ansari, head of this particular church, have already started addressing the crowd for the rally procession. The bishop is wearing a white gown with a white drape, which bears an insignia of the cross. There is a tall cap on his head and a long golden staff in his hand, forming a cross at the top. Young children training to be priests stand behind him in a queue, with the first child in the line also carrying a golden staff similar to the bishop's.

Father Ansari, in his late fifties, is dark-complexioned and bald. The few strands of hair that have remained on his lower head are grey. He is wearing a white gown as well, but with a red drape. After the bishop, he addresses the crowd, without a loudspeaker. On a table covered in a white cloth in front of them, there are small branches of palm trees which the attendees pick up. Almost everyone in the crowd has one waving as the bishop and Father Ansari address them. Almost unconsciously, the standing crowd gets divided into sections; one male and the other female. Both Father Ansari and the bishop talk about the religious significance of Palm Sunday. At the end of the speech, a passionate devotee says, '*Bolo Khudawan Yesu Masih ki* (Say, to the Lord Jesus Christ),' to which the crowd responds in a loud roar '*Jai* (Glory).' He then repeats, '*Badshaon ke Badshah ki* (the King of Kings),' '*Jai*' responds the crowd in a louder roar this time. '*David ke bete ki* (the son of David),' '*Jai*'.

Waving their palm fronds, the crowd starts to head towards the church, while random men from the crowd occasionally raise these slogans. The bishop and Father Ansari follow at the end. A devotee touches the back of the bishop and presses the hand that touched him all over his face seeking the blessing of the bishop through physical contact. In Catholicism, the clergy is elevated to a particular status and even physical contact with its members becomes blessed. This is one of the reasons why devotees kneel down before the bishop and kiss his hand before addressing him. This semi-divinity of the Catholic clergy was the major reason why a group of clergymen protested against Catholicism and founded the Protestant Church.

* * *

'Before 9/11, a huge procession used to leave from the Don Bosco School (another church school) on the railway road and used to travel on foot till this church, about 20 km from there. There used to be thousands of people singing and chanting the names of Jesus Christ while holding up palm tree branches. All the Catholic churches in the city would merge into that one procession. It would take us over an hour to get here. However, after the rise of terrorism, the Government of Pakistan forbade us from taking out that rally. Thousands of Christians together in a procession became too difficult for the government to protect,' says Javed Aftab, a fifty-two-year-old Catholic. Holding a palm branch, he walks with the procession, shouting '*Jai*' every time a slogan is raised. Wearing a yellow shirt with off-white trousers and a maroon tie, Aftab is neatly dressed. He comes to church usually with his family but they today they could not come. 'Now all that has left of that procession is this short walk within the compounds of the church.'

Aftab explains how this rally is not the only tradition that has suffered because of the deteriorating security of the country. Every year, there used to be religious conferences around the city, which attracted different Christian religious leaders and scholars. About 3000 people attended them. 'There used to be stalls for food, books and Christian paraphernalia, like cross necklaces,' he says. Tents used to be raised for people coming from outside of the city to sleep in the night. Following the threats of rising terrorism, the Christian community of the country has been asked by the government to refrain from arranging those conferences as well.

* * *

The atmosphere inside the church is festive. A band has set up its instruments and is singing an Urdu song near the entrance. There are separate choirs for men and women, sharing pieces of paper with each other to follow the lyrics. A man in his mid-forties standing opposite them is playing African bongo drums with his hands, while a young man in his late twenties sitting next to him is playing the piano. This is in complete contrast to the atmosphere earlier in the day during the English procession, which lacked musical instruments. This is much more alive, but indigenous in its element. With the help of large speakers, the acoustics are resonating from the hall. The tune more Eastern than Western is easy to follow and the lyrics easy to remember with '*Jai Yesu* (Long live Jesus)' as the chorus. The bishop and Father Ansari have been escorted to the altar, where the bishop has taken his 'throne', while the priest is sitting beside him on a smaller chair.

The administration is struggling to contain the crowd as there is no more seating left. Even the benches behind the altar have been occupied while the rest of the people have taken up the empty space on the floor, blocking any passage in or out of the church.

This session will be conducted by the bishop himself and the service would include similar chapters from the

Bible that were read out in the morning: the last supper, the betrayal, the capture, the trial, the persecution and then the crucifixion of Jesus Christ. The only difference is that of language.

* * *

Sebastian Francis makes his way through the crowd and manages to find an empty spot on the floor. One of the priests monitoring the crowd from the side looks at him and asks him to move to one of the benches, but Sebastian refuses. He is a democrat at heart, part of the masses. In his late forties, Sebastian is an articulate proponent of minority rights and also happens to be a prolific writer. At the moment he is serving as the president of the Pakistan Congress for Equality and Harmony (PPCEH), an organization that works for the equal rights of minorities and comes under the purview of the Roman Catholic Church, Pakistan. Fluent in English, he still prefers attending the Urdu service. 'The one in English is too boring,' he says.

'I believe it was around the 1960s that the Catholic Church all over the world still used Latin for prayers, reading and service. The problem with that is that the majority of the Catholics do not understand it, which was resulting in them distancing themselves from their religion. After much discussion, which was no less than a revolution in itself, the Catholic Church agreed that the Bible could be translated into other languages besides Latin and the service at the church could be conducted in these languages. The response has been phenomenal. All the people can now understand their religion and relate it with it. There is now a Bible in Urdu which all of us can understand here,' he explains.

'Ripples of these changes were also felt in Pakistan. Till that point all the clergy positions here were filled by Europeans. There was not a single Pakistani priest! In 1960, Bishop John Joseph became the first Punjabi priest after graduating from a religious seminary. He later became the first local bishop. Now, four decades later, all the clergy positions are with locals.'

GOOD FRIDAY AT SACRED HEART CATHEDRAL, LAHORE

The sound of the generator resonates in the large hall of the church. Power outages in the city have become worse forcing the church administration to keep a generator on standby for such gatherings. The bishop, Sebastian Shaw, is addressing the crowd. His sermon is in Urdu, interjected with a few Punjabi phrases to stress a particular point and make a connection with the people. He talks about how Christ was betrayed by his disciple Judas, as well as other city dwellers out of fear of retribution. They accused our beloved Christ of blasphemy. According to the tradition of that time, he was made to carry his cross which was used to crucify him through the entire city. Murderers and other criminals at that time were made to carry their crosses in the manner that our beloved Christ was. But he bore all this patiently. He did that for you; to give you a lesson in patience and humility. If he wanted he could have punished those people right there and then, proving to them that he is indeed the King of Heaven. But he did not because he wanted to save us. He taught us that no matter how bad the situation gets, we should bear it patiently. He knew that non-believers would attack his followers like they attacked him till the end. But remember, they would only be testing our commitment to our Lord. Christ wants us to be patient in this ordeal.'

* * *

On the morning of 6 May 1998, the then Bishop of Lahore, John Joseph asked his driver to prepare the car earlier than usual. In a couple of hours they reached the Sahiwal civil court about 150 km from Lahore. The bishop had visited the court several times prior to this visit as he was following the case of a young Christian man by the name of Ayub Masih who had been accused of blasphemy. The twenty-six-year-old man had been languishing in Sahiwal Jail and his case was being heard in the civil court that day. He had been accused of blasphemy by his Muslim neighbour. Throughout the proceedings, the bishop maintained that the motivation behind the case was a property dispute between the Christian and the Muslim neighbour but as the case headed towards its conclusion, it became increasingly clear that the judge was likely to rule against the Christian accused. The punishment for blasphemy in Pakistan is death!

Bishop John Joseph, who was the first Punjabi priest and then the first native bishop of the Roman Catholic Church in Pakistan, had spent a life dedicated to political activism along with his religious commitments. Over the years, he had represented several blasphemy accused, helping them with their cases and finding them lawyers. In 1993, the bishop had been involved in another high-profile case. That case concerned an eleven-year-old boy, Salamat

Masih, and a thirty-eight-year-old man, Manzoor Masih, who were accused of scribbling blasphemous material on a neighbourhood wall. The bishop argued that the accused were illiterate. Using that evidence the high court judge, Arif Bhatti, acquitted the blasphemy accused. Later, however, the judge was gunned down in his own chamber for supporting a blasphemer, a blasphemy in itself. Before the assassination of the judge, Manzoor Masih was also shot down in front of the civil and session courts while Salamat Masih sustained injuries. After the death of Manzoor Masih, the bishop promised himself that there would be no more deaths to the blasphemy laws as long as he was alive. A celebrated figure in his community, throughout his political activism days, the bishop maintained that blasphemy laws be revoked.

Outside the Sahiwal civil court, the driver and the junior priest who were accompanying the bishop wondered why they were there. Only ten days prior to that day, the court had sentenced Ayub Masih to death, having found him guilty of blasphemy. What happened next was shocking, to say the least. Standing outside the gates of the court, the bishop using a handgun shot himself in the head as a protest against the sentence of Ayub Masih. In a letter that was found after his protest suicide, Bishop John Joseph stated:

'I shall count myself extremely fortunate if in this mission of breaking the barriers, our Lord accepts the sacrifice of my blood for the benefit of his people.'

He hoped that his protest suicide would ultimately turn public opinion against the outrageous blasphemy laws and the government would be forced to revoke them. His sacrifice, like that of Christ, was meant to be the reason for the salvation of millions of Christians living in Pakistan. However, nothing changed.

* * *

Sitting inside the sunlit hall, members listen with devotion, their heads lowered in respect. Volunteers sitting outside are not allowing any more people inside the hall, which is overflowing well beyond its capacity. Father Ansari sitting behind the bishop monitors the crowd as if checking as to who is paying attention and who is not. In front of them, a couple of cameramen from local television channels record the proceedings, moving from spot to spot trying to capture as many angles as possible, unaware and unconcerned of the protocol one is expected to follow in front of the bishop. These are concluding proceedings of Good Friday, the day when Jesus Christ, the founder of Christianity, was crucified for committing 'blasphemy' and fomenting dissent against the Roman Empire, which ruled over the region at that time. 'This was the sacrifice of the Christ for the people,' says the bishop.

The relevance of the holy day is not lost on the members of the audience. They know that they are a persecuted minority with members from the community often accused of committing blasphemy. The bishop doesn't make that connection between the blasphemy of their saviour and today's Christian 'blasphemers'; he doesn't need to. The atmosphere in the church is sombre, as if the bishop is not making a religious speech but a poignant political one. Despite its religious references, his sermon is politically relevant to the Christian community today in Pakistan.

The 'blasphemer' Christ could be seen as a symbol for all those individuals who have suffered as blasphemy accused. The Christian community understands that they weren't really blasphemers, they were victims of the wrath of the majority. The patience that the bishop extolls during his speech is for this persecuted minority targeted because of its religious beliefs.

* * *

Forty-six-year-old Aslam Nayamat is standing next to the gate wearing a crisp white shalwar kameez, supporting black Ray-Ban glasses. He is a tall, well-built man with a short moustache and grey hair. Standing next to the gate, he monitors the security of the church. Usually lax, the guards are particularly attentive today, checking the National Identity Cards (NIC) of all the visitors. Once again, no Muslim is allowed.

On being questioned, he doesn't explain the exact nature of his job at the church, giving instead a vague answer. 'A few years ago, there was a scandal within the clergy regarding property. There is vast property associated with the church, which was allegedly sold by someone. So in 2010, I was called in to look after it and devise a system for greater transparency.' He doesn't want to share what that scandal was or who was involved. He enjoys a particular reputation in the church and often interacts with the bishop.

For a decade before he joined the church, he was employed at the Pakistan Congress for Equality and Harmony (PPCEH), an organization that reports to the church. Here, Nayamat was responsible for working with persecuted segments of the religious minorities, focusing on but not limited to the Christian community. He spent most of his time interacting with blasphemy-accused victims and under the guidance of Bishop John Joseph initially and subsequent bishops, he helped them with lawyers and looking after their family. 'Once someone is accused of blasphemy, his/her life can never return to normalcy. Even if the court acquits them, they constantly remain under the fear of extrajudicial murder. Not only the accused, but even their families also come under threat. In a lot of instances, we have had to hide the families of the accused as well. I would do so undertaking personal risk. There is an environment of fear because of which the blasphemy accused, even if innocent, is doomed. No lawyer wants to risk taking the case. The judges feel threatened. I have visited the accused in the jails and I can't even tell you the conditions they live in. They are harassed by their fellow inmates. The police officials physically torture them. They are not even given proper food or bedding like the other prisoners. Those in the death cells are treated better compared to the blasphemy accused. They all become psychological patients, who find it very hard to reintegrate into mainstream society. A majority of those cases are those which are fabricated as a result of personal enmities or property issues. I remember an old woman who I worked with. She had rented out some property to a Muslim prayer leader of a mosque, who was very bad with paying rent. Often, the Christian landlord and the tenant would argue and the prayer leader would threaten her. Then one day, he went to the police station and registered a case of blasphemy against her stating that she had insulted the Holy Prophet of Islam (PBUH), whereas there was no such thing. Knowing well enough that submitting herself to the police and expecting justice in this highly charged atmosphere would be ridiculous, she fled and has been on the run ever since. It has been three years since she left her home. Tired, she now wants to stop running but I don't let her. Even if the court acquits her, some fanatic would gun her down like they have so many other such innocent people.'

'Let them in,' says Nayamat, gesturing to the security guards to allow a group of young Christian devotees to enter the church carrying cartons of juice and other eatables. Politely declining the offer of juice or chips, he instructs the boys to move along the passage leading to the bishop's house and distribute it amongst the people in the ground. 'This is to avoid the accumulation of too many people at this spot which is being used for entry and exit,' he explains. As the boys unload their cartons and start distributing it to the crowd gathered in the lawns of the church, a rush of people gather around them, screaming, snatching and pulling to get their share of this free offering in the name of God.

'There is no such tradition of distributing food on holy days,' says Nayamat as he looks on at the scramble for free food. 'This is a new tradition that has started recently. Young members of the community look at how Muslims distribute free food at Islamic shrines to seek the blessings of the saint and get inspired by these non-Christian practices.'

'I used to be a businessman and had no intention of ever being involved in political activism,' says Nayamat. 'My house was in a Christian-dominated village near Khanewal. In 1997, after the Shanti Nagar incident, I wrapped up my business and moved to Lahore. That incident was my introduction into the world of religious fanaticism, something I had never experienced prior to that. Neighbours and friends who had known us for years were driven crazy by the passion of religion. The incident broke my heart and I could no longer live there.'

* * *

About a kilometre from the village of Shanti Nagar, next to the canal that is the lifeline of the village and the reason why it is the most prosperous village in the surroundings, there is an abandoned white mosque under the shade of a peepal tree—the tree of peace and spirituality. On the night of 5 February 1997, a couple of days after the national elections of Pakistan, in an unusual series of events, a few Muslims decided to offer their evening prayers at this abandoned mosque. However, before they could bow down before Allah, they discovered charred pages from the Holy Book of Quran lying in the courtyard of this mosque with the names of the seven culprits conveniently noted down on the margins of one of the pages. A note scribbled down on an empty space next to the names mentioned defiantly that these seven people were responsible for the burning of the pages of the Holy Quran—an act of blasphemy and punishable by death—and also urged Muslims to take revenge if they dared.

The news spread like wildfire as mosques all around the neighbouring villages and the city of Khanewal, a few kilometres from here, started spewing hatred and sought revenge against the Christians. Within hours, Muslims from all over the area started gathering at this mosque, the site of the blasphemous act. In the meantime, a First Information Report (FIR) was also registered against the seven accused culprits, one of whom was Ahmad Gill, a cousin of Aslam Nayamat.

Unaware of the simmering situation, Ahmad Gill was returning from a wedding ceremony in Khanewal along with his family—two children and wife—late in the night. 'There was a huge gathering of people on the canal numbering in the several thousands. They had blocked the road with burning tyres and were gesturing at me to stop. I knew that something was wrong but would have stopped the car had my wife Mary not asked me to keep on driving. I sped up the car and slamming against the people who were falling on my windscreen and thundering at the windows, I dug through the crowd. You can imagine our condition at that moment. Our children were crying and we were scared. Taking a brick, one of the protestors smashed my windscreen. My children's eyes could have been permanently damaged by the impact of the glass but thank God, nothing happened. Another man leapt into the car through the windscreen and jumped at me with a knife. I held it with my hand and averted the attack. I felt at that moment as if my time had come and started praying to Jesus Christ. Right then out of nowhere, four Christian boys emerged and shielded the car and my family from the angry mob and got us through. I don't know where those boys came from and how were they able to rescue us safely in the midst of a raging crowd. I later realized that they were angels. I don't think the crowd knew that I was Ahmad Gill, otherwise they would have never allowed me to pass through alive.'

All through the night, the crowd swelled as Christians in the twin villages of Shanti Nagar and Tibba could only observe the situation from a safe distance. A message was conveyed to the villagers to hand over the seven blasphemers upon which the crowd would disperse peacefully. However, the villagers were aware of the fact that if that was done, those men, whom they regarded as innocent, would be lynched by the mob, something the villagers were not willing to concede despite the looming threat of the mob descending upon the village in a fury.

Early in the morning, scared for their lives, the villagers from Tibba, an almost entirely Christian village, abandoned their homes and took refuge in Shanti Nagar, a much larger village. At the centre of this village, elders from the community gathered to discuss the approaching danger. Here they were assured by police representatives who had by now arrived from Khanewal that the crowd was peaceful and only wanted to pass through the village venting their anger at the act of blasphemy. The police officials assured them that no one would be attacked. To make sure that no untoward incident occurred while the protesting crowd passed through these Christian villages, the police managed to convince the elders to submit all private arms and ammunition to the authorities. Satisfied by the promises of the police, the elders of the village were able to convince most of the villagers to hand over their weapons. A few, however, refused to follow these instructions. They were the lucky ones.

Ahmad Gill, who still resides in the village, is of the opinion that this was not a sporadic event, a result of a few burnt pages of the Quran. This had been building up for quite some time. On 17 January, about fifteen days before the incident, the police raided the house of a Christian man from the village called Baba Raji. They alleged that he was involved in the illegal business of making and selling liquor. During the raid, as a result of the callousness of the police, a copy of the Bible which was placed on one of the shelves fell on the ground. The police used to raid different houses of the village randomly on one pretext or the other. The truth is that the Muslims of the surrounding areas are jealous of the prosperity of this village. Compared to the water supply of the neighbouring villages, the water from the canal that passes through Shanti Nagar is particularly suitable for agriculture, which is why the yield here is much better than that of the neighbouring Muslim village. A Christian landlord from Shanti Nagar does much better than a Muslim landlord with the same landholding from the neighbouring village. This is something that Muslims could never come to terms with. The police would frequently take our men and lock them up knowing well enough that other members from the community would be able to pay bribes for them.'

Shanti Nagar, which literally means the land of peace, was established in 1916 by a Christian missionary by the name of William Youth Tucker, a representative of the Salvation Army. Purchasing vast tracts of land around the village, he distributed it to the native Christian families. Based on its strategic location next to the canal, the Christian landlords of the village have thrived, making this village a unique case study in the social fabric of the Punjab. Whereas in most of the villages across the province Muslims are the dominant landowners, while Christians are confined to menial jobs associated with the untouchable caste, here the Christians are the dominant landowners, while the few Muslims who remain are economically vulnerable. In a regular village where Christians are on the lower rung of the social and economic hierarchy, they would be treated as untouchables.

In Shanti Nagar, however, the low-caste Muslims are not treated as untouchables. The only *tandoor* in the village is run by a Muslim, a profession unacceptable for a Christian in a Muslim-dominated village.

'Our villagers were also aware of the general persecution of the Christian community by Muslims and how they are often accused of blasphemy on the basis of alleged desecration of the Quran. When our holy book, the Bible, was mistreated by the Muslim police officials raiding Baba Raji's house, members of the community felt that it was time to give the Muslims a dose of their own medicine. They decided to report a blasphemy case against a police constable responsible for the fall of the Holy Book. That was the fatal blow to our community.'

Most of the residents of Shanti Nagar feel that the burning of pages from the Quran and the names of the seven culprits on the edge was orchestrated by the police to seek revenge for the humiliation they had suffered at the hands of the Christian villagers, considered a lowly caste. The concerned constable who had been accused of blasphemy was suspended from service after the interference of high-ranking police officials. They also believe that disarming the villagers just before the attack of the Muslim mob was part of the plan to deal a severe blow to the Christian community.

An angry mob first turned towards the empty village of Tibba and burned several buildings down. 'There were about 50–60,000 people,' recalls forty-five-year-old Saima Rabnawaz, a resident of the village and a teacher at the Salvation Army School. 'Some of the boys in the mob were no older than thirteen or fourteen. A few of them were Muslim students of the same school that they were now burning. There is a church behind the school which was also burned.' Saima shivers in agony as she recalls that fateful day. 'It was people we knew who attacked us. We had relationships with them, interacting with them on deaths and marriages. I regarded some of them as my friends; but not any more.

I don't interact with Muslims now having realized that no matter how sweet they are to you, they can never be trusted. They can harm us any day when it comes to their religion.'

After the havoc at Tibba, the mob turned towards Shanti Nagar, destroying agricultural fields on the way and stealing animals. 'There was a beautiful mango orchard at the entrance of the village. The mob burned it down. It successfully burned half of the village down before the army arrived from Khanewal to restore order. When they came, they caught many people stealing our animals. So much for religious fervour,' jokes Ahmad Gill. The damage at this village would have been worse had a few members of the community not held on to their weapons defying the orders of the police. From within their houses, they fired threatening shots into the crowd and this kept the angry mob away from certain quarters of the village. Order was restored and the crowd scattered within hours after the arrival of the army. As news of this attack spread, both national and international media descended upon this village, forcing the newly elected Prime Minister Mian Nawaz Sharif and his brother Mian Shahbaz Sharif, the chief minister of Punjab, to also visit the village and speed up the recovery process. Funds were allocated for the reconstruction of the burnt houses and shops.

However, while Shanti Nagar was physically reconstructed, the traumatic components of the attack and underlining prejudices that spurred the attacks were left unattended, leaving room for similar attacks in the future. In 2005, an identical attack was launched against a Christian settlement in Sangla Hill, followed by attacks on Gojra and Bahmniwala, Kasur, in 2009, all of which happen to be located in Punjab. The story of a few burnt pages from the Quran found in local mosques seems to happen often.

Sher Khursheed was another person blamed in the FIR for blasphemy. After the attack, his six-year-old son started suffering from schizophrenia and now lives in the Lahore Mental Hospital, where his father visits him regularly. Another child from the community who is now a young man has not left his home since the attack. A number of elderly from the village passed away due to heart attacks as the mob came raging in. Most importantly, the attack has destroyed the relationship between the Muslims and Christians of the area. 'For at least three or four years after the event, we served the Muslims in separate utensils giving them a taste of their own biases,' says Khursheed staring with his bloodshot eyes suppressing inexpressible anger and frustration. 'Every time I go to the neighbouring Muslim village, which I have to often,' says Mary, the wife of Ahmad Gill, 'I feel afraid. Even though I enjoy a friendly relationship with them, I still feel that I cannot trust them.' Lying in the obscurity of rural Punjab more than 300 km from Lahore, the Christian-dominated village of Shanti Nagar is still there, trying to put together its shattered rhythm and trying to come to terms with the events of 6 February 1997.

* * *

'We love Pakistan because it is our country,' says the bishop as he prepares to conclude the sermon. He has the lost the passion that had gripped him while talking about the persecution of Christ. His words now sound hollow, losing their effect and grip on the audience that he commanded only a few minutes ago. This part is now for the media, its rhetoric a reaffirmation of the loyalty that members of the religious minorities are deprived of often in Muslim Pakistan. 'And no matter how bad the situation gets, we will face all persecution with compassion, with love. That was the message of Christ. That is what he wanted to teach us through his crucifixion.'

EASTER SUNDAY AT CATHEDRAL CHURCH OF THE RESURRECTION, LAHORE

The Cathedral Church of Resurrection, head church of the Church of Pakistan, Lahore diocese, stands opposite the Lahore High Court. Lights have been set up at the iron bar gate and fence, raised much after the construction of the church as a result of the increasing need for security in changing times. At about four in the morning, people start entering the gate, where they are greeted by seventy-two-year-old Yousuf Khan, wearing an off-white shalwar kameez. His long white beard implies that he is a Muslim but one is not sure. Zigzagging along the newly placed roadblocks inside the gate, most members of the community arrive on bikes and in cars, while those arriving in a rickshaw take a drop a few yards away from the entrance. Greeting and allowing most of them to enter without checking their identity cards, Khan, it seems, knows most of them. A lone structure built of big grey bricks lies to the left. This is the bishop's house.

* * *

'A cathedral is that church which houses the bishop,' explains Dr Ammar Farooqi, a seventy-three-year-old poet from Lahore. 'When I use the word "church", I can either mean the building which is a church, of course, or the Church as an institution under which several other churches function. It is a whole organization of churches that looks after the Christian parish or a community of a particular region. The Church as an organization heads schools, colleges, hospitals, missionary work, etc. This organizational church is headed by the bishop, under whom come all the churches that are subjected to that head church like the cathedral here. A particular church is a building headed by a dean, who is a priest.'

Dr Farooqi is a PhD in Urdu literature and has penned several books. He is a Protestant Christian and regularly visits the church, mostly all by himself. His wife passed away a few years ago and all his children have migrated abroad. He lives alone in Allama Iqbal Town. 'My children ask me to leave the country all the time. They say they are afraid for my safety. But why should I leave? This is my country. I have as much right over it as anyone else. We Christians were living here before Lahore became a part of Pakistan. If they want to kill me for my political views then let them. I am not scared of anyone and I will continue to speak the truth.'

Dr Ammar Farooqi, an otherwise fragile-looking man, is a strong critic of the blasphemy laws of Pakistan, which are often used to persecute members of the religious minorities. 'We are not against the law. It is important to protect all religions from malicious propaganda, but care should be taken to protect the innocent. Almost all the time, the laws are used for personal vendetta.' This is indeed a strong position to take given the current political situation in the country. Following the assassinations of Salman Taseer and Shahbaz Bhatti, two of the most vocal critics of the laws, and death threats to a lady parliamentarian, Sherry Rehman, after she introduced a private bill in the Parliament for amendment of this law, no one is left to raise a voice against the persecution of the religious minorities through the blasphemy laws. On the other hand, the religious right continues to exert its street muscle for greater Islamization of the society and the government. They maintain that they would uphold the laws against this onslaught of the 'liberals', a derogatory word in contemporary Pakistan with connotations similar to calling someone 'bourgeois' in a communist society.

The assassination of Salman Taseer in January 2011 was the turning point in this struggle for a liberal Pakistan as opposed to a theocratic state. Historically, none of the religious parties of the country have ever gained enough votes to acquire a majority in the Parliament except when they were used as proxies and as political stooges by the military dictators, General Zia-ul-Haq in the 1980s and General Pervez Musharraf in first decade of the second millennium. For this particular reason, it has long been argued in the liberal section of the Pakistani media that the silent majority of the country holds liberal values and shuns political Islam. As opposed to the silent majority, the religious right wing is a vocal minority who come out on the streets often and disrupt daily life, protesting sometimes against the secularization of the country and on other occasions against the nefarious plans of the Pakistani version of the axis of evil—India, the US and Israel. It was believed that due to their nuisance value, these religious political parties have been able to put across their agenda to the state despite a low count in terms of the vote.

However, after the assassination of the Governor of Punjab, this perception was shattered as thousands rallied in support of Mumtaz Qadri, the security guard of the Governor responsible for his assassination. Overnight, web pages dedicated to the heroic act of the assassin were created and joined by thousands of tech-savvy, educated people. An overwhelming majority of the lawyers' community expressed their admiration for the warrior of Islam, showering him with rose petals as he arrived for his hearing. A number of them offered to represent him free of any charge, one of who was the former chief justice of the Lahore High Court, Khawaja Muhammad Sharif. On the other hand, Salman Taseer was portrayed by the supporters of Qadri as a corrupt 'liberal' who drank alcohol and supported blasphemy against the Prophet of Islam and was therefore liable to be murdered. As opposed to gatherings of thousands in favour of Qadri, when the liberals tried organizing candlelight vigils for the slain Governor, no more than a handful of people gathered. The myth of the silent liberal majority had burst and the liberal politicians and writers of the country accepted their defeat in silence, refraining from further discussion on the blasphemy laws. The silence was strengthened after the assassination of Federal Minister for Minority Affairs Shahbaz Bhatti, only a few months after Salman Taseer.

In such a charged environment, the strong opinions articulated by Dr Ammar Farooqi, a member of the religious minority, are indeed an act of defiant bravery. But there is a subtle caution in his statements as well. Whereas earlier the demand had been scrapping of the blasphemy laws, a law that was introduced by the Islamist dictator General Zia-ul-Haq, now the demand has changed to the wrong manipulation of the law without directly challenging the presence of the law itself.

'The current bishop, Alexander John Malik, is an excellent man,' says Dr Kanwal Feroze. 'He is the head of the church in perhaps the most demanding circumstances and is a critic of the exploitation of the blasphemy laws. The situation has changed ever since the assassination of Salman Taseer. The bishop has confided in me that since these two assassinations, he has been confined to his house. This is because his life is also threatened. Earlier, he was constantly on the move meeting dignitaries, politicians and engaging with the media. The bishop organized a prayer in remembrance of Salman Taseer at this particular church after his assassination. In fact, several services were held all across, in the churches of Pakistan. Salmeen Taseer is a hero of the Christian community of the country.'

* * *

Parking his Vespa scooter in the parking lot facing the building of the church, Dr Farooqi joins a group of people that have gathered outside in the courtyard. Spotting the dean, Shahid Miraj (head of this particular church) walks up to him, handing him a copy of his monthly magazine, *Shama*. Dr Farooqi is a well-known figure in the Protestant community because of his journalism. He publishes a monthly magazine, which he distributes to members of the Christian community. The dean, who is wearing a white gown with a yellow scarf around his neck, hands it over to a young priest assisting him and continues monitoring the preparation for the early morning ritual.

The main building of the church, a tall structure, was constructed in 1887, following the Gothic architectural tradition with its skyward-pointing spire and was affiliated with the Anglican Church in England. In 1970, the church left that order and formed the order of the Church of Pakistan. 'During the late sixties, there was a worldwide movement to unite the various denominations of the Protestant Church under one system. However, that failed internationally and only succeeded in Pakistan, where four different sects within Protestantism combined to form the Church of Pakistan with a common administrative body. This happened in 1970,' explains Dr Farooqi.

The trees are decorated with lights shining in the darkness of early morning. The young priest asks the people to pick up a candle from the porch of the church and light it with a matchbox placed next to them as they approach for the ceremony. As people collect, the dean organizes them in a line. The children are made to stand in front, the women behind them, followed by older boys and men. A young man in his twenties, wearing a blue shirt and light blue jeans, is instructed to stand in front of the children holding a staff shaped like a cross. Lifting it with both his hands, he makes sure that its base doesn't touch the ground.

In a matter of minutes, there are about 300 people in the line. Satisfied with the numbers, the dean asks the man standing at the front to start walking, while everyone follows him. The procession intends to circle around the church thrice. Shahid Miraj walks next to the young man with the staff. Reading from a blue book which contains various gospels he begins singing an Urdu song, which the crowd joins in. In this long line, the song scatters into various parts as the group in front sings a different part of the gospel while those at the end follow their own timing. At one point, a loud voice from the end yells, '*Bolo Yesu Masih ki*,' to which the crowd yells back, '*Jai*'.

* * *

'What the Muslims here do not understand is that we do not like to be called *Eesai*. We are Masih,' says Dr Farooqi. Christians all over the country are referred to as Eesai, a name that derives from the Arabic rendition of the name for Jesus Christ—Hazrat Isa. Followers of Hazrat Isa become Eesai just like Muslims are occasionally wrongly referred to as Mohammedans or the followers of Prophet Mohammed (PBUH), a title that Muslims don't ascribe to themselves. 'The correct name for Jesus Christ mentioned in the Bible is that of Yesu Masih translated into Jesus Christ in English. I am not sure about the exact language but I believe that Yesu Masih is a combination of Arabic, Hebrew and maybe Armenian as well, as these were the dominant languages spoken at that time in that area. Yesu is the name and Masih the title used for the role of Jesus as the saviour—Jesus the Christ. The name Isa is mentioned nowhere in the Bible and only comes in the Quran which is why we don't accept the title of Eesai. On the other hand Jesus Christ is referred to as Yesu Masih in the Quran more times than he is called Isa, so it makes sense for the Muslims to call us Masih, but they insist on using Eesai. Eesai is a derogatory word. This is just like how the Sikhs before Partition used to call the Muslims, 'Musla'.' However, unaware of this differentiation and without intending harm, the majority of the population of Pakistan continues to call Christians Eesai against their wishes. In order to exert their identity, on the other hand, a lot of Christians use the surname of Masih.

* * *

'This is the time when Jesus Christ was resurrected,' says Dean Shahid Miraj as he walks with the procession. It will soon be dawn. 'The candle and the light is a symbol of life. Christ came back from death on this day, which is why we celebrate Easter Sunday. It is celebrated three days after he was crucified. He took three days to resurrect.' Completing their third and final round, the crowd, singing and chanting, heads inside the church after placing their candles in a small niche in front taking care that the light continues to burn. A few latecomers too sleepy to take part in the initial ritual are already sitting inside.

The interior of this Protestant church for the most part is the same as that of a Catholic church with the significant absence being that of the iconic statues so prevalent in Catholic setups. The Protestants regard prostration in front of statues of Christ, Mother Mary or the saints, as idol worship. They satisfy their iconic needs by the cross which symbolizes the Holy Trinity: the Father (God), the Son (Jesus Christ) and the Holy Spirit. The Protestants also look down upon wearing religious symbols as jewellery like cross necklaces, which one often finds round the necks of many Catholics. Usually outside Catholic churches, one finds small stalls selling religious items, including posters, statues and necklaces, but this is highly unlikely next to Protestant churches.

Dr Farooqi, a devout Protestant, goes a step forward in explaining the sociological differences between Catholics and Protestants.

* * *

'During the Partition, when the Hindus, Sikhs and Muslims were at each other's throats, the Christian community was seen as a neutral community,' says Dr Farooqi. A lot of Hindus from the Punjab at that time who couldn't afford to migrate or belonged to the lowest rung of the caste hierarchy either started passing themselves off as Christians by wearing crosses around their necks and displaying them to the bloodthirsty mob or actually converted as a matter of convenience. 'Most of those people converted to Catholicism,' he elaborates. One cannot be entirely certain if the conversion to Catholicism is a historically verifiable statement; however, there is no denying the fact that in that polarized society, where either one of the above-mentioned three religions could have been reason enough for losing one's life, a lot of Hindus and Sikhs who found themselves on the wrong side of the Radcliffe Award (boundary demarcation line between India and Pakistan upon the Partition of India) opted for this marriage of convenience with Christianity. Dr Farooqi's statement may be true but one cannot discount the fact that it may also be a product of his own prejudices against the Catholics. While this conversion was a matter of prudence as opposed to religious conviction, their descendants now are fully recognized Christians. It probably hurts his own religious sentiments to acknowledge the fact that a lot of Protestant Christians around him too converted in this particular manner. Conversion to Catholicism on the other hand is convenient history.

Mary is an eighty-three-year-old widowed, childless woman living on the outskirts of Lahore. 'We were untouchable Hindus and used to live near Shahjamal on the canal that now divides Lahore into two parts. Its source lies somewhere in India. As children I remember playing on its banks. During the days close to the Partition, we would frequently sight mutilated bodies floating in the water. It was really scary. Afraid, our mother made us wear a cross around our necks and told us to show it to anyone who would come asking for our religion.' Mary today is a hybrid of Christianity and Hinduism with a tinge of Islam in her practice living in a Muslim Pakistan, defying the very notions of separate categorization of religion that Partition and the creation of Pakistan are products of. Widowed and without any progeny, she has taken refuge at the house of another Christianized Hindu woman called Raj Kumari. Every morning, Raj Kumari stands in front of the idols and pictures of Hindu pantheon singing Christian hymns. Born only a few years before Partition, she never learnt Hindu prayers but kept a connection with the deities as she retained some part of her religious heritage. Officially Christian, she joined a missionary school where she learned Christian prayers and hymns. While she stands in front of an idol of Kali Mata holding both her hands in front of her, eyes closed in devotion, she prays for mercy from her Lord—Jesus Christ.

* * *

The church has filled to its capacity and the members of the clergy have taken their places at the altar. There is no water bowl here from which a devotee needs to purify himself or herself before sitting; neither do they kneel in front of the altar as people do at a Catholic church. There is also no cushion support at the back of the benches used for kneeling otherwise. Most of the women are seated on one side and men on the other; however, there is no rigid boundary. The women are wearing shalwar kameez with their heads covered. The bishop sitting behind a desk on the podium is wearing a light brown drape with the border decorated in green and brown embroidery with a long hat of similar design and is ready to lead the prayers on this holy day. He gestures empathically with his hand, displaying the ring bearing a cross mark that he was gifted on the day of his anointment as the bishop. His silver necklace with a huge cross dangles on his chest. The choir composed of boys and girls of different ages stand ready on his right with a pianist accompanying them. A banner behind the bishop reads 'He has risen', with no pictures of Christ to be found anywhere. In front of him on a table covered with a neat white cloth, white roses are placed in a green vase along with a golden statue of an eagle, an emblem from the church when it was a symbol of the British colonial authority here.

At the end of the sermon, which is a combination of recitations from the Bible and holy hymns, a few men walking around the hall collect money from the gathering and present it to the bishop who accepts it with authority. This donation will be used to run the expenses of the church, the clergy and other philanthropic work that the church undertakes. Like Palm Sunday, the proceedings of the day also conclude with the consumption of the wafer and holy water.

* * *

Every year on the occasion of Easter Sunday, the church arranges for a communal breakfast, open for all at the end of the prayers. Outside, the sun is already out. A few tables have been organized on the ground next to the church building. At one end of the lawn a few men are busy preparing breakfast: halwa puri and channa, typical Lahori *nashta*.

A huge stone cross erected at one end casts a shadow across the lawn. 'This cross was found in the ancient city of Taxila, near Islamabad, during the colonial era. This discovery proves that Christianity was present in this part of the world much before the advent of the British as is the general perception,' says Dr Feroze. He is eager to prove that Christianity, like other religions, also has its roots here dating back several centuries. However, the fact of the matter remains that Christianity as a mainstream religion that it has now become in South Asia never existed on such a scale here before British colonialism.

Done with breakfast, people slowly begin to slip out of the church. Families excited on the occasion of a religious day, will now head to parks, the zoo or to visit their families celebrating the holy day. In the meanwhile, the clergy and the administration of the church prepare for the next service of the day—an English version of the same service, a remnant from colonial days.

ZOROASTRIAN

NAVROZ IN LAHORE

Just off M.M. Alam Road, the modern food street of Lahore, hidden from the thousands of people who visit this area on a daily basis, is the only functional Fire Temple in Lahore, a sacred shrine for the microscopic Zoroastrian community of the city. So unknown is this place and so easy to disappear in the shining lights of this modern locality that not even the locals are aware of the presence of this small shrine.

'At the time of Partition, there were quite a few Parsis (a title specific to the South-Asian Zoroastrians) living in Lahore and Amritsar,' says Farah Desai, an eighty-two-year-old Zoroastrian woman living in Lahore. 'They were all well-to-do, most of whom ran their own businesses. However, over the years, majority of the Parsis emigrated, settling in the States or Europe. There are only a handful of us left here. There used to be a priest at the temple but he has now moved to Karachi, hence there is no one left to lead the prayers here any more.' The absence of a priest becomes an issue particularly on the occasion of religious festivals and events. Traditionally, the community would gather at the fire temple in the morning to take part in a communal prayer, after which they would prepare for the evening celebrations. However, now that there is no one to lead the prayer, attendance at the temple has shrunk.

* * *

'It has been months since we've been to the Fire Temple,' says Hamdast, as he sits back at the table after helping himself to some rice and chicken. He is not too sure about the quality of the salad and fish so he refrains from eating them. Hamdast, twenty-two, is a student of law at TILS University, Lahore. He is one of the youngest members of the community in this city.

Wearing a black T-shirt and matching jeans, he is sitting at a round table surrounded by ten other people, all of whom are in their late teens or early twenties. His two sisters, one of whom is a student at the Lahore Grammar School (LGS), an elite institution of the city, are accompanying him. Sitting next to Hamdast is twenty-five-year-old Saba Chinoy, a graduate from the National College of Arts (NCA), who has now taken up a teaching job at the LGS Defence Branch. 'Hardly anyone follows the tradition any more,' she says. 'None of us sitting here went to the temple in the morning.' Everyone nods. 'Our family might stop on the way back, or so they say. I doubt we will.'

The food has just been served and everyone has helped themselves to their first serving. There are no traditional Parsi dishes, only regular Lahori ones. Members of the community heap chicken kabab, rice and fish on their plates. Waiters in white shirts and black trousers stand attentively, distributing plates to the guests. A few women adjust their saris and hair in front of the mirror situated in the corner. This is a big hall and it is quite empty. The food laid out on the tables is at one end of the hall and the seating at the other. There are about seven round tables here, each occupied by five to six people. Most of the women are wearing sleeveless blouses and saris, with their *pallu* draped across their right shoulder, a traditional feature of the Gujarati tradition. The men are wearing trousers and dress shirts while the younger girls are clad in jeans or shalwar kameez.

Hamdast's father, a tall man with glasses, wearing a blue shirt with black trousers, walks up to the table of the youngsters and standing behind Hamdast's chair listens to the conversation. He is in his late forties. 'What are you doing here?' jokes his son. 'This is no place for old people.' His father smiles and replies in Gujarati, a language that all the youngsters here are comfortable with. They laugh at the joke. The date is 21 March 2011 and the feast is in honour of Navroz, the Iranian and Parsi New Year.

* * *

Zoroastrianism is believed to be one of the oldest religions of the world, its origin lost in the obscurity of ancient history. The religion is focused around the teachings of Prophet Zarathusthra or Zoroaster, who is believed to have lived in Iran during the sixth and fifth century BCE. 'Once the Prophet created fire out of nothing and ever since then, fire has become a sacred symbol of divinity for the Parsis,' explains Farah. 'But now we know that that area around the Caspian Sea in Iran, where this miracle took place is rich in oil. I think the miracle was in fact a natural phenomenon, which the people of that time did not understand.'

Fire is an essential feature of the religion. There is a chamber at the temple which holds the sacred fire in a silver container. A few senior members of the community visit the temple regularly to attend to it, making sure that it remains lit, using oil and other material. 'The fire at the Fire Temple of Lahore is more than a century old,' says Sadaf, Farah's sister, a seventy-three-year-old woman who lives with Farah. 'By that, I mean that it has been continuously lit for more than a hundred years. There are a few temples in India where the fire is several centuries old. The oldest fire in this region is at the temple of Udvada in Gujarat. This is the most important pilgrimage site for the Parsis. It holds the original fire that was brought by the community when they came from Persia.'

Zoroastrianism was the dominant religion of Persia before the advent of Islam. According to Parsi legend, when Islam spread to Persia in the seventh century CE, a small band of Zoroastrians set out in three boats and ended up at Sanjan, a city in present-day Gujarat, India. On their arrival, the leader of the community sent a message to the king of the city, a Rajput Rana, asking for permission to be allowed to live there. The Rana turned down his request. The leader of the Parsi community then asked for a bowl of milk and some sugar. Taking a handful of sugar, he mixed it into the milk and sent it back to the Rana with the message that the Parsi community in his kingdom would be like sugar in this milk; invisible yet present and adding colour to the community. The Parsi leader further promised that they would adopt the local customs and culture of that region and would never proselytize. The Rana, impressed by the sagacity of the leader and his promises, allowed them to settle within his kingdom. Here, they eventually earned the title of 'Parsi', the community that came from Persia.

Adhering to its promise, the Parsi community adopted the Gujarati language, a language that they still use and treat as their mother tongue. They also adopted traditional Gujarati clothes with the women wearing the pallu of the sari on the right as Gujarati women do, as opposed to the conventional left. Even today, living in Pakistan, they sing traditional Gujarati songs on the occasion of their weddings and make traditional Gujarati food. Their integration into the local culture in fact was so strong that the original language, Avestan, which the community spoke when it arrived, has disappeared, with no one able to understand it. Even though the community still recites its prayers in Avestan, it does so without understanding, reading it in the Gujarati script.

* * *

On an accompanying table, Sadaf Dhodi helps Farah to her feet and guides her to the food table. For Farah, the sari is an everyday dress but Sadaf usually wears shalwar kameez. She was born after Partition and thus born into a Lahore that was different from the multi-religious city that Farah grew up in. The sari by the time Sadaf grew up had become the symbol of an Indian woman and wasn't encouraged in Lahore any more. Today, however, given that it is an auspicious day, she is wearing one. She has recently retired from the Kinnaird College where she taught for more than two decades and also headed their dramatics society. It was here that she made a few ever-lasting friendships with progressive Muslim women.

During the 1980s, while her Muslim female colleagues protested out on the roads against the Islamization of the country by the military dictator General Zia-ul-Haq, she refrained from taking part in any politics. During that decade, several religious laws were passed that restricted the freedom of religious minorities and women, a few of which are part of the Hudood Ordinance and Law of Evidence. For example, a law was passed that since women were emotionally weaker than men, their testimony would be half of that of a man. Another law that was passed stated that in order to prove rape, a victim needs to produce four honest Muslim men as witness. Critics of the law suggested that if a victim failed to produce the witnesses, then having reported the case, she would be liable to be punished as a fornicator having admitted to sexual conduct. Women all around the country rallied against these laws. Sadaf too felt strongly about the cause but she couldn't participate in the protest, upholding a promise that her ancestors made to the Rana of Sanjan about thirteen centuries ago.

Like the Christians, the Parsis too remained a neutral community during the riots of Partition. 'Our father used to say, "We will remain in Pakistan and accept any government that comes to power." Most of our family based in Bombay continued staying in India after Partition. We visit often but it has now become increasingly difficult to do that,' says Sadaf. Since the past many months, both the sisters have been trying to travel to India to meet their relatives, but every time the sisters apply for a visa, Indian officials based in Islamabad ask for a whole new set of documents from their sponsors in India. 'We returned three times with our visa application and on each new visit they wanted more documents. We cannot bother our friends in India to run around for more documents now. They too are old women. So we have just dropped the plan.' In the conflict between Muslims, Sikhs and Hindus,

Zoroastrian families were divided against their wishes and politics.

One of the reasons why the Fire Temple in Lahore functions in oblivion, despite the prominent locality that it is situated in is that the Parsi community tends to play down its religious identity. Following a strict code of conduct, they do not allow any non-Parsi to enter the temple. This is a tradition that developed after having promised the Rana that they would never proselytize. 'There is a Muslim caretaker at the shrine who looks after the cleanliness and runs other errands but he is not allowed to enter the room that contains the fire. Only members of the Parsi community tend to the sacred fire,' says Sadaf. She recalls that the Fire Temple, which was earlier situated on Rettigan Road, a prominent locality in colonial Lahore, now taken over by small businesses and shops and no longer the clean spacious area that it once was, moved to its current location sometime in the 1960s. Following the required protocol, the sacred fire was carried in a pavilion covered from all sides to avoid the gaze of any non-Parsi while on the road.

The temple is divided into two main sections; one room which is reserved for the fire and another hall where non-Parsis are allowed but reluctantly. Next to the temple, a compound has been raised to accommodate Parsi families who cannot afford to live elsewhere. Here, flats are leased out to them at subsidized rates. These administrative tasks on the part of the community are handled by an organization called the Anjuman, an elected body.

'In the hall next to the room where the sacred fire is kept, you will find a picture of the Prophet Zoroaster and other senior members of the community who have passed away,' says Sadaf. 'Well, actually, the Zoroastrians are an ancestor-worshipping community. On all religious occasions and other days, we try to remember all of our ancestors who are no longer with us,' elaborates her sister. Their house, located in a posh locality of the city, is a living history museum with pictures more than a century old decorating the walls. 'That's my great-grandmother and father along with their children. That little child on the right corner, no older than ten is my mother. You can calculate how old this picture must be,' points out Farah talking about a picture on the wall. In the middle of the conversation, a giant clock indicates that it is noon which is signalled by a bell. 'That belonged to my mother,' she says. Outside on their lawn, an iron swing neatly painted in white swings in the spring breeze as if the spirits of her ancestors are still sitting on it. 'That also belonged to my parents. Every evening they would have siesta on it while we were living on Waris Road.'

Explaining Parsi beliefs, Farah explains, 'The Parsis are a liberal people. We enjoy celebrations and parties, which is why we celebrate all festivals irrespective of religion. On every Eid, we visit our Muslim friends with a cake, while on every Christmas we do the same for our Christian friends. We also do not bind members of the community to marry only within the Zoroastrian community. They can marry anyone they chose: Muslim, Hindu, Christian, whoever they want. And if they want to convert to any one of these religions, no one would object to that. In fact, over the years, so many Parsi people have married non-Zoroastrians and converted to other religions that it has resulted in a steep decline in the population of the Zoroastrian community the world over. There are only thirty-five Parsis left in Lahore, but that's all right. Religion is the private matter of an individual. It is really sad though that people enforce it so forcefully. That's not the purpose of religion. However, what we do not allow is for any non-Parsi to convert to Zoroastrianism. To be one, one has to have a Parsi mother and father.'

* * *

Sitting quietly at this talkative table, with a round face and eyes, and dimpled cheeks, is a young girl wearing a black shalwar kameez. She is wearing a pendant probably containing verses from the Holy Quran round her neck. Moving his attention away from Hamdast, his father talks to her in Gujarati, asking her about the food. With a shy smile and downcast eyes, she responds politely as a few other comments in Gujarati come from other members at the table. A woman in her mid-forties, sitting on the neighbouring table, follows the conversation attentively for a little while after which she once again starts talking and laughing with the people at her table. Sitting next to her, a man as oddly quiet as this young woman in this room full of merry, giggly people, gets up to help himself to another serving of the food.

'Not all the Parsis of the city are present at Navroz this year,' whispers Hamdast watchfully looking around to make sure no one else is listening, as he helps himself to a serving of dessert, a yellow custard with chocolate mousse. 'A few years ago, there was a debate within the community that since the number of attendees at Navroz has reduced over the years, the community should also invite those Parsis who have converted to other religions. There was one small group who was against that idea. After the majority of the community agreed on inviting the former Parsis, those who were against the idea were dropped.'

Done with his dessert, a waiter offers him green tea, which he politely refuses.

'You see that woman on the other table, laughing and talking with everyone. She married a Shiia-Muslim and became a Muslim herself. Her husband is the one helping himself to food right there. He is not from within the community. This girl here is their only child. She is a non-Parsi as well.'

Sitting on Rati and Sadaf's table, a tall woman wearing a sari with a sleeveless blouse, sporting a golden frame on her eyes, gestures to one of the waiters. She whispers secretively into his ears while he listens attentively, nods obediently and then disappears. This woman is sixty-four-year-old Daria Boatwala.

* * *

When Daria moved to Lahore sometime in the 1980s after her wedding to Mahavir Boatwala, she knew that she had to work somewhere to keep herself busy. She approached Byram Dinshawji Avari, the owner of the Avari chain of hotels and a Parsi himself. She was employed immediately and has been working here ever since. Every year on the occasion of Navroz, Avari throws a lavish dinner party for the Parsi community of the city in his hotel, considered to be one of the best in the country. As a senior employee here, Daria looks after the preparations.

'Moving to Lahore was a cultural shock for me,' recalls Daria. 'It took me a long time to adjust here. Karachi is a much more happening city with a huge population of Zoroastrians and other non-Muslims. One interacts with Hindus, Christians, etc. in several social forums. But here in the Punjab, the situation is much different. There are hardly any Zoroastrians here and I have never come across any Hindu. The only Christians that you see are those who are cleaners and sweepers. Lahore is much more monolithic and I would say religiously conservative. There in Karachi I would wear dresses everywhere but here it is an issue. I still wear dresses to work, but there are a few people who object to it. I ignore their comments. A lot of people are also curious about our religion. They think that we worship fire, which is not true. We regard it as a symbol of divinity.

'In the beginning, I loved the fact that Lahore was a quiet, peaceful place with lots of greenery, as opposed to Karachi, which is really a desert, but then I started missing my friends and family. Besides, there are thousands of Parsis in Karachi, which makes occasions like Navroz a lot of fun there. Nothing really happens here as you can see. While I was in Karachi, on the morning of Navroz, all members of the community would gather at the Fire Temple where there would be a communal prayer. In the evening, we would gather at the Beach Luxury Hotel (part of the Avari chain of hotels) where there would be various games for the children and adults, organized on the lawns of the hotel. One of the games I remember used to be a race that one had to run clasping a spoon with one's teeth while trying to balance a lemon. Another race involved tying one's leg with that of a partner. There would be several stalls for eatables serving Pakistani as well as traditional Parsi food. In the evenings after dinner, we would gather inside the hall to dance. '

* * *

Before the waiter places a cup of green tea in front of Farah, he removes the Tambola sheets that the community played before dinner. This is the only game they play in Lahore now. Each participant is handed a sheet of paper that contains rows and columns with a few numbers. Picking numbers blindly from a bowl the host announces the number and the participants strike it off their sheets if they have it. The first one to cross out all of his/her numbers is the winner.

'You know dear, when the children were younger, we would have several games but now that they have grown up, they are not interested in games any more,' laments Farah.

On the other table, Hamdast and other youngsters remember when they used to play games on the occasion of Navroz. 'When I was about thirteen or fourteen, all the children used to come dressed up according to a theme for the fancy-dress competition that used to be organized every year. I remember that once I dressed up as an Arab sheikh and my sister dressed up as a towel.' Sitting nearby, his sister does not enjoy this recollection and looks at Hamdast disapprovingly, but he ignores her. 'My other sister dressed up as a goldfish that year. We would also have musical chairs and 'Pass the Pillow'. Even the adults used to participate. There was one game particularly for adults in which married couples were made to stand on two opposite ends of the hall, with a distance of about 20 metres between them. At a signal, the husband would run to his wife and put make-up on her. After completing the task, they would run together towards the other end of the room, where there was a line drawn on the floor. The first one to cross would win.'

'I really don't know why we don't have games any more,' jumps in Saba, eager to share her perspective. 'I know some of the games were silly and we cannot possibly dress up as goldfish or towels,' she jokes catching a glimpse of Hamdast's sister, who refuses to look up and continues eating, 'but we can have games like musical chairs or the make-up game.'

'Honestly, I don't think even the adults are keen on doing it now.' Hamdast responds. 'Who cares about traditions any more?' comments another young girl sitting across him. 'Most of these people sitting around this table, I hardly meet except on occasions like these. The last time we all sat together was probably on the occasion of last Navroz.'

* * *

The celebration of Navroz is not the only tradition that has suffered because of the dwindling numbers of the Parsi community. Because of no priest, there is no way to perform a traditional Parsi marriage in Lahore. The same applies for the rites after death. Traditionally, the Parsi communities place the bodies of the deceased at the Tower of Silence, an enclosed space where animals roam and eat the last remains of the departed, a tradition that dates back several centuries. There is a Tower of Silence in Karachi but none in Lahore. Here, instead, the Parsi community buries its dead in a graveyard next to the Minar-e-Pakistan facing the ancient walled city of Lahore. 'If we want to organize a traditional wedding, we either invite the priest up here or just travel down south to Karachi,' says Farah.

* * *

Finishing off their green teas, the families begin slipping out of the hall as the waiters stand in line seeing them off. Sadaf supports Farah as she walks around and exchanges niceties with everyone. On the way back, Saba's family might or might not stop at the Fire Temple.

BAHA'I

HAZRAT BAB'S BIRTHDAY IN LAHORE

'And that's the garden with the shrine. Isn't it beautiful? Hazrat Shogi Effendi designed it himself. He would walk around and instruct which trees should be planted where,' says forty-year-old Ayesha, a science teacher at Lahore Grammar School. She is dressed up in a pink shalwar kameez, her hair all tied up. She is wearing some make-up on this auspicious day. Her son, Haider Saeed, is sitting on the podium staring at the projector screen, which takes the audience through an aerial tour of the shrine of Hazrat Bab, the founder of the Baha'i religion. It is a tall white structure, standing in the midst of neatly and symmetrically maintained gardens, with a golden dome on the tomb. Situated on Mount Carmel and facing the Haifa Bay, terraces have been cut on both sides of the shrine for the garden.

* * *

Hazrat Bab's body was moved to this particular spot sixty years after his death. His spiritual successor, Hazrat

Abdul Baha, made the move in 1909 after which a basic structure was constructed for the tomb. This structure was expanded by Hazrat Abdul Baha's grandson, Hazrat Shogi Effendi. Hazrat Abdul Baha is buried in one of the rooms at the shrine. The Universal House of Justice, which is the governing organization of the Baha'i community the world over, is situated on the same mount as well. Just about 15 km from this port city is Acre, the holiest city in the Baha'i religion. This is where Hazrat Bahaullah is buried. Hazrat Bab, Hazrat Bahaullah, Hazrat Abdul Baha and Hazrat Shogi Effendi are the four most important people in the Baha'i faith, and a pilgrimage to their shrine is a pious act. All of them have remained spiritual and political heads of the Baha'i community, which is now governed by the Universal House of Justice, founded by Hazrat Abdul Baha and developed by his grandson. All of these places are in present-day Israel; a forbidden place for a Pakistani. It is the only country in the world that Pakistan doesn't recognize. Every page of the green booklet reads, 'This passport is valid for all the countries of the world except ISRAEL.' This is one pilgrimage that Pakistani Baha'is cannot perform, at least in the foreseeable future.

* * *

'There will be a huge gathering there today. Baha'is would have come from all over the world to pay their tributes to the founder of the religion,' adds Ayesha, as the scene on the projector changes into a night-time vision of the shrine, illuminated with lights. The lights of the city can be seen at some distance from the shrine with dramatic music accompanying the clip. It is only since the social media revolution that all the Pakistani Baha'is can catch a glimpse of their most sacred shrines, prior to which only a few people had seen pictures of it. Ayesha's son, Haider, has picked out this clip from several available ones on the Internet. Haider, wearing a grey shirt and black trousers, is twenty-two years of age and along with his father, is responsible for the arrangement of this function. They are the only two members of the Programme Committee for 2011, appointed by the Local Spiritual Assembly (LSA); the local administrative body of the Baha'is. Haider is a student at the Lahore University of Management Sciences (LUMS), a premier business school in the country.

Facing him, the audience is divided into two sections as per the seating arrangements, with the men and the boys occupying the right side, and the women and girls on the left. There are only about forty-odd people in this hall at the moment out of the 150 Baha'is registered with the LSA. A few are sitting downstairs in the garage socializing, while a family is busy in the kitchen giving final touches to the feast for the night. A feast concludes all the religious gatherings here of which tonight is one of the most important ones — the birthday of Hazrat Bab. The date is 20 October 2011.

* * *

Hazrat Bab was born into a Syed Shiia family in Sheraz, present day Iran, in 1819. His real name was Syed Ali Muhammad Shirazi. As a young man, he became a merchant and at the age of twenty-four declared himself to be the promised messiah, known as Imam Mahdi in Shiia parlance. This attracted the wrath of the Shiia-Muslim state, resulting in his persecution and that of his followers. He took up the title of Bab, which means gate, and his followers came to be known as Babis. He was executed in 1850 by the government on the charge of being a blasphemer.

After his death, one of his followers, Mirza Husayn Ali, declared himself to be the second messiah in line at the young age of twenty-seven and took up the title of Bahaullah, which means glory of Allah (Babis, who were later to be called Baha'is, also use the name Allah to refer to their God, amongst many others). The majority of the Babis accepted him as the second messiah and came to be known as Baha'is. Like Hazrat Bab, Hazrat Bahaullah also had to face religious persecution, which led to his exile from Iran. He went to Turkey, but was forced to leave from there as well. He eventually settled in Acre, where he is now buried. He was succeeded by his son, Hazrat Abdul Baha, as the spiritual and political leader of the community, who was then succeeded by his grandson, Hazrat Shogi Effendi. According to the law laid down by Hazrat Bahaullah, only a male successor from the messiah's family could be the head of the Baha'i community. In 1957, Hazrat Shogi Effendi died without any male progeny, thus putting an end to the lineage of Hazrat Bahaullah. After his death, the Universal House of Justice became the spiritual and the administrative head of the community.

Using references from other religions as well, both Hazrat Bab and Hazrat Bahaullah declared themselves to be the messiahs promised not only in Islam but also Christianity, Hinduism and Buddhism. One of the youngest and latest religions to emerge on the world stage, the Baha'is regard their faith to be the unifying factor of all these religions. It's a monotheistic faith, which says that all the religions and the prophets were sent by God, therefore no religion or prophet is false. Following this line of thought, the Baha'is allow intermarriage between different religions.

* * *

'Hazrat Bab declared himself to be the messiah at the age of twenty-four, while Hazrat Bahaullah did so at the age of twenty-seven. They were both appointed by God at a young age. It is because of this that the Baha'is give a lot of responsibility and respect to youth. By trusting them, they encourage them to channel their vitality and energy in constructive activities,' says Rasikh Zarin, who at the age of twenty-seven, is a member of the LSA and takes part in discussions pertinent to all decisions. 'The youth has a lot of energy but no direction. We believe that if we show them the right path, they can achieve wonders. We try to incorporate them in all administrative and religious matters,' says seventy-year-old Professor Bahari, a member of the National Spiritual Assembly (NSA), the national administrative body of the Baha'i community in Pakistan, with its office in Islamabad.

* * *

The arrangements for the religious proceedings have been organized in the hall situated on the first floor of the Baha'i centre. This can accommodate about 100 people. There is a small platform at one end of the hall, used as a stage on such occasions with a table and wooden chairs placed on it. Behind the chairs, a frame hanging on the wall contains a symbol of the Baha'i faith called the ring stone symbol. This calligraphic design, created by Hazrat Abdul Baha himself, has a three-tier meaning—the world of God, the world of His Manifestations (prophets) and the world of man (human). Many Baha'is wear this insignia as a ring.

This purpose-built hall has nine corners. If viewed from the top, the room appears to be a nine-sided star. The nine-sided star is another symbol of the Baha'i faith, nine considered to be an auspicious number representing the highest individual integer. There are nine members of the Universal House of Justice. Similarly, there are nine members of the LSA and the NSA. As per the requirements of Baha'i law, the Baha'is are urged to set up an LSA at any city, village or town, where there are nine or more members.

The LSA at Lahore was established before Partition. There are LSAs in Rawalpindi, Multan, Quetta, Karachi, Hyderabad, Sargodha, Mirpur Khas and several other cities of the country. The LSA acts as a platform for Baha'is through which they represent themselves as a community. It is also responsible for media, administrative, civic, political, educational and philanthropic activities. It's an elective body, which then forms other bodies like the programme committee or the educational committee (which provides spiritual and secular education to the young members of the community as well as non-Baha'is). It comes under the NSA, which then falls under the Universal House of Justice.

In Lahore, the LSA meets at the Baha'i Centre, which is near the Ganga Ram Hospital. This building was purchased by the community sometime in the 1980s, before which the centre was located in a rented space elsewhere. From the outside, it looks like any other house in the residential area that it is situated in. However, a blue board at the top of the gate distinguishes it. It reads 'Baha'i Centre' in English as well as Urdu. There is a quotation by Hazrat Bahaullah on it that reads, 'The Earth is but one country and Mankind its citizens.' Hazrat Bahaullah believed in the unification of the world through a world government, which represented all countries. He was also in favour of recognizing a universal language, which would have its speakers all over the world in order to facilitate the intermingling of people from various nationalities. The Baha'i religion developed in the second half of the nineteenth century at a time when the first steps towards globalization were being taken and therefore its philosophy reflects the sensibilities of its era.

The gate is open and anyone can walk in. The Centre is usually empty with just one person at the office. There is no security guard. The community is closely knit so any outsider is easily identifiable. Upon entering, there is a small room on the right side, next to which stairs lead up to this hall. There is a small garden adjacent to the staircase while an empty garage lies right in front of it, where meetings are held during pleasant seasons. The kitchen is in a room within the garage.

* * *

The clip finishes in fifteen minutes marking the beginning of the proceedings for the night. Haider's brother, Aakil Saeed, comes to the stage with his Spanish guitar accompanied by two other people, a boy of about eighteen and a woman in her forties. Aakil sits on a chair that Haider drags from the crowd, and starts to pluck his fingers on his guitar, playing chord D. His companions position themselves to face the crowd, both of them holding a white book. Following a head signal from the guitarist, they start singing a religious song. Ayesha, sitting in the crowd, takes out a small book from her black bag and sings along as do a few other people. Some who remember the song by heart sing with their heads bowed and eyes closed attentively. The projector on the wall now shows a daytime picture of Hazrat Bab's shrine.

No one claps at the end of the song. The performers quietly return to their chairs. From a seat in the second row of the men's section, a man about seventy years of age and dark complexioned, wearing a white shirt and matching pants stands up and heads to the podium, as if following a cue. His name is Rehan Behzadi and he is one of the few Baha'is in the city who has converted to the Baha'i faith instead of being born into it like the majority of the people here.

* * *

'I was still in college at that time and about twenty years old, when an uncle of mine, who was a Baha'i, gave me a book on the Baha'i religion. That was my first encounter with this faith, before which I hadn't even heard of it. I was born a Muslim and was a devoted believer. That book introduced me to the Baha'i faith and the lives of Hazrat Bab and Hazrat Bahaullah. It argued that both of them were the messiahs promised in Islam, highlighting signs in the Islamic tradition that these two prophets fulfilled. I then read Islamic books, including the Quran, and was convinced that indeed their claims were correct. I found all the signs in these books. I also studied Christian and Judaist books and found that the arrival of these two messiahs was also mentioned in their books as well as those of the Hindus and the Buddhists. I had found the right religion, so I converted at the age of twenty,' says Behzadi in a calm, calculated manner, the way he usually talks.

For the initial few months, unsure about what their response would be, he didn't tell his parents about his conversion. 'Finally, when I told them, naturally they were upset. They tried convincing me otherwise but I would have answers to all their questions. Soon they realized that I was firm in belief and would not budge. They gave up on the cause and I continued living with them normally. We stopped talking about religion. However, there were other family members who stopped talking to me altogether. I haven't met my uncles and aunts ever since because they are Muslims, or should I say because I am a Baha'i.'

Behzadi is nervous about sharing these intimate details from his life. He feels that by doing so he might be transgressing the social laws laid down by the Baha'i community. A board in the garage of the Baha'i centre reads 'It is forbidden for Baha'is to take part in politics' and nothing is more political in Pakistan than religion. The creation of the country was based on religious identity. Behzadi is not sure where religion ends and politics begins. 'Hazrat Bahaullah said that it is forbidden for the Baha'is to take part in politics. It is the duty of every Baha'i to show allegiance to the government of any state he or she is living in, Hazrat Bahaullah further stated,' justifies Behzadi. He is also confused about the distinction between individual identity and that of the community. According to the laws laid down by the administrative authority of the Baha'i community, any statement about the community needs to come after the approval of the LSA. Behzadi is not sure if by sharing the story of his conversion he is transgressing Baha'i laws. Like a typical convert, he is much more scrupulous about the new religion and its laws compared to its older believers. Ostracized from his extended family, he married a Kashmiri Baha'i girl of Iranian origin who his uncle introduced him to. Grandparents now, both of them have a perfect Baha'i family.

Unlike Behzadi, Anwar Ahmed, seventy-five, is not shy about his non-Baha'i past. Sitting one row behind Behzadi, he was an Ahmadiyya and converted to the Baha'i faith about ten years ago. Earlier considered to be a sect within the fold of Islam, the Ahmadiyya community was declared non-Muslim in Pakistan after the National Assembly passed a law in 1974. In 1984, further Ahmadiyya' laws were adopted into the constitution inhibiting their religious and social freedom. Considered heretical, the community has been vulnerable to religious persecution over the years. On 28 May 2010, two houses of worship of the Ahmadiyya community in Lahore were attacked, resulting in the death of ninety-four people and all political leaders refrained from visiting the site or sympathizing with the community because of the backlash that it was likely to invite. Major cities of the country have wall graffiti inciting violence against the Ahmadiyyas, to which the concerned authorities have turned a blind eye. As a result, a lot of Ahmadiyyas have migrated out of the country. It is also believed that in the recent years a lot of Ahmadiyyas have adopted the Baha'i faith to avoid social discrimination. However, that is an inconvenient 'truth' that neither of the communities is willing to admit. Anwar insists that he converted out of conviction instead of any political consideration and denies the fact that anyone who has become a Baha'i from Ahmadiyya has done so to avoid persecution. His family, including his wife and children, are still Ahmadiyya.

Another story of conversion is that of Usman Nawaz, a sixty-two-year-old man living in Shahdara, Lahore. 'I was a Sunni Muslim by birth and was living in district Gujrat at that time. I was working at a factory when I heard of the Baha'i faith. I wanted to read more about it. Whereas on the one hand, Hazrat Bab and Bahaullah claim to be the promised messiahs, the followers of Mirza Ghulam Ahmad (Ahmaddiya) also regard him as the promised messiah. I started reading about Ahmadiyya teachings as well. After reading a little, I decided to interact with both communities. I first went to the NSA in Islamabad. They asked me why I wanted to convert to the Baha'i faith. After a few more questions they told me to go back and return after reading up more on the faith. They also encouraged me to read up more about other religions, including the Ahmaddiya faith. The Ahmaddiya community, on the other hand, told me that I had come to the right place. They got a little uneasy when I raised a few questions about Hazrat Bab and Hazrat Bahaullah. From my interaction with the Baha'i community, I realized that the Baha'is were sincere, so I adopted their religion. When I went to the centre this time, they gave me a certification and entered me as registered Baha'i,' says Nawaz. However, unlike Behzadi and Anwar, Nawaz had to face stiff opposition. He was married at the time of conversion. His wife refused to convert with him and instead pressed him to come back to Islam. 'Things got so bad once that we almost got separated. However, our elders intervened and we both decided to let each other live. But she remained unhappy with my conversion till her death.'

A few years later, he moved to Lahore, where he started working at the Sohrab Cycle Factory, located across the road from his home in Shahdrah. He worked there for eight years, but was eventually forced to resign because of the hostile attitude of his colleagues. Things got worse when a Muslim worker threw a stone at him and injured him because he was a Baha'i. The Muslim fanatics would call him a kafir, a derogatory word used by Muslims to refer to any non-Muslim. 'I reported the case to the higher management but they were afraid to take any action against the culprit. So I resigned.' Nawaz is also the only Baha'i from his house. His son chose the religion of his mother and married a Muslim; hence their children are also Muslim. His son cooperates with him when he can, bringing him to the Baha'i centre on special days. 'However, a lot of times he is busy because of which I cannot attend many religious days.' Nawaz has been losing his eyesight for quite sometime and is now almost blind.

While there have been a few particular incidents of hostilities, the Baha'is in general have been spared the religious persecution in Pakistan unlike most of the other minorities. A majority of the Baha'is are economically well established and reasonably educated. Many people in the country are unaware of this religion whereas others think it is a sect within Islam. On the other hand, the condition of the Baha'is in the country of their origin is that of a persecuted lot like the Ahmadiyya in Pakistan. In 1979, after the Iranian revolution, a systematic persecution against the Baha'is began in the country, similar to what took place at the time of the religion's inception. As a result of this treatment, there was a large influx of Iranian refugees into Pakistan. Here they were helped by the local Baha'i community, many of who opened up their homes to welcome them. An Iranian family lived in Behzadi's house for years before migrating to Australia. Various LSAs gathered money and used it for the welfare of the Iranian refugees. Over the years, most of them have migrated to other countries; however the state of Baha'is in Iran remains the same.

* * *

Standing on the podium, Behzadi opens the Kitab-i-Aqdas, the holiest book of the Baha'is. Written by Hazrat Bahaullah, it lists the basic principles of the religion. Announcing that he would read a chapter from it, he begins to recite: 'Indeed, it is obligatory that in each city a House of Justice is established comprising nine persons. There is no problem if the number of persons are more.' The crowd nods in agreement as if reinforcing their commitment.

Sitting on his right is the twenty-six-year-old Haytham Zarin, wearing a white shalwar kameez. The pink glow of her fair skin is reflective of her Iranian origin. Most of the Baha'is here have similar complexions as most of them trace their roots back to that ancient land. Haytham's grandfather moved to Pakistan years before Partition and continued living here after the creation of the country. She is currently working at the Fatima Memorial Hospital, Lahore, doing a house job after completing her MBBS. Keeping the tradition of giving young people authority she has been appointed by the LSA as the head of the study circle.

Hazrat Bahaullah has given particular importance to universal education. In the Kitab-i-Aqdas, he has ordered the parents that it is their religious duty to provide education to their children. In line with this philosophy, the Baha'i community the world over gives special attention to the education of children and youth. Along with secular education, they give a lot of importance to spiritual and civic education, held to be important for the development of a society. In this regard, the community regularly arranges study groups in different areas, imparting secular, spiritual and civic education to the young members of the community. 'This is not only reserved for Baha'is. We invite members of different religious communities to attend the classes. Most of the children come from Muslim backgrounds,' says Haytham. Every month at the monthly festival held at the Baha'i centre, she gives a report on the progress of the study circles.

Behzadi's recitation also concludes without any applause from the crowd, as he returns to his chair quietly. Haytham walks up to the podium and greets everyone with 'Allah-u-Abha,' which means 'God is all glorious' in Arabic. This is the traditional Baha'i greeting. Her visit to the podium is short, only meant to call in the next speaker: Atiya Saeed, one of the senior-most members of the community in Lahore. Atiya is the daughter of the famed Baha'i scholar, Syed Mahfooz-ul-Haq Ilmi, who migrated to Pakistan at the time of Partition. Here he travelled all over the country spreading the message of Hazrat Bahaullah and engaging with the community for philanthropic work. Atiya's family is one of the oldest Baha'i families in South Asia and is held in high esteem by the local as well as the international community.

Baha'i functions do not follow a fixed agenda. The stage is open for anyone who wants to come up and speak, sing, or recite something concerning religion or ethics. After Atiya, her son, an aspiring musician, performs an original song to which the younger members of the community sing along. Following this, Nawaz expresses his desire to read out an original poem that he has written. He is helped on to the stage by Aaftab, Behzadi's son.

The audience enjoys his poem, smiling and interacting with him as he recites. At the conclusion of the poem, Haytham brings a little girl about eight years old wearing a yellow dress, on to the stage, who recites a poem that she has learnt at school. The singing and recitation continue as Aakil, and later Behzadi, come back for further performances. Behzadi's son Aaftab, forty-two, also volunteers to sing a devotional song.

At the end of the ceremony, the community gathers in the garage, where a long table has been set up with food. Two round tables with chairs have also been arranged at one corner of the garage for the older members of the community. The food is chicken qorma, roti and salad. This marks the conclusion of the event. The community will head back after dinner but will congregate again a few days later to celebrate the birthday of Hazrat Bahaullah. The event will be similar to this, with the only difference being that Hazrat Bahaullah will replace Hazrat Bab as the focus of the recitation and readings.

Sikh

BAISAKHI AT HASSAN ABDAL

Surrounded by mountains on one side and the entire city of Hassan Abdal on the other, the Gurdwara Panja Sahib is one of the most important Sikh shrines in the country. It is home to about fifty to sixty Sikh families, who have moved here in the last few years from the tribal areas due to the rise of insurgency there, while the rest of the city is Muslim. Most of the Sikhs only know Pashtu, which just a handful of Punjabi/Hindko-speaking people here can understand. The Sikhs are mostly confined within the boundaries of the gurdwara, protected by police officials, tall walls and barbed wire on all sides; only occasionally do they venture out. A few pilgrims visit all year round to pay their respects to the shrine associated with the founder of the Sikh religion, Guru Nanak (1469–1539).

Hassan Abdal is a historic city which has managed to retain its character. The streets are narrow and curved with wooden balconies leaning into them providing shade to the passersby. Situated on hillocks, the city descends and ascends in different parts. A few Hindu temples are still present here, standing tall above the other buildings and visible from afar, but are now being used as improvised houses or in some cases wandering grounds for stray animals, abandoned by the people of the city. The remains of a Mughal garden in a dilapidated state still survive facing the gurdwara referred to in the sixteenth century court treatise written during the reign of the third Mughal Emperor, Akbar (1542–1605) by Abu-Fazl, *Ain-i-Akbari*. For three days and nights in the month of April, everything changes here. The streets around the shrine are cordoned off and no Muslim is allowed to venture near the Gurdwara. The local schools are shut down and their classrooms converted into hostels for the pilgrims coming for the festival of Baisakhi. After spending three nights here—13, 14 and 15 April—most of the pilgrims go to the other holy Sikh shrines, while some stay for a few more days. The demographics of the city changes in these days as thousands of turbaned Sikhs are seen haggling with the shopkeepers in the market; most of them Indian Punjabis speaking a language that is understood here. Most of the Sikhs here are fair-skinned and blue-eyed Pathans, from the regions of Khyber-Pakhtunkhwa and tribal areas and they are more alien to this place than the Indian Punjabi Sikhs who are more or less at home when they visit. A third category of the pilgrims are those who do not sport a turban and are clean-shaven—Hindus from the different regions of Pakistan.

The date is 13 April 2011 and the scorching sun of late spring burns the tar road that a few pilgrims walk on without shoes as an expression of extreme respect to a city that is associated with the founder of the Sikh religion. According to local media reports, about 7000 pilgrims have arrived for the festival this year—about 2000 from India and the rest from within Pakistan.

* * *

There is a long queue outside the main entrance. A police officer stands in front of a small gate, checking everyone's security cards and only permits entry to one person at a time. Even until last year, pilgrims were allowed to enter without any such identification, their turbans or head covers proof enough of their non-Muslimness. Those who looked more 'Muslim' were asked for an identity and if proven Muslim were barred from entering. This year, however, the security has been intensified due to the deteriorating security conditions of the country. Even till recently, Muslims were allowed to pay their respects to the shrine of Baba Guru Nanak, much in line with the Sikh philosophy but not any more. All pilgrims and other visitors like journalists, etc. are allotted a security card from the 'Special Branch' which they have to exhibit every time they enter the gurdwara.

At the end of the line, a television crew argues with the police official at the entrance. Shoving his media card in the officer's face, the representative demands that he be let in, but the officer refuses to do so without the security card. The cameraman threatens to record the treatment meted out to them and telecast it on national television. Blackmailed, the police officer finally lets them pass.

There are more than 200 people standing in the line waiting to be ushered in. The façade of the building is pink, the view inside closed off by an iron gate. On the opposite building, a police officer stands on the top of a shop looking out for any suspicious activity. Behind the shop, ant-like lines of pilgrims can be seen heading towards the summit of the mountain. From here one cannot tell if they are Muslim pilgrims or non-Muslims, as the shrine on the top of the mountain is visited by both; for religious reasons by Muslims (this is a Muslim shrine by the name of Wali Qandhari) and because of its historical significance by non-Muslims.

* * *

About 500 years ago, on the same date, the first day of Vaisakh, Guru Nanak came here along with his two companions, Bhai Mardana—a Muslim, and Bhai Bala—a Hindu. At this spot, which was not a city at that time, he settled down under a peepal tree, the very spot where the gurdwara was built later. Having walked for several kilometres under the scorching sun, Bhai Mardana felt thirsty. Nanak, possessing special powers, knew that there was a *wali*, a saint sitting on top of the mountain facing them who had access to a fresh pool of water and told Mardana so. Ascending this steep slope stepping over sharp stones, Mardana got to the top, where he encountered Wali Qandhari, guarding a fresh pool of water, supplied by a stream. Initially, the wali agreed to provide Mardana with water but when he was told that Mardana was a companion of another saint, the wali, feeling rather insecure, refused him the water. He, in fact, mocked Mardana saying that if Nanak was such a pious man, then he should instead arrange for the water himself. A dejected Mardana came back and explained the situation to Nanak. Nanak instructed him to go back again and ask for water. Mardana did what he was told but in vain. The third time, Nanak told him to ask for water in the name of God. Having failed to yield results this time as well, Nanak moved a stone from the ground close to where they were seated and miraculously water started to gush out.

* * *

The main shrine is a splendid grey building adorned with three white and yellow domes on the top. Colourful cloths hanging from the building are tied to a railing around the shrine. On a small platform in front of the main shrine, the pilgrims have laid out their clothes to dry off, while others lie sunbathing. Double-storey buildings surround the shrine on all four sides; these contain rooms for the pilgrims to stay. Children are running around the courtyard while others sit under the shade of the building socializing. This place became a site of devotion after the miracle of Nanak. It was then extended during the tenure of the Sikh ruler of Punjab, Maharaja Ranjit Singh (1780–1839).

A hymn being sung in Punjabi along with the harmonium and tabla resonates all over the complex. This is the sound of *kirtan*, a religious song being performed in one of the rooms, heard everywhere through a system of speakers. Kirtan usually includes verses from the Sikh holy book, the Guru Granth Sahib. This tradition goes back to Nanak's Muslim devotee, Bhai Mardana; Bhai being a title given to him due to the exalted status he enjoys in the religion and Mardana being his real name. There are several paintings depicting a serene Nanak listening to the songs of Bhai Mardana holding a *rubab* (a traditional stringed instrument), while Bhai Bala stands behind them holding a fly-whisk. The depiction of this scene is particularly popular in Sikh hagiography.

The sacred pool said to have been created after the miracle of Nanak lies in the shadow of the main shrine. Several male devotees stand in this turquoise-coloured pool holding both of their hands together deeply engrossed in prayers while an old man swims around them practising his freestyle strokes. A few children standing on the stairs look at the pool longingly, eager to dive in but reluctant, perhaps due to the sacredness of the water.

A dark young man wearing a pink T-shirt and blue jeans fills out a bucket of water from the pool and hands it over to another man standing a few steps above him; who then hands it over to a man standing on the first step. Taking the bucket, he splashes the water on the white marble floor of the courtyard cleaning off the filth that has accumulated from the bare feet of the pilgrims. He hands the bucket back in this chain of human labour and the cycle is repeated. Next to him, a woman using a broom squatting on the floor directs the water to the drain on the edge of the residential buildings. This is no mundane activity, but a sacred duty called *sewa* (service). According to the Sikh religion, everyone is obliged to spend 10 per cent of their time or money in the performance of sewa. Following this principle, volunteers take it upon themselves to clean the shrine, while others volunteer to serve food, clean dishes and help with the cooking at the langar hall.

The stairs leading into the pool have also been made out of white marble with several of them bearing the names of the people or organizations who have donated money or other things to the shrine. 'Kulvinder Kaur, Malkit Kaur, Canada Maple ridge (1100), 11.3.2007, Pray for family,' says one of the inscriptions. 'Jaspreet Singh Atwal (Jesse), Sept 1, 1991 to May 10, 2008, s/o Sadhu Singh Atwal, Seattle, USA,' reads another inscription.

Facing the main shrine, inside the pool, in a small niche whose protective arch is made of ivory, there is a grey stone with parts of it immersed in the water. There is a small line in front of the stone as several devotees wait for the darshan of the stone. On their turn, they place their hand on a black mark in the middle of the rock that looks like a handprint, while pouring water on it with their other hand. Some even kiss it. Flanking the stone on both sides, there is a window from where women offer their devotion to the sacred rock. A marble plaque next to it describes its significance in Gurmukhi, the script used to write Punjabi in East Punjab.

* * *

According to the legend, when Nanak removed the stone and water started gushing out of this place, the reservoir of the wali dried out as all the water was directed here. Infuriated at having lost his vantage point, the wali hurled a huge rock towards the saint which he stopped with his hand leaving a permanent mark on it. The stone in the niche is that rock that Nanak stopped. This particular shrine derives its name from that incident—Gurdwara Panja Sahib, Panja meaning palm, in this case, Nanak's palm.

* * *

Water still gushes into this pool through a stream, flowing into the complex from under the protective walls recently raised by the Government of Pakistan. Next to the sacred pool, a section of the stream can be seen temporarily, before it once again disappears under the building. Stairs constructed recently lead one directly to the stream where children are seen diving and swimming.

Standing on the stairs of the sacred pool, one of the boys from a group of children decides to jump into the water, having played long enough in the shallow stream. Another one follows him but the rest are too scared to follow suit.

Out of nowhere, a sturdy Pathan-Sikh man rushes towards them, cane in hand. 'Get out, you little rascals,' he shouts in Pashtu-accented Punjabi. 'This is no place to play!' The boys standing on the stairs flee, while the other two drag themselves out of the pool sheepishly and walk away.

The Pathan-Sikh is thirty-five-year-old Surjeet Singh from the city of Peshawar, a city on the western border of Pakistan. His family belongs to a small village in the Khyber Agency which is part of the Tribal Areas of Pakistan and in focus internationally due to the war on terror. His elders lived with their Muslim neighbours peacefully for several generations before moving to Peshawar for better economic opportunities, while Surjeet was still a child.

During his reign, Maharaja Ranjit Singh captured the Pathan regions of Khyber-Pakhtunkhwa and the tribal areas, as a result of which several people converted to Sikhism. At the time of Partition, unlike Punjab, this area was spared bloodshed primarily due to the influence of the *Sarhadi* (Frontier) Gandhi—Abdul Ghaffar Khan, an ally of the Indian National Congress and a proponent of the non-violence philosophy. Whereas millions of Hindus and Sikhs were uprooted from the plains of Punjab following the religious division between India and Pakistan, several Hindus and Sikhs stayed rooted in Khyber-Pakhtunkhwa because of the comparatively peaceful political situation here. Surjeet's family was one such family which never migrated.

After appearing for his matriculation exams, Surjeet joined his father's business of cloth trading. Standing on the steps with a stick in his hand making sure that the children do not use this sacred pool for a recreational bath is his way of performing sewa. There is a thick bangle on his right wrist, and his jeans are folded up to his knees and soaked on the edges. His white shirt reads, 'Never forget 1984' accompanied by a black and white picture of a man with a long beard, holding an arrow in his hand with a bullet belt strung across his chest. This is a picture of Sant Jarnail Singh Bhindranwale, a charismatic leader from the late 1970s and early 1980s. Based in East Punjab, India, Bhindranwale is a symbol for Sikh separatists fighting against the Indian state to carve out Khalistan—a pure land.

* * *

Bhindranwale was killed in an army operation that began on 3 June 1984 and lasted till 6 June 1984 at the Golden Temple in Amritsar, the holiest Sikh shrine in the world. Codenamed Operation Blue Star, it was launched on a day when thousands of Sikhs from all over Punjab had gathered at the shrine to commemorate the death anniversary of the fifth Sikh Guru, Guru Arjan. The symbolic value of the operation and the loss of life of thousands of Sikh pilgrims were not lost on the Sikh community who had gathered to remember the first Sikh martyr, assassinated by the fourth Mughal Emperor, Jahangir (1569–1627). In a long list of martyrs who followed Guru Arjan, the victims of the operation, including Bhindranwale, became the latest entry in Sikh tradition.

After becoming the head of the Damdami Taksal, a Sikh religious organization founded by the tenth Sikh Guru, Guru Gobind Singh (1666–1708), to impart religious education to people, Bhindranwale rose to prominence when he launched a movement of Sikh revivalism, encouraging people to revert to the roots of Sikhism. In his speeches, he passionately claimed that the new generation of Sikhs do not respect the Sikh way of life as taught by Guru Gobind Singh. He also took up a staunch stance against the Congress-led Indian government which he branded as a Hindu lobby thus gaining immense popularity amongst the youth of Punjab. On the other hand, the Indian government alleged that Bhindranwale and his followers were the reason why there was a law and order situation in Punjab. Even though he denied any involvement, during that time several Hindus and members of minority sects were targeted in Punjab resulting in their exodus from the region. The government also objected to the fact that Bhindranwale and his group were arming themselves while also fortifying a religious sanctuary—the Golden Temple, for a final showdown with the government.

As the government braced itself for the conclusive attack, it imposed a curfew in the state, escorting all foreign correspondents out of Punjab. At a shrine teeming with pilgrims not any different from Gurdwara Panja Sahib today, the Indian army unleashed its military assault. After an initial delay when they couldn't break through the militants' defence, they brought in tanks and fired at the most sacred of Sikh shrines. Bhindranwale and several of his compatriots lost their life in that battle with hundreds of pilgrims as collateral damage according to state figures. However, some eyewitnesses claim that more than 8000 people were killed.

The operation sent ripples through the Sikh community the world over, who felt a strong sense of resentment at the desecration of their holiest shrine. Sikhs in Canada, the US, the UK, Malaysia, Pakistan and all over the world took to the streets protesting against the Indian government and

Indira Gandhi in particular who was the prime minister at that time and responsible for approving the operation. This operation furthered fuelled insurgency against the Indian state as young Sikhs took up arms against the government.

On 31 October 1984, while Indira Gandhi was walking in her garden, she was gunned down by her two Sikh bodyguards in retaliation for the desecration of the Golden Temple. The assassination further divided the Sikh and the Hindu community as Delhi saw its worst riots since Partition. Thousands of Hindu vigilantes took to the streets seeking revenge for the death of 'their' prime minister, lynching and burning to death thousands of Sikhs residing in the capital. Sikh-owned shops and taxis were looted and burnt. In Punjab where there was a burning insurgency, the authorities clamped down harshly as numerous innocent Sikh boys were picked up on the slightest of suspicions, tortured and sometimes even killed. As a result of these severe anti-insurgency steps taken by the government, most of the separatists were either killed or chased out of the country by the end of the decade and the insurgency lost its momentum.

However, this dark chapter has not been erased from the minds of the people of Punjab. Bhindranwale is still seen by several Sikhs as a martyr for the cause of the Sikh religion. His pictures and shirts are available readily in East Punjab and many websites dedicated to him and the Khalistan movement are up and running.

* * *

'This shirt represents the passion of Baisakhi,' says a charged-up Surjeet. 'Sant Jarnail Singh Bhindranwale was a great Sikh warrior who died for the Sikh religion. He took forward the message of Guru Gobind Singh. Guru Gobind told us that we should keep a *kirpan* (sword) with us at all times for our protection as well as for those who are being victimized. Sant Jarnail Singh Bhindranwale told us that we should upgrade our weapons according to the need of the times and keep a gun instead. Guru Gobind Singh founded the Khalsa on the occasion of Baisakhi, giving the Sikh community a separate identity. Sant Jarnail Singh Bhindranwale asserted that separate identity. Bhindranwale represents the passion of Baisakhi.'

* * *

On the first of Vaisakh 1699, thousands of Sikhs gathered at the city of Anandpur Sahib, East Punjab, India, a holy Sikh city founded by the ninth Sikh Guru, Guru Tegh Bahadur (1621–75). Here addressing the crowd, the tenth Sikh Guru asked if anyone present was willing to give up his or her life for the Guru. This was a few years after the assassination of Guru Tegh Bahadur at the hands of another Mughal Emperor, Aurangzeb (1618–1707); hence the passion of sacrifice was high. One volunteer offered to sacrifice his head and was taken behind a tent from where Guru Gobind Singh emerged alone with his sword dripping blood, clearly implying that the head of the volunteer had been severed from his body. In that state of confusion, he asked for another volunteer from the crowd.

In this manner, he led away a total of five volunteers every time returning with a blood-soaked sword. In reality however, all were safe, hidden behind the tent and the act was only meant to arouse the fervour of sacrifice in the Sikh community. These five volunteers are now referred to as the *Panj Pyare* (the five beloved ones) and they became the first members of the Guru's Khalsa.

Khalsa, literally translated to mean pure, was a term that the Guru used to refer to his followers. On this particular day, he made it compulsory for all the Sikhs to identify themselves with the five Ks. These are: *Kesh*; the Guru forbade his followers from cutting off hair from any part of their body choosing to stay in the pure form that God created them. *Kanga*; all the followers must keep a wooden comb in their hair symbolizing cleanliness. *Kara*; an iron bracelet is to be worn by a devotee on the hand at all times to remind him/her of the bond they have made with the Guru and hence protect them from evil doings. *Kachera*; underwear which represents modesty and finally, *kirpan*; a dagger or a sword meant to be kept with one at all times and to be used for self-defence or for the protection of an innocent person. In order to dilute caste identities made prominent by the use of surnames, the Guru also instructed all male members to use the surname of Singh meaning lion, whereas to women he gave the surname of Kaur, lioness. The state of Khalistan which the separatists were fighting for derives its name from the word 'Khalsa'.

The formation of the Khalsa on the first of Vaisakh marked by the five Ks was meant to distinguish the followers of the Guru from the rest of the community. It is a symbol of a separate Sikh identity, an identity that the proponents of Khalistan felt had come under threat in a post-Partition India dominated by Hindu culture.

* * *

'Never forget 1984' is a popular T-shirt here, being sold in a stall behind the main shrine. A small table has been set up behind the gurdwara, next to an alley which leads to another open area, where there are more residential quarters. The place is teeming with visitors. Several T-shirts packed in plastic covers are lying on the table. There is a black wire hanging behind the vendor, who is a young dark boy from the southern part of the country. A pink-coloured 'Never forget 1984' T-shirt hangs on the wire. There is a white one next to it just like Surjeet's. A long stick with a protruding nail is resting on the adjacent tent. The vendor takes off the pink shirt with this stick and presents it to a woman in a sari, whose eyes are fixed upon it.

'How much?' she asks. 'Two hundred only.' 'Are you crazy! Look at the material!' she shouts back. 'Madam, take it or leave it!' The vendor is in no mood to bargain. There are several other clients, checking the sizes of the shirts on the backs of their children. The vendor's partner is packing four shirts that he has just sold to a woman. 'I want it for fifty,' the woman says, but the vendor doesn't reply. 'Oyeee, I want it for fifty!' He takes the shirt from her and puts it back on the wire without saying anything. 'Ok, ok. Here take a hundred and give me that shirt.' Her authoritative tone has given way to that of submission. 'One-fifty. Final price.' She takes out a red note and stares at it for a little while, making sure it is a hundred-rupee note. 'I don't understand this currency,' she says, her voice laced with irritation.

Her son, for whom she is buying the shirt, is least interested in the process. Busy play-acting a plane with his right hand, he lands it on a few CDs lying on a table adjacent to this one. His whistle fades away as the plane comes to a complete halt. 'Sikh Gurdwaras in Pakistan' reads his landing strip, a government-sanctioned propaganda documentary on the famous Sikh shrines in the country, most of which are associated with Guru Nanak. There is a poster next to it with a large picture of Gurdwara Janamasthan in the middle, a long yellow building with a white outline, with pictures of other mango-coloured yellow buildings in bubbles around it. This is a picture of all the functional gurdwaras of Pakistan. Only 16 out of 135 historical gurdwaras are functional in Pakistan, according to Iqbal Qaiser, an expert on Sikh gurdwaras in the country. The rest are being used as houses, farms, stables or isolated make-out spots for villagers. Two large speakers flank this table, playing kirtan music. 'Take this CD—Ravinder Singh's latest collection of kirtan. Only a few left,' says a young Sikh man, wearing a pink turban, to the pilgrims even as the young pilot stares at him intently.

Suddenly, a number of people run into the alley, almost crushing the boy. From behind an iron-bar gate, a man with a thin moustache and a handkerchief covering his head is throwing *nimko* into the crowd. Several hands rise, trying to catch one as the smarter ones push and snatch as soon as someone catches and then disappear into the crowd.

The alley ends in an open space, surrounded by more buildings for the residence of the pilgrims. A garden in the centre covered by tents provides makeshift rooms to pilgrims who have not been able to find a place indoors. Women and children stand on the balconies of the buildings looking at the activities unfolding on the ground. Several vendors have laid out their items wherever they have been able to find a place, most of them selling religious paraphernalia; head covers with Khalsa symbols, plates for aarti, posters of Hindu deities and Sikh gurus. Most of these vendors are Pakistanis who travel all over the country throughout the year attending Hindu and Sikh festivals, selling their items and also performing pilgrimage. One can see their bags and bedding lying around their temporary shops. In the night after packing up their items, they sleep right there, under the stars.

* * *

Vishal Chand, a dark, handsome young man with a French beard, sits on a bag behind his display of religious paraphernalia. He sits peacefully as his brother nearby attends to a few customers. Next to him, his brother's wife and children are having lunch. 'I belong to the city of Multan but I live in Quetta (Baluchistan).' He moved there to live with his brother who works in the Anti-Terrorism Force (ATF). Currently a student, he takes time off at the time of a festival to help his family out. Almost all of their items on display are from India, brought by their friends and relatives every time they visit Pakistan on a pilgrimage like this. The tradition of making idols and other religious items practised in this part of the world for thousands of years died an untimely death after the Partition.

* * *

There are four entrances into the main shrine, one from all sides, symbolizing the openness of the religion. Anyone and everyone is allowed inside a Sikh gurdwara according to the tradition, a practice that doesn't exist in Pakistan any more though. The political and religious realities here don't allow any blur in religious distinctions, which would be implied when a 'Muslim' pays his or her respects to a 'Sikh' shrine. It does not matter any more that Guru Nanak visited the shrine of Baba Fareed, a famous Muslim saint from Pakpattan or that Mian Meer, another Muslim saint laid the foundation of one of the holiest Sikh shrines of the world, the Golden Temple. The strict compartmentalization of religious practices and identity which Pakistan is a product of leaves no room for the historical religious syncretism that was once part of this land's religious traditions.

The building inside is decorated with gaudy glass patterns put up recently by the government of Pakistan as renovation work to cover the fading frescoes, part of the original complex built by Maharaja Ranjit Singh. In the centre of the room, there is a wooden palanquin behind which a young Pathan-Sikh man is busy reading the holy Sikh book, the Guru Granth Sahib, while several pilgrims lie around the room resting on this warm day. Others sit around him, listening to the recitation while a few read from their pocket Granths.

For the Sikhs, the Granth Sahib is not just a holy book, but a living guru, equivalent to a living leader. In 1699, when Guru Gobind Singh founded the Khalsa, he also declared that no other person after him would succeed him as Guru. He had four sons, all of whom were martyred fighting the Mughal army, with which the Sikh community remained in a constant battle after the assassination of the fourth Sikh Guru, Guru Arjan, while he was still alive. He instructed that after his demise the Granth Sahib, which contains the writings of various saints, including Baba Fareed, Guru Nanak and Bhagat Kabir, should be revered as the Guru, as it contains everything a devotee needs to know about the religion. Unlike the Quran or Bible, the Granth Sahib is not regarded as a God-sent book but rather as the word of holy people, divinely inspired nonetheless.

Standing behind the Granthi (one who is reading the Granth at the palanquin), devotees pick up a fly-whisk, after having prostrated in front of the Granth upon entering the gurdwara and fan for a little while before making way for the next pilgrim in the line. This is a tradition that comes from Bhai Bala, the Hindu devotee of Guru Nanak.

At the moment, the final chapters of the Granth Sahib are being read. This procedure marks the conclusion of *Akhand Path*. Held on auspicious occasions, this is the continuous recitation of the Granth Sahib, from beginning to the end without a break. Usually three or more readers are assigned to the job, one of whom is always reading. The entire reading takes about two and a half days during which the readers take shifts. At the end of one's shift, the other reader joins him/her and starts reading along, as the first reader identifies his spot by pointing to the relevant line with his/her finger, while continuing to read at the same time. When the second reader catches up, the first one leaves having made sure that the reading does not stop even for a second. The first-ever *Akhand Path* was arranged by Guru Gobind Singh, after compiling the final version of the Guru Granth Sahib. He made five readers read it to him as he stood at one place throughout the reading.

* * *

Sitting next to the door that opens towards the sacred pool is fifty-five-year-old Avtar Kaur, wearing a pink shalwar kameez, her head covered with a dupatta. Her husband is sleeping next to her, a handkerchief spread over his face. Head bowed, she is listening to the recitation. This is her first trip to the country.

'I have always wanted to come to Pakistan. This is the land of Guru Nanak,' she says. And it is true. Guru Nanak was born in a city now called Nankana Sahib, Pakistan. He passed away in a small village called Kartarpur also in present day Pakistan. He spent most of his time here, and there are several sites all over the country where Nanak stayed or performed miracles. Gurdwaras that were built there later by the devotees still stand tall.

Kaur belongs to the Indian city of Amritsar and is visiting with her husband. She is the managing director of a well-established school there. A soft-spoken lady, she speaks with a warm smile. 'After the *Akhand Path*, there will be a procession of *Nagar Kirtan*. In Amritsar, a huge procession leaves from the Golden Temple and travels all around the city, while smaller processions from other gurdwaras join it on the way. After travelling around the whole city, it heads back to the Golden Temple. The entire city takes part in this celebration and there are decorations all over. This happens in all the other cities of Punjab. However, here I have heard that the procession will not be allowed to leave the premises of this gurdwara. That is sad.'

Till a few years ago, the procession marched around the city of Hassan Abdal as local Muslim onlookers, too insecure about their own religious identity to join them like they used to before Partition, looked on from the side, intrigued by the strange spectacle. But now that has changed due to the growing threat from the Islamic extremists happy to blow up anyone or curb any practice that doesn't ft their definition of the true religion; the procession now remains within the protected confines of the gurdwara.

* * *

Throughout the day, the sound of kirtan being performed in a hall behind the main shrine resonates in all the corners of the gurdwara. At its entrances, statues of two Sikh soldiers stand guard holding spears, dressed up in yellow clothes and blue turbans. The stage is set at one end of this long hall with a picture of this particular gurdwara in the centre and that of Guru Gobind Singh on the top left corner. Two musicians, one a young boy and other a man, sit on the stage playing and singing, while another man sits next to them reading the Granth Sahib. Behind him there is a picture of Guru Gobind Singh collecting money for langar. A few notes and coins lie in front of the musicians offered to them by devotees listening to their devotional music.

Next to the hall, a staircase disappears into the underground leading to two spacious corridors with a number of doors. This place is teeming with pilgrims; a few, who have not been able to find any space inside the rooms, live in these corridors. Usually, foreign pilgrims are accommodated in rooms, while Pakistanis are allowed to settle wherever there is space. In one corner here, a group of old Indian pilgrims having just returned from langar are sitting in the corridors socializing with the other pilgrims. All of them have vivid memories from the Khalistan days of insurgency.

* * *

Sixty-five-year-old Harvinder Singh was living in Delhi when Indira Gandhi was assassinated. Resting against a wall, squatted on the floor, holding both of his folded legs against his chest, he stares into emptiness as he recalls those days. 'I had a cloth shop in Lajpat Nagar (Delhi). It was burnt down by the mob. My son and I cut our beards and hair, removing our turbans to avoid identification.' He now has re-grown his beard and is wearing a pink turban. 'We could not live in Delhi any more so we decided to move to Amritsar after the event.' During his narration, his emotion vacillates between remorse and anger. One of his companions sitting next to him places his hand on Harvinder's knee to console him. A dark-complexioned Punjabi, his name is Jasdeep Singh and he is fifty-four years old. 'They were the sort of days when anyone sporting the Khalsa (5 Ks) was picked up by the authorities.' Harvinder goes back to staring into oblivion.

'My husband was picked up by the authorities and killed,' jumps in Virinder Kaur. Wearing a loose shalwar kameez, she is wrapped in a red shawl and there is thin layer of hair on her upper lip, showing that she has been baptized into the Khalsa. She is fifty-five years old and belongs to a village near Amritsar District. 'Both my sons were picked up after my husband, also without any warrant. They were missing for three years during which time I ran from pillar to post to find out about them. I sold whatever little property I had to make ends meet during that time. Finally they were released, because like my husband, they too had nothing to with the separatists.'

* * *

The langar hall is a newly built double-storey construction, situated behind these residential quarters. The stream that supplies water to the holy pool emerges from under the buildings here, and then flows out of the complex. Next to the hall, a few Sikh boys having set up a stall are serving doodh-soda, a drink prepared by mixing milk with a carbonated drink, popular in this part of the world. Another group of volunteers stand guarding the entrance of the langar hall as people fight and argue with them to be allowed to enter. There are too many people inside, which is why they are not allowing anyone else to enter at the moment. Facing the building, opposite the stall, is a small garden where several pilgrims are resting under the sun. Most of them have had food and are now taking a nap. One of the people lying on the grass is forty-four-year-old Maninder Singh.

* * *

Maninder is a photographer from Amritsar city. He has a round face with a round nose. His thick black beard is now greying. He is wearing a faded white cotton kurta and has pulled his pajamas up to his knees. 'I actually belong to Pakistan,' he says. 'This is where my heart is. I don't ever want to go back. I don't understand these artificial borders. They don't exist for wind or birds. Some politicians make a living out of perpetuating these differences.

'My parents died with a heavy heart. Both of them belonged to this side of the border, moving to Amritsar at the time of Partition. My father is from a village in Gujrat (a city in Punjab, Pakistan) and my mother belonged to the city of Shah Alamgir (also Punjab, Pakistan). They longed to come see their homes before their death but couldn't.

After my mother passed away a couple of years ago, I decided to visit her ancestral home on her behalf. So last year, when I came for Guru Nanak's festival, I got special permission to go to her village. I walked around it trying to make sense, according to the stories my mother had told me, but I couldn't. It had changed a lot. Just as I was about to return, an old Muslim woman called me and asked me about my whereabouts. When I told her about my mother she started crying and told me that she was her neighbour. She held me tightly, refusing to let go. I felt as if my mother was hugging me. We both started crying like babies. She then took me to my mother's ancestral house, where a Muslim family from Ferozepur had moved after the Partition. They were sweet enough to allow us to have a look. At the end I asked them if I could take a brick from the house which they allowed. Now that brick is in my living room in Amritsar. I look at it every day and think of my mother.' Maninder's eyes swell up as tears stream down his eyes.

GURU GOBIND SINGH'S BIRTHDAY AT NANKANA SAHIB

Guru Nanak is celebrated all over Nankana Sahib. There is a Guru Nanak High School, a Guru Nanak grocery store and a Guru Nanak cloth shop, all run by Sikhs. The Muslims generally refrain from eulogizing Guru Nanak in this particular way. Near the Gurdwara Janamasthan, next to the office of the *nazim*, the former elected head of the district, is the Government College rechristened recently as Guru Nanak Government College. Currently, there are only a few Sikh boys studying here; the majority of the students are Muslim.

There is an open ground at the back of the building, which serves as the cricket, football, hockey, and any other sporting ground. It is also used for college fun fairs. On this particular day, the ground of the college has been reserved for the Sikh community of the city. There are various carts selling ice cream, French fries, shaker kandi (sweet potato), challi (corn) and aloo chat at the boundary of the ground. Young Sikh boys stand around them wearing black cloths (*dastar*) on their heads, with a lump in the middle holding their hair (*kesh*), more interested in what is being served as opposed to what is happening at the ground. A scream from the loudspeaker distracts them temporarily. They look in the direction of the ground for a few seconds, before returning to their eating.

'And in this way, Khalsa XI has lost its second wicket. What a lovely ball by Sukhvinder Singh,' was the announcement that had sidetracked them temporarily. Two Sikh boys, seated on a single seat, are engaged in a live commentary of the cricket match which is being played in front of them in the ground. Their seat is situated amongst others on a raised platform on one side of the ground. The rest of the seats are occupied by elder members of the community. The boys have been given a seat because of their job. Everyone is basking in the sun of the cold winter afternoon. The date is 10 January 2011 and the occasion is the birthday celebration of Guru Gobind Singh, the tenth Guru of the Sikh community and the founder of the Khalsa. There is a blackboard behind the commentators, borrowed from one of the classrooms. Khalsa XI and Nankana XI are written on two sides of the board, separated by a chalk line in the middle. One of the boys gets up from the seat and picks up a piece of chalk to update the scorecard.

Sikh boys and a few Muslims from the college are sitting around the ground watching the match. A white boundary has been drawn with a chalk. On the opposite end, facing the stage, another group of Sikh boys have taken up seats, while the rest of them sit on the ground. Most of them are dressed in a black cricket kit, which reads Khalsa XI in golden letters in front. They have matched their black dastars with the colour. This is the team batting at the moment. The other team wearing a yellow kit is called

Nankana XI, according to the name written in green on their shirts. A few players from this team are sitting with the Khalsa XI members, while the rest of them are in the field, bowling and fielding. There are two boys wearing a blue cricket kit in their midst, with their team name, Singh XI, written in red. They lost the semi-final to Nankana XI. A dark-complexioned dhol-wala, with long oiled hair falling on his shoulders and a thick beard, is sitting on a seat next to the boys. His assistant, a young boy wearing a red kurta, stands next to him, intrigued by the sight of so many Sikhs. Daljeet Singh, a young man in his early twenties, just dismissed by Sukhvinder, is walking back from the ground. The dhol is playing in celebration of the dismissal. A few steps before the boundary, Daljeet looks up and lifts his bat with both his hands, performing *bhangra* with a broad smile on his face. His teammates, who had been quiet and disappointed until now, rejoice at his gesture and reciprocate by lifting their fists, raising one forefinger each and moving their shoulders in rhythm to the beat of the dhol. 'Horarara,' shouts a bulky Khalsa XI player, standing up and dancing. The dhol-wala, excited by the response of his audience, stands up from his seat and revolves with the dhol, continuing his playing. The boys in the ground, whose victory is being celebrated, join the fiesta. Children, dressed in plainclothes, engaged in their own game of cricket behind the older boys, stop playing for a little while to see the celebration. A few other young ones ignoring their play stand next to the boys, pretending to take an interest in the match being played on the ground, hoping against all odds that they would also be given a chance. Under a tent raised next to the boundary wall of the ground, where rows of seats have been laid out, most of them empty at the moment, a few women and girls are sitting in the front row watching the proceedings. This is a twenty-overs match.

Surjeet Singh is the captain of Khalsa XI. He is training to be a *hakeem*, a traditional medical practitioner, with his father. Their 'shop' is in Nankana Sahib. A number of Sikhs living here are engaged in this profession, following a practice that goes back several generations. 'I completed my matriculation at the Guru Nanak High School, after which I joined my profession,' he says. 'There was no point of studying any further as I was eventually going to do this anyway,' he comments as he makes himself comfortable on one of the vacant seats after his little jig. He shouts at his teammates to cheer for the batsman in the field. The dhol-wala has stopped playing, the celebration halted as the match resumes.

'However, now there is a growing understanding in the members of the community that education is important,' he continues. 'More Sikh boys are venturing into different fields. That's my cousin, Manjeet,' he says as he points to a young Sikh man wearing a black uniform, busy talking on his cell phone. Not knowing the context, Manjeet smiles politely and walks away, continuing to talk on the phone. 'He has done his MBA and is now working in Lahore. Other boys are also doing their MBAs and other computer degrees.'

There has been a growing migration of Sikh boys and men from Nankana Sahib to bigger cities like Lahore, Faisalabad and Gujranawala in recent years. Even there, they continue to engage in their family businesses, which are primarily grocery shops, cloth trading and *hikmaat* (traditional medicine). But then there is also a growing trend of young men training to become professionals.

'The uniforms for the tournament have been arranged by Udham Singh,' says Surjeet. 'You can think of him as my cousin as well,' Surjeet adds, implying that they are close friends. Udham, wearing a pink turban and a dark brown sweater over a cream shalwar kameez, comes and sits next to Surjeet after hearing his name. He doesn't talk but listens intently. 'He, along with his brother, runs a cloth shop in Gujranawala. They sponsored the uniforms this year,' says Surjeet.

'I am originally from Nankana but we have our business there,' explains Udham, finally speaking up. 'We travel often between the two cities.'

Both Surjeet and Udham speak Urdu with a Pasthu accent. Their families moved to Nankana a few years ago, which has allowed them to pick up the languages of Urdu and Punjabi that were earlier alien to them. However, not all Sikhs here can speak Urdu or Punjabi. The commentator shifts between Urdu and Pashtu throughout the match. A vast percentage of Sikhs living in Nankana moved to Punjab only recently. In the past ten years, the population has increased almost sevenfold. There were only about thirty to forty Sikh houses in Nankana ten years ago, consisting of families who had moved here gradually over the years, following the alienation after the wars of 1965 and 1971 as well as the demolition of the Babri Mosque in 1992.

Until a few years ago, the vast population of Sikhs was living peacefully in the tribal areas. But as the influence of the religiously hardline Taliban increased there and especially after the onset of the War on Terror, the delicate balance between the Muslims and non-Muslims shifted. The Taliban demanded *jaziya*, a tax imposed on non-Muslims, from the Sikh community if they wanted to live in a Muslim-dominated area. There had been no such issue prior to the arrival of the Taliban. In 2009, eleven Sikh houses were destroyed in the Orkazi Agency because they refused to pay the tax. In 2010, Jaspal Singh, a young man from Khyber Agency was beheaded after his family failed to pay the hefty amount asked as jaziya.

'Baljeet over there can tell you the story of his family,' Udham says, pointing to a dark-complexioned chubby boy, sitting on the ground next to the seats. 'Come here, Baljeetay, tell them the story of your village.' Baljeet is about sixteen years old with a thin layer of hair covering his cheeks and upper lip, yet to form into a proper beard. He is wearing a green shalwar kameez with a black dastar and belongs to one of the latest families to have moved to Nankana. Udham makes some space on his chair for Baljeet to share.

'We had a small cloth shop at Ghariza, Jamrud (Khyber Agency, Tribal Areas). It was a good thriving business. The shop had been set up by my grandfather. One day, these men with long beards and the latest weapons came on a jeep and parked in front of our shop. I was present there along with my father. They told my father that if we wanted to continue working here, we would have to pay them two crore rupees (20,000,000) within a month. We knew it was time to leave. We locked our shops and houses and came away that very night,' says Baljeet.

'Many families moved in these conditions,' adds Udham. 'You will find many such stories here.' Surjeet is no longer interested in the conversation and is busy following the progress of the match.

For the new refugees, there was no better option than to move to cities where there was already a considerable Sikh population. Families moved to Peshawar, Hassan Abdal and

Nankana Sahib, and started living at gurdwaras, just like the migrants before them. In about ten years, the population in Nankana Sahib increased to about 200 houses.

The drastic increase in the number of Sikhs has had various impacts on the local Sikh community. Most of the newcomers were incorporated within the gurdwaras, in rooms which were generally reserved for pilgrims. Others, who already had friends and families living here, were adjusted in their houses. Migrating suddenly, most of them were also financially weak when they arrived, and so the local community collectively helped them in setting up small businesses or facilitated their rent. Whereas on one hand, the incoming migrants were supported by the locals, such a large influx also strengthened the existing community. All of a sudden, they had the numerical strength of young people, giving a confidence boost to the Sikhs who were until now dominated by the Muslim majority in a city with a population of over a million. This allowed them to exert their Sikh identity and culture, which was otherwise downplayed.

'Earlier for smaller festivals like Guru Gobind's birthday or Lohri we would just visit a few houses of our friends and relatives, or go to the gurdwara for prayers, but now we actually celebrate them,' says Surjeet. 'For the first time, this year we have arranged this cricket tournament. We wanted to have other sports and games as well, like hockey, volleyball, etc. but there was no time.' The migrations have infused a new energy into the community.

Engaging in sports on the occasion of Guru Gobind Singh's birthday has always been an essential feature of the celebration. Traditionally, the Sikhs organized war games, including exhibitions of horse-riding, swordsmanship, archery, spearing and the use of the stick. War games are significant because Guru Gobind Singh was a warrior himself who challenged the mighty Mughal Empire and set up a Sikh army, meant to preserve the Khalsa. Exhibition of war games is a tribute to the warrior, Guru Gobind Singh. However, this tradition ended here at the time of Partition. The small number of Sikhs that remained in Pakistan were spread over a vast geographical area and thereby unable to form a cohesive entity. There were a few religious events which were kept alive by the foreign pilgrims including Baisakhi at Hassan Abdal and Guru Nanak's birthday at Nankana Sahib. But other festivals, like Lohri and Guru Gobind Singh's birthday, which had no historical significance to particular shrines on this side of the border, were neglected. However, now that a considerable population of the community has concentrated in particular cities, the traditions which were earlier downplayed are once again being claimed. An interesting feature, with regard to this particular festival, is that whereas on the one hand it is a tradition which has been reclaimed, on the other it has also been contemporized. War games have been replaced by cricket.

'Last year, we held a small event at Gurdwara Balila (this is near Gurdwara Janamasthan),' says Surjeet. 'This was solely for the younger children. There were games like racing and tug of war, amongst others. However, we couldn't do it this year because the gurdwara is being renovated. That's why these children look so sad,' jokes Surjeet, gesturing towards a child resting on the back of his chair, interested in the conversation. The child blushes and removes his arms from the top of the chair. The selection of Gurdwara Balila for children's games is a natural choice. Situated across the road from Gurdwara Patti Sahib, this gurdwara is constructed to mark the spot where Guru Nanak used to play as a child. Winking at the blushing kid, Surjeet adds that the children would be allowed to show off their talent in the evening.

* * *

As night falls, the temperature drops to near freezing point and it becomes foggy. A cold breeze blows occasionally as people walk towards Gurdwara Janamasthan, shivering each step of the way. The guard at the entrance is too cold to check for any suspicious people trying to enter. Lalit Singh, a young man in his late thirties, the head Granthi at the gurdwara, has already taken his place on the stage next to the shrine and is playing the tabla. Two female vocalists accompany him, one of whom is also playing the harmonium.

Lalit's family has been living here since the late 1970s. He is considered to be the most learned (religious) person in this Sikh circle. He leads the community prayers most of the time. Wearing a blue turban over a white kurta-pajama, covered in a brown sweater with a white scarf around his neck, he plays sternly without smiling. The girls follow his lead and refrain from smiling as well. Lalit is a serious man, who rarely smiles. The teenage girls, singing a song dedicated to Guru Gobind Singh, are wearing white shalwar kameez and orange dupattas, their heads covered with a black cloth with an orange Khalsa symbol in the front. They are amateurs, struggling to maintain their tune. People listen patiently, as they repeat the chorus expressing their devotion to the Guru. It is evident soon that the evening is dedicated to the children. Young boys and girls walk in groups, dressed up like one another. Some are holding pages with which they disappear into a corner, memorizing the lines after prostrating to the Granth Sahib. Others sit with their parents in the crowd, waiting for the kirtan to end. All the children are dressed in white shalwar kurta, wearing the 5 Ks for this special day, even though most of them have not been baptized as yet. A group of young boys are wearing orange turbans, while another slightly older group wears blue ones. A few boys have decorated their turbans with quoits of steel, brandishing the Khalsa symbol on the top. The oldest group is that of young teenagers, all of whom are wearing black turbans complemented with matching sweaters. The girls are also wearing white shalwar kameez, covering their heads with blue or orange dupattas according to their groups.

Surjeet has arrived, dressed appropriately for the occasion. Wearing a red turban on an off-white shalwar kameez and a dark brown sleeveless jacket, he is also holding a piece of paper in his hand. Parents throng to him, to get the names of their children on to the list that he holds. He will be conducting the show tonight, inviting groups of children to demonstrate their skills. Holding the paper against his friend's back, he jots down the names as parents call them out.

The performance begins after the conclusion of the kirtan. Surjeet starts by congratulating Khalsa XI for winning the cricket tournament. Placing the paper on the pulpit, he announces the names of the children who would be performing. As the first group, the young boys with orange turbans, make their way to the fore of the crowd, Surjeet kneels on the ground and holds the microphone in front of them. The boys start reciting poetry from a piece of paper that one of them holds in the middle. This is a recitation from the holy book, the Guru Granth Sahib. Following this, he invites a group of teenage girls. One of the girls asks Lalit Singh to accompany them on the tabla. They would be singing a religious song, dedicated to the bravery of Guru Gobind Singh, with an emphasis on the valour of the Singh. In fact, all the recitations from the night are dedicated to the Guru and the significance of the Khalsa. A fourteen-year-old girl wearing a white shalwar kameez and a blue dupatta over her head, passionately reads out a poem about how the younger community is now cutting their hair and their turbans are being replaced with caps. Her glasses slip off her nose repeatedly as she uses her hands to express herself during the recitation. She emphasizes that there is a greater need for the Sikh community to follow the rules of the Khalsa, especially in this era of degeneration. Inspired by her poem, Udham, who is sitting in the crowd, makes an emotional call, '*Jo bole so nihal*!' '*Sat Sri Akal*!' shouts back the audience. The girl smiles at the success of her performance.

Throughout the performances, Surjeet is occupied in dealing with the parents who want their children's names added to the list. He argues with them patiently stating that he cannot accommodate so many performances in one night. 'You should have come earlier,' he says, but the parents are persistent. He tries to include as many names as he can, resulting in the show running over the scheduled time. It is now eleven in the night and there are still quite a few children interested in showing off their skills. Finally, Surjeet announces that the show needs to end. He apologizes to all those who could not perform, but promises that they would be accommodated in the morning. However, he tells them strictly that only those children whose names are entered tonight would be invited tomorrow and he would accept no new requests in the morning. Following his announcement, the tired congregation heads back to their warm houses, while parents surround Surjeet once again.

* * *

The concluding ceremony of the festival is held on the morning of 11 January 2011, which is when the actual birthday is, according to the Sikh calendar formulated by Pal Singh Purewal. It's a beautiful morning, crisp sunlight providing much needed relief on a cold day. People start gathering at the gurdwara at eight in the morning. Young men, dressed up in their cricket kits yesterday, are wearing shining new shalwar kameez today. They are still under the spell of cricket, discussing matches and performances from yesterday. People working out of station have come to Nankana for this auspicious day. They are greeted by their friends, as they tell them about the success of the cricket tournament.

Women and older men sit on the carpet inside the pavilion. Surjeet will be conducting the proceedings again. He invites two groups of girls who had returned home disappointed last night. They come to the stage and start reciting a poem from a piece of paper, still angry at the treatment meted out to them the night before. Surjeet, also irritated by the delay in prayers, stands next to them looking at his watch after every few seconds. However, this doesn't make the performance go any faster and the girls take their time. After satisfying all the disgruntled parents and children from last night, Surjeet announces the results of the cricket match. His friends bring out several trophies, in different sizes, from the main shrine and place them next to him on the ground. Group of boys, standing in the courtyard, uninterested in the proceedings so far, turn their attention towards the pulpit. Announcements of best bowler, best batsmen and man of the tournament are followed by joyous shouts and hooting from the young people. Surjeet invites his entire team, Khalsa XI, to come to the stage and receive the trophy. This is the tallest award, golden in colour, with a picture of a batsman playing a cover drive. The award ceremony will be followed by a communal prayer.

LOHRI AT NANKANA SAHIB

Kartar Singh Kartar picks up a saffron cloth from inside the gurdwara. Tearing it into small pieces, he hands each bit over to everyone present there. He ties his bit to one of the tree branches and reads out a small prayer, his eyes closed and his hands together in prayer. His Muslim friends also tie the cloth and say out a prayer making sure though that they don't hold their hands together, instead letting them hang loosely on their sides. Tolerant and progressive they might be but holding their hands in front of their chests during a prayer is getting too close to 'Hindu' culture, a culture they have learnt to hate from their birth.

There are already many prayer cloths tied to the several branches of this tree, which is spread out like a tent. This is an ancient tree, called *waan* in Punjabi. It is short, but can live up to several centuries. This one stretches over a large area and is protected by a boundary fence. There is only one gate and visitors are required to take off their shoes before entering. It looks as if the tree is now lying on the ground, slowly preparing itself to pass over to another world. Behind the tree, there is a small mango-coloured building with a small dome on the top. A board at the entrance reads,

'Gurdwara Tambu Sahib.' The word *tambu* comes from the tent-like cover of this tree. *Tambu* means 'tent' in Punjabi. The saffron-coloured *Nishan Sahib* (the Sikh flag) stands in the courtyard.

The colour of the sky starts to change. The orange stream diminishes and dark blue takes over. It is almost symbolic of what it taking place in Pakistan. The dark blue sky is the 'monolithic' Muslim culture whereas the diminishing orange light is the multi-religious, pluralistic society that Pakistan was at her onset.

There is a tractor parked near the tree, partially covering the single-storey building that stands behind it, which is used by the farmers who till this land. There is vast land lying vacant on both sides of the shrine which is used for agriculture. A tall, barbwire wall covers the area from all sides. Beyond the walls, there is the hustle-bustle of the city. Only one gate is used to enter this compound, the one from the main market. A brown board on the road points towards the gate, spelling out its name in three scripts, English, Shahmukhi (the Arabian script which is used for Urdu) and Gurmukhi (a script used to write Punjabi in Indian Punjab). There is another blue gate on the other side of the complex, kept permanently locked for security reasons.

The sound of the muezzin reciting the azaan echoes from the sky. The birds begin chirping in competition. Another muezzin calls as if exhorting followers to come to his mosque instead. This battle continues for a little while as they raise their voices, each trying to outdo the other. It starts to get extremely cold. The night of 13 January is considered to be the coldest night of the season.

* * *

According to the legend, when Baba Guru Nanak turned eighteen, his father asked him to take up a trade. He gave him twenty rupees for this purpose, instructing him to buy something useful and then sell it profitably. Baba Guru Nanak left the city (present-day Nankana Sahib) along with his companion Bhai Mardana (who also belonged to the same city). Outside a place called Mandi Chuharkhana in district Sheikhupura, about 46 km from here, the young Guru ran into a group of starving *jogis* (an order of religious mendicants, similar to the Sufi dervish in Islam). Unable to bear their starvation, Guru Nanak purchased food for them using the twenty rupees. On his way back home, he realized that his father would be angry with him, so he hid under this tree, where Kartar Singh tied the piece of cloth.

When Nanak didn't return home for a long time, his family started to look for him and eventually found him hidden under this tree. Nanak told his father that he had spent the money for a *Sacha Sauda*, a true deal (which was feeding the jogis). Initially angered, his father eventually forgave him. Now there are two gurdwaras to commemorate this event. One is this gurdwara, Tambu Sahib, and the other is situated in Chuharkhana at the spot where the Guru fed the starving jogis.

* * *

'We believe that by tying a cloth on the branches of this sacred tree, our wishes come true. There is no place to tie a cloth on these branches at the time of the larger festival (Guru Nanak's birthday, for which thousands of people come to Nankana Sahib from all over the world). People tie over each other's cloth,' says Kartar as he kneels down to point towards a red flower growing from the ground. 'This is also a sacred flower. It grows nowhere else in the world except in this enclosed compound. Scientists have made various attempts to plant it at other places but all have failed. This is a miracle of the Guru.'

Adjusting his red turban, he rubs both his hands together and blows into them for warmth. 'Let's go inside. The ceremony is about to begin.' He heads towards the gurdwara, walking with his hands in the pockets of his sleeveless red jacket, matching in colour with his red turban. He is wearing a grey baggy shalwar kameez, traditional wear of the residents of the province of Khyber Pakhtunkhwa.

* * *

Kartar, thirty-two, was born and raised in Nankana Sahib, a city considered to be one of the holiest cities in the world for the Sikhs, as the founder of their religion, Nanak, was born here. Kartar lives in Lahore now, where he is enrolled in a PhD programme at the University of Punjab. His father moved from Tirat Valley (Tribal Area) after the 1971 Indo-Pak war and settled here, inside Gurdwara Janamasthan, the main gurdwara of the city where Nanak was born. They have never gone back but still retain a few of their traditions.

His father can speak only Pushtu, the language spoken in the Tribal Areas. However, other family members including Kartar's mother, Tarvinder Kaur, have learned Urdu and Punjabi.

'Ours was the only Sikh house in the village,' says Kaur, Kartar's mother. She covers her head with a dupatta all the time. 'The nearest gurdwara was a walk of three to four hours. There was no other medium of transport.

'We used to go there for important religious festivals like Guru Nanak's birthday or Baisakhi. However, we used to celebrate our smaller festivals inside the house. There was a separate room for the Granth Sahib, where we would arrange prayers. We had friendly relationships with our neighbours. They used to invite us to their events, and we did so on ours. Their women used to come to our prayers and even take part in them, whereas we used to send food to their houses and receive *tabarak* on their holy days.'

But then the situation turned for the worse when war broke out between India and Pakistan in 1971 over the issue of East Pakistan, which resulted in the creation of Bangladesh. For a lot of people who defined the two countries as Muslim and Hindu, the war was seen as Muslims being pitted against Hindus and Sikhs. Pakistani Hindus and Sikhs who had lived with their Muslim neighbours for centuries became 'Indians' overnight, as the ideological distinctions between Indian, Hindu and Sikh became blurred. Just like at the time of Partition, Hindus and Sikhs in different parts of the country were attacked. They were accused of being Indian agents.

'Once we were returning home after a wedding,' recalls Kaur, who until the 1970s had never stepped out of FATA. 'We were only women and children. A group of men carrying weapons surrounded us. It was clear that they wanted to kill us. Fortunately, our men came to our rescue with weapons and we were able to escape. For weeks after, we remained imprisoned inside our own houses as the Muslims had enclosed us from all sides. One night, while they were sleeping, we managed to sneak out and fled to Peshawar, where there was a considerable Sikh population.'

They stayed at Peshawar for a few months, after which the family decided to move to Nankana Sahib.

* * *

Kartar takes out a white candle from a pack of new candles placed at the base of the *Nishan Sahib*. He asks one of his Muslim smoker friends to hand him a matchbox. Kartar and all the other Sikhs are forbidden from consuming tobacco by their religion. He lights the candle and puts it in place.

* * *

'Ours was one of the first families to move to Nankana Sahib,' says Kartar. 'There was no Sikh left here after Partition. Our gurdwaras became barren and were in a bad state. There was only one Sikh living here and even he had come from India. His name was Giani Pratap. He was part of a pilgrimage party from India which had come here sometime in the 1960s. When he saw the condition the shrines were in, he decided to stay back and look after the gurdwara. He died recently in Lahore. When our family moved here, he allowed us to live inside the gurdwara for a little while and gave my father the job of a *sewaadar* (worker) at the gurdwara.' After a few months, his family was able to move out of the gurdwara and live at their own rented place.

* * *

He stops at the entrance of the gurdwara and digs his hand into a bucket of caps placed next to the door. These are green and white caps, similar to the ones found in mosques.

He hands them over to his friends and walks in with his head bowed and hands joined in front of his chest. He stands in front of the *Thara Sahib* (a wooden pavilion which hosts the Granth Sahib) and bends, prostrating to the Guru Granth Sahib. Standing up, he takes out a ten-rupee note from the pocket of his kameez and puts it in a small enclosure in front of the Thara Sahib. There are a few other notes there as well, the highest one being that of fifty. Two swords are placed in the enclosure covered in their blue velvet sheaths. Walking around the Granth Sahib, Kartar sits on the right side. There are three other doors leading into the building. All of them are closed at the moment; this is a Sikh-only affair.

It's completely dark outside by now. People start coming in and the room fills up. There are as many men as there are women. The women are covered in shawls, while the men wear jackets and sweaters. Everyone bows down before the Granth Sahib and takes a seat. Some donate money while others don't. The money will be used for the renovation of the gurdwara.

The crowd swells up to about fifty people. A Granthi, in his mid-sixties, takes his seat behind the pavilion. He carefully removes the white cloth covering the holy book and starts to recite from it. People in the room listen to him attentively. The language of the Granth Sahib is classical Punjabi, difficult for the people of today to comprehend. The reading continues for half an hour after which the attendees stand up. It is time for the community prayer. At the end of every line uttered by the Granthi, the audience cries out in unison, '*Waheguru.*' Everyone takes part in the prayer with their hands held in front of them. The children mimic the elders, looking around to make sure that they are doing what is expected.

At the end of the prayer, a man and a child walk around the room carrying a silver tray with naan and a sweet cooked in desi ghee. They place the sweet on top of the naan and hand it over to the supplicant. It is important that he/she receive it with both hands. 'This is prasad,' Kartar whispers into the ear of his Muslim friend. 'It is rude to say no to prasad.' He signals to a little boy carrying one of the trays to bring him some more, amused at his mischief.

* * *

Taking their prasad, people start to leave the room. There are a number of candles lit at the base of the Nishan Sahib by now, held up in a circle around the aarti that carries lit incense. People walking out seek their blessings from the fire. They place their hand on top of the fire and rub their faces. A few women stand there lighting more candles. The procession will now head towards the main gurdwara—Gurdwara Janamasthan.

There is one main road that runs through the entire city of Nankana Sahib. It begins or ends, depending on where one is coming from, at Gurdwara Janamasthan, the most famous place here. There are shops on both sides of this street. At this time of the day, about an hour after sunset, it is teeming with people; a last burst of activity before everything shuts down. A few shops are closed already. The entire city needs a major uplift. The buildings are old and the road has potholes. Traffic flows both ways. Most of the buildings are from the late British or the early Pakistan era.

The Sikhs are walking in several groups. The men share greetings with several other men on the way as they pass along, whereas the women giggle to each other. Kartar stops at a juice shop, at a junction which heads out of the city. The shop is run by a teenage Muslim boy. Neatly placing fresh fruits on display, the vendor tries to entice customers. Kartar greets the boy in Punjabi and asks him to show the glasses kept underneath the counter. The boy understands what he is asking for and takes out the glasses, handing them over to Kartar. One of them is a clean glass with a handle, while the other appears to be an old one, not even properly rinsed. Lifting the hand that carries the clean glass, Kartar says, 'This one is for Muslims. And this one for us,' he comments as he raises the other hand. 'There are a few shopkeepers here who keep this distinction between Muslim and non-Muslim utensils. They believe that if we eat from their plates, they will become impure.' Kartar laughs at the concept. Placing the glasses over the counter, he starts walking towards the gurdwara.

'Once I walked into a restaurant in Model Town,' recalls Kartar, talking about his experience in a Lahore locality. 'This is not a low-end place like Shah Alami. This is Model Town I am talking about. I was waiting for the bus, which was running late and so I decided to have food in the meantime. I was about to sit when a man came to me and apologized, saying that they cannot serve me. He told me they did not have "our" utensils,' says Kartar, staring piercingly into the eyes of his Muslim friend. His eyes are a little moist now. He slips his fingers into the hands of his Muslim companion and leads the group. The rest follow.

This practice of not allowing Sikhs to share utensils with Muslims is a unique practice adopted from the Hindu concept of untouchability. In a post-Partition Pakistan, unified under the banner of Islam, caste identities moved to the periphery as religious distinctions became prominent.

The concept of untouchability that was earlier practised only against low-caste Hindus by the Muslims was then extended to high-caste Hindus as well as Christians, who were seen as Hindu converts to begin with. Taking a life of its own, the concept was extended to all non-Muslims and is now practised by an overwhelming majority of the people here, ignorant of the practice's cultural origin.

* * *

Kartar walks proudly, taking long strides, as if he is the king of this kingdom. The main gate of the gurdwara appears at the end of the road. Kartar stops short and waves to a Sikh sitting behind a desk in his shop. Speaking quietly, he asks his friends to notice the tall minaret right in front of Gurdwara Janamasthan. It's a tall structure, the tallest in the city. There are spiral stairs that lead to the top. A mosque accompanies the minaret. It is grey, not painted as yet. 'What does constructing such a tall minaret in front of the gurdwara say?' asks Kartar. Then, without waiting for anyone to answer, he responds himself. 'It is a show of strength. They want to tell us who the real inhabitants of Nankana Sahib are.' He laughs again, mockingly, and heads over to the gurdwara.

The main gate is closed. Only a small door, that doesn't allow many people to pass through, is open. Kartar waits for a Sikh family to enter. He and his friends follow one by one. There are two police officials sitting inside. Both of them are wrapped in brown shawls, their faces half-covered. Their hands emerge from under the shawls to warm up in front of the gas heater which is burning at full blast. They are alarmed at the sight of the new visitors, who clearly don't look Sikh. One of them starts to get up to inquire but Kartar extends his hand, asking him to remain seated. 'These are my guests.' The police officials are satisfied with the answer and let the group proceed.

Facing them is the entrance to the gurdwara. There are buildings on the right, where visitors stay when they come for the larger events. There is a small garden next to the walkway, with two parallel ways going around it. There are streetlights on the edges of the garden, illuminating the walkway. The yellow light is hazy due to the mist that has now started to descend.

As they get closer to the gurdwara, Kartar asks them to take off their shoes and hand them over to a child standing behind a bar cage. The first-timers are instructed to take their socks off as well.

The cage is a small enclave with shelves for shoes. The child doesn't work here but is a volunteer. He has been instructed by the elders to do his sewa in this particular way. The child takes the shoes and puts the entire set in one shelf. Picking up two coins from the shelf, he places one of them on top of the shoes and hands the other one to Kartar. It reads '22'. The one on top of the shoes also reads the same number. On the way back, Kartar will hand over this coin to whoever is volunteering at the shoe section and collect the shoes.

There is a small niche within the ground at the entrance of the gurdwara containing water. Kartar lifts his shalwar up from his thighs and steps into it. Standing there for a little while, he rubs his right foot over the left one, and vice versa, to make sure that both of them are clean. His friends follow suit. There are two sinks on both sides after crossing this niche. An old Sikh stands on one of them, rinsing his face and hands. Kartar moves on without doing so.

The gurdwara is two steps higher from the ground. It has a gilded door, with depictions of Guru Nanak and scenes from a langar. It is believed that the tradition of langar began with Guru Nanak, when he fed the poor jogis at Mandi Chuharkhana. There are other floral and geometric patterns as well. Inside, there is a small passageway which leads one to the courtyard of the gurdwara. There are two framed pictures on the left. The first one is of a Muslim saint from the twelfth century, popularly known as Baba Fareed Ganjshakar, depicted kneeling on the floor in a green shawl, both his hands raised towards the sky in prayer. The next picture is that of Baba Guru Nanak, wearing a saffron-coloured dress, his head covered with a matching cloth, a white beard, and a rosary around his neck. Sitting on a rock, he looks straight out of the picture with his serene eyes.

Guru Nanak was a spiritual follower of Baba Fareed. He traveled to Pak Pattan where he met the spiritual descendants of Baba Fareed and collected the poetry of the saint. This poetry was later incorporated into the Guru Granth Sahib, when it was first compiled by the fifth Sikh Guru, Guru Arjan. Being part of the Granth, Baba Fareed is also given a special status in the Sikh religion and revered like the Gurus.

There is an orange bin at the end of the passageway containing cloth of various colours. Some are decorated with golden embroidery at the edge. Kartar's friends take out these cloths and tie them on their heads. There is a railing dividing the walkway to the main room of the shrine. The passage on the left is for going in, while that on the right is for those coming out. It is useful when there are huge crowds. This, however, is a smaller festival and there isn't much of a crowd. Little children run from underneath the railings and disappear into the darkness of the courtyard. A green cloth has been spread out throughout the passageway. There are footprints of wet feet on the cloth.

Just a few steps into the walk, there is a well covered with an iron-railing. Little children have climbed on it and are peeping inside. A board alongside reads, 'This well was part of Guru Nanak's house.'

On the other side of the railing is the Nishan Sahib where women and children are gathered, some lost in prayers while others are busy lighting candles at the base. Some children pick up the lit candles from here and place them on the mouth of the well.

The short walk ends at a small room surrounded by a portico. About a hundred people are sitting here on the carpets that have been laid out on the cold marble floor and are listening to the kirtan being performed here. Kartar bends before the window and prostrates to the Granth. His Muslim friends stand behind him awkwardly, not knowing what to do. Prostrating in front of anyone or anything besides Allah is blasphemy. They have been taught this all their lives. This room, where the Granth is being recited, is the room where Nanak was born.

Whereas the majority of the devotees are listening to the kirtan, there are a few who are paying their respects to the other important places around the shrine. One of them is a historical tree, next to the portico. A woman lights up an unlit candle from one of the many that have been placed at the base of the tree and puts its next to the several candles and lamps. There is a bar fence around the tree with a plaque in front that recalls its significance: 'Sikh Martyrdom'—'20th February 1921 at Gurdwara Janamasthan, Nankana Sahib.'

* * *

On 20 February 1921, a group of unarmed Sikhs, some of whom had come from other districts, including Lyallpur (Faisalabad), Lahore, Sialkot and Gujranwala, gathered at Gurdwara Tambu Sahib. This was a group of about 200 people, protesting against the control of the Hindu priests (*mahants*) at major gurdwaras like Janamasthan.

As a result of sectarian divisions between the Sikh communities and the takeover of Punjab by the British, a large number of important Sikh gurdwaras were being administered by Hindu mahants. The mahants used to organize the prayers in accordance with their religious traditions, offending the Sikhs, who demanded that the administration of the gurdwaras be handed over to them, so that all non-Sikh practices were stopped.

The Sikhs gathered at Gurdwara Tambu Sahib and accused the current mahant of Gurdwara Janamasthan, Narayan Das, of corruption. He was alleged to have sold parts of the vast property connected with the gurdwara. After taking part in a small prayer, they decided that they would walk to Gurdwara Janamasthan and hold a prayer there as well, in accordance with Sikh traditions. In the meantime, Mahant Narayan Das found out about the situation and gathered his supporters. Muslim Pathans from the tribal areas guarded him. Other Hindus from the vicinity who supported him also gathered at the gurdwara.

The group of Sikhs was being led by Bhai Daleep Singh and Bhai Lachman Singh. When these peaceful Sikhs entered the gurdwara, Mahant Narayan Das's supporters fired at them, killing about a hundred people and injuring several others. Bhai Lachman Singh was taken into the courtyard of the main shrine. Here he was hung upside down on this tree and burnt. Bhai Daleep Singh was thrown inside a brick kiln, which once used to exist within the premises of the gurdwaras.

This act of brutality invited condemnation from all over India. Major political parties, including the Indian National Congress, threw their weight behind the protestors. Under pressure, the British government took action against Narayan Das and his accomplices, some of whom were sentenced to death, while others were sentenced to life imprisonment in the notorious jail at the islands known as Kala Pani (Andaman Islands). This event formed the basis of a larger movement to take control of all the major gurdwaras of the country from the Hindu mahants.

This movement, which began in 1921, ended in 1924–25. By the end, the Sikh community was able to gain control of all the major Sikh gurdwaras in Pakistan and India. This movement resulted in the formation of the Shiromani Gurdwara Parbandhak Committee (SGPC), an organization responsible for the control of all the important Sikh gurdwaras across India. Till the formation of the Pakistan Sikh Gurdwara Prabandhak Committee, the Sikh Gurdwara Prabandhak Committee (SGPC), looked after the gurdwaras of Pakistan as well. As a result of this political struggle, a Sikh political party also emerged by the name of the Akali Dal. Master Tara Singh, the famous Sikh politician who was vehemently opposed to the creation of Pakistan at the time of Partition, belonged to this party.

* * *

There are a number of rooms in the courtyard of the gurdwara which are allotted to Sikh pilgrims at the time of major festivals. One of the rooms behind the shrine is reserved for the Granth. There is a bed here where the Granth is kept. There is an air-conditioner which is turned on during the summers for the Granth. A thick blanket lies on the bed, which is put over the holy book in winters. The Granth Sahib is treated as a living object. No other activity can take place in this room.

Next to the tree there is another small portico, similar to the one around the main room. There is a glass room at the centre, which contains a golden palanquin. This portico marks the spot where the martyrs from the deadly day of 20 February 1921 were cremated in one big pile. The golden palanquin was gifted to the gurdwara by the former chief minister of Indian Punjab, Captain Amarinder Singh.

Two paintings depicting two different scenes from the life of Guru Nanak rest inside the glass wall. One of them portrays Baba Nanak with his companions, Bhai Mardana and Bhai Bala. Mardana is playing the rubab and Bhai Bala is holding the fly-whisk standing behind Baba Nanak. Another is a depiction of an episode from Guru Nanak's life. Nanak is shown as a young boy sleeping while a cobra is sitting next to him, with its hood distended. This painting depicts the occasion when once Baba Guru Nanak fell asleep under a shady tree while out grazing his buffaloes. After a little while, the sun moved and Nanak was exposed to the light. A cobra then emerged and stood next to Nanak, providing him shade with its hood for as long as Guru Nanak slept. There is a gurdwara about 500 metres from Gurdwara Janamasthan that commemorates this spot. It is called Mal Ji Sahib, and is situated near the Nankana Sahib railway station.

After about an hour of kirtan recitation, there is a communal prayer which is led by the head Granthi of the shrine, Lalit Singh. The entire community stands behind him, listening and responding to his calls of *'Wahe Guruji ka Khalsa, wahe Guruji ki fateh.'* At the end of the prayer, an elderly man picks up the Granth and placing it on his head, walks out of the room using the exit door. As he encircles the shrine, the community follows him to the Granth's bedroom chanting *'Waheguru, Waheguru.'* The Granth is placed on the bed and covered in a blanket to protect it from the cold. This marks the end of the prayer and the beginning of the Lohri festival.

* * *

Following the conclusion of the prayers, the entire community gathers in the outer courtyard of the gurdwara where there is a flame in front of the main building. Everyone is trying to get close to it. The spots closest to the fire have been taken up by young Sikh men. Women and children struggle to catch a glimpse of the fire from the side, an integral part of the Lohri celebration.

Kartar goes to the shoe counter and gets everyone's shoes. He doesn't want anyone to be late for the next step, which would be the burning of another fire at Gurdwara Patti Sahib, where Kartar also happens to live. In one large group, the entire community heads out of Gurdwara Janamasthan and walks towards the next gurdwara, which is only a few hundred metres away.

Gurdwara Patti Sahib is constructed where Guru Nanak learnt Hindi and then Sanskrit from his teacher as a child. There are seven gurdwaras in Nankana Sahib, most of which are associated with incidents from the life of Baba Guru Nanak. The gurdwara has a number of rooms which have been taken over by local Sikhs with Kartar's family being one of them. Muslims, standing in their shops or on their bikes, look at the pilgrimage of the Sikhs with burning curiosity.

Unlike Gurdwara Janamasthan, there is no security at this particular shrine. An arch entrance leads into the complex facing which there is a double-storey yellow structure with a white dome, standing in the middle of the courtyard on a platform raised a few steps above the ground. The Nishan Sahib, next to the building, signifies the presence of the Khalsa in the vicinity. Candles, lamps and incense are burning at its base.

Standing in the middle of the courtyard, Kartar picks up a window made out of wood and breaks it with his feet. He throws it into the centre, where there are already other broken items of wood. There are also some branches from trees that children and boys have collected on their way to the shrine. One of his friends pours oil on to the piles of wood and then, burning a piece of paper, he throws it on the wood, which catches fire in an instant. Children and young men amused at the rising flames throw more items into it. The community gathers around the fire, comfortable in the piercing cold of the night.

* * *

Lohri like Vaisakhi or Basant, is an ancient festival of the Punjab that commemorates the change of season. It is celebrated on 13 January, which is generally the last night of the month of *Poh*, according to the indigenous calendar. Poh is considered to be the coldest season of the year followed by the month of *Maghi* that heralds the arrival of spring. Historically this festival, like other season-celebrating festivals, has been celebrated by all the religious communities based in India. Traditionally, the entire village would gather at an open space outside the village and settle around a bonfire, eating dry fruit throughout the night, sharing folk songs and stories with each other, praying for the cold spell to end. Children would go from house to house collecting wood and other items that could be used to keep the fire alive the entire night. Women of the household would prepare kheer, a traditional sweet dish, which would be put out in the open to cool overnight. In the morning after performing their ablutions, the community would eat the kheer prepared overnight.

For the Sikhs though, Lohri is not just a cultural festival but also a religious one, associated with a historical event. On this day the Sikhs were able to defeat a large Mughal army under the command of the tenth Sikh Guru, Guru Gobind Singh, in a battle fought in Muktsar, India. In memory of the victory, special prayers are held in all gurdwaras. The festival of Lohri also falls close to the celebration of Guru Gobind Singh's birthday, celebrated only a few days before the festival.

After the creation of Pakistan, as a newly independent Muslim country grappled with issues of its identity, it began to shun all cultural festivals that reminded it of its past conjoined with the Hindu and Sikh communities. Over the years, this indigenous festival of the Punjab died down as the Muslims here shaped for themselves a religious identity inspired by the puritanical version of Islam imported from Arabia. Living under the shadow of a Muslim majority, the Sikh and the Hindu minorities of central Punjab also stopped this celebration.

* * *

On one side of the courtyard, a man wearing a maroon turban with a white shalwar kameez distributes kheer to the community in small steel cups and bowls. Given the change in lifestyle over the years, no one can afford to spend the entire night waiting for the kheer to prepare any more. The fire will be extinguished soon and people will head back to their homes.

* * *

'Celebration of Lohri and other events like celebrating the birthday of Guru Gobind Singh have only begun in the last couple of years,' says Kartar. 'They have been made possible by the increase in the Sikh population as a result of the migration from the tribal areas after the war. Just a few years ago, there were only about fifty Sikh houses, but now there are almost two hundred to two hundred and fifty Sikh homes. We have become much more confident with enough numerical strength to exert our identity. Earlier, there was only a prayer at the gurdwara.' The celebration of Lohri at Nankana Sahib this year is an attempt to revive this cultural tradition of Punjab, earlier celebrated on a large scale throughout the province. It is ironical, though, that this Punjabi tradition shunned by Punjab is now being revived by a group of Pathan men residing in Punjab.

* * *

The consumption of kheer marks the end of the celebration for women and children, who start heading back to their homes. The older boys, however, make small groups and prepare to visit the homes of various members of the community. Here, they will be offered more kheer and other eatables that women of the community have prepared for the wandering group. Kartar joins a group of young men as they head towards the nearest Sikh house from the gurdwara; meanwhile his Muslim friends head back to Lahore.

COMMEMORATION OF GURU ARJAN'S MARTYRDOM AT GURDWARA DERA SAHIB, LAHORE

Outside the Alamgiri gate of the Lahore Fort, the Guru was forced to sit in a cauldron of boiling water. Burning sand was poured on him to add to the torture. According to legend, the Guru bore all this patiently. His Muslim Sufi friend, Mian Meer (1550–1635), whose shrine now attracts thousands of devotees in Lahore, was incensed by the treatment meted out to his friend by the Mughal cronies and asked the Guru if he should destroy his oppressors. The Guru replied that he should not. On the fifth day of the torture, the Guru requested a bath in the River Ravi, flowing next to the fort. His wish was granted. Guru Arjan (1563–1606) stepped into the river, joined his hands in supplication and took a dip. Onlookers waited for him to emerge, but he didn't. The Mughal cronies sent search parties but to no avail. His followers realized that the Guru had performed a miracle. Legend has it that the Guru was lifted alive into the sky by God.

* * *

The river has changed its course, moving a few kilometres away. The Mughals no longer rule the country. The fort, which was once the emblem of their power and wealth, is now a tourist destination. For twenty Pakistani rupees, one can visit it and even tour the private chambers of the mighty Mughal Emperor, Jahangir, who ordered the Guru's assassination. Facing the fort is a small yellow building with a golden dome. A thick yellow wall protects it from its surroundings. Several street vendors are usually sighted there, sitting on the base of the wall, busy selling cheap toys and other artefacts from the city. This place is teeming with visitors on any given day. Facing the fort, adjacent to the yellow building, is the Badshahi Mosque, constructed by the Mughal Emperor, Aurangzeb. The Hazuri Bagh in the middle of the mosque and the fort is another historical site. This is where the Sikh ruler of Punjab, Maharaja Ranjit Singh, used to meet his subjects. A Mughal *baradari* (a pavilion with twelve pillars) stands in the middle of the garden. All of these three places are famous with the tourists. A giant gateway leading into the yellow building from here facing the garden is permanently locked.

Today, this place is deserted. The only road that leads up to these historical monuments is cordoned off by the police. A barricade, fortified with barbwire, has been put up at the start of the road. Only people carrying special cards, which have been made for them by the ETPB, are allowed to pass this checkpost. Many local tourists return disappointed at not being able to visit the fort or the other sites. The security intensifies at the large iron bar gate from where the yellow wall begins. A metal detector door has been placed at the entrance that reads 'Out'. The entry gate that says

'In' is shut. The date is 6 June 2011 and the occasion is the commemoration of Guru Arjan's death anniversary.

A few security officials in plain shalwar kameez are seated in front of the gate, while police personnel are standing across them checking the security cards of all those coming to the gurdwara. About 300 pilgrims from India have come to Lahore for this event, while several hundred have come from other parts of the country. The Indians will stay here for three days, after which some will return while others will visit sacred shrines in Nankana Sahib and Hassan Abdal.

* * *

On regular days, hundreds of local visitors pass this building, peeking in and trying to get a glimpse of what lies beyond all the protection. They know it has something to do with the Sikhs. Overwhelmed by their curiosity, a few tourists show up at the reception window, asking if they can visit it from the inside. The answer from the security men employed is blunt, 'If you are a Muslim, you are not allowed.' Rarely do they catch the sight of some Sikh man coming out or going in. This turns a lot of heads for it is now rare that one runs into a Sikh in this city, a city which was once ruled by a Sikh and the seat of their political strength. 'Children wave at me. Some men come and hug me. Others want group photographs. For them, I am a langur (a species of monkey),' jokes Kartar Singh Kartar. He is temporarily residing at this gurdwara for his education and being given free accommodation and food at the shrine.

* * *

Before being ushered into the courtyard, one has to pass through a final security check. Male and female police personnel physically search the person, while all the bags pass through an X-ray machine. The structure inside is of the same colour as the protecting wall; yellow was commonly used for buildings in Punjab during the older days. A couple of rooms at the entrance have been taken over by the security officials. They monitor who enters and leaves the gurdwara from here.

Straight ahead one can see Kartar, clad only in a vest and a shalwar standing behind a stall serving drinks to the pilgrims. A tent covers this courtyard from the top, warding off the intense heat of June, and carpets have been spread out over the floor for the pilgrims to sit on, facing the Granthi. The recitation of the Granth Sahib can be heard through a small speaker that is attached to the building. There are several devotees sitting inside while others have gathered outside, surrounding the shrine from both sides. Most of the pilgrims are Sikhs, bearing the 5 Ks; however, a few are clean-shaven, their heads covered with a cloth. These people belong to the areas of south Punjab and Sindh and are called Nanak Panthi Sikhs. These are Hindus who believe in the teachings of Guru Nanak, but not in the Khalsa founded by Guru Gobind. They are also referred to as Nanak Panthi Hindus, or those Hindus who believe in the teachings of Guru Nanak. Inside their temples in Sindh and southern Punjab, one will find portraits of Guru Nanak, along with Krishna, Kali Mata and other Hindu deities. They are found in very large numbers in the province of Sindh.

The Khalsa flag, also known as the Nishan Sahib, stands at the edge of the courtyard. The flag is hoisted on top of a long pole, its saffron-coloured cloth visible from far away.

The flag is saffron as well. It is triangular and contains the symbol of the Khalsa, a double-edged dagger. There is a circular shape in the middle, called *chakker*. Two single-edged swords or kirpan flank it. The entire symbol is called *Khanda* and is hoisted high up to signify the presence of the Khalsa in the surroundings. A couple of men are standing at the base of the flag, which is a circular platform about 5 feet from the ground. With their hands held out together in front of their chests, they look up at the khanda and recite a silent prayer. Some touch the base at the end of the prayer and then kiss their hands, while others pray and then touch their eyes one by one on the platform before moving on.

Adjacent to the courtyard, there are a couple of stairs that lead one into another space covered from the top. It is open from one side and protected by a wall from the other, beyond which is the langar hall. There is a small room in the middle of the area with windows on all sides, protected by iron bars. There is a humming sound coming from here, which is the result of the combined muted prayers being recited by the devotees. The voice of the Granthi echoes from the courtyard in the background. People climb over each other to get a glimpse of what's going on inside the room.

A small door facing the side of the langar hall leads into this structure and is jam-packed with visitors. About twenty attendees are stuck inside this tiny room, which has a capacity of no more than five people. A few women sit inside with their heads covered, wearing shalwar kameez; the traditional dress of Punjabi women on both sides of the border, reciting from their pocket Granths, their small kirpans dangling out of their black belts. A man desperate to go into the room shouts at the people inside to come out after having performed darshan. A few women oblige and make way for the others, but most of them continue to sit. In the centre of this room, there is a small bulge which is covered by a velvet cloth on the top, hung from the roof. This is the main attraction; the samadhi of Guru Arjan. According to the legend, this place marks the spot where Guru Arjan disappeared into the river.

* * *

Guru Arjan was the fifth Sikh Guru of Sikhism and the son of the fourth Sikh Guru, Guru Ram Das. One of his major contributions towards the development of the Sikh religion is the compilation into the Granth Sahib of the writings of all the previous Sikh Gurus and other non-Sikh saints collected by the earlier Gurus from diverse sources. He was assassinated on the orders of the fourth Mughal Emperor, Jahangir, in Lahore, where his gurdwara stands, by the name of Gurdwara Dera Sahib. Emperor Jahangir records the events leading up to his assassination in his memoir *Tuzuk-i-Jahangiri*. He says:

> 'At last when Khusrau passed along this road, this insignificant fellow (Guru Arjan) proposed to wait upon him. Khusrau happened to halt at the place where he was, and he came out and did homage to him. He behaved to Khusrau in certain special ways, and made on his forehead a finger-mark in saffron, which the Hinduwan (the people of India) call qashqa, (Tilak) and is considered propitious. When this came to my ears and I clearly understood his folly, I ordered them to produce him and handed over his houses, dwelling-places, and children to Murtaza Khan, and having confiscated his property commanded that he should be put to death.'[1]

Khusrau was Jahangir's rebellious son who fought against him for the throne. During his campaign, he stopped over at the langar of the Guru in Amritsar and sought blessings for his victory. The tilak on the forehead, mentioned in the passage above, was that blessing. This action of the Guru was considered treason by the emperor.

The persecution of Guru Arjan at the hand of Mughal authorities played a crucial role in the development of the Sikh religion. It also defined future relations between the Mughals and the Sikhs, which remained hostile until the end of the Mughal Empire. Several battles were fought between the two groups in the subsequent years. Sometimes the Mughals routed the Sikhs, while at other times the Sikhs caused damage. The Mughals later assassinated the eighth Sikh Guru, Guru Tegh Bahadur and the four sons of the tenth Sikh Guru, Guru Gobind Singh.

It was the assassination of Guru Arjan that transformed the Sikhs from a peaceful religious reforming group into a political community that took up martial arts and other forms of self-defence mechanisms, eventually leading to the formation of the Khalsa. Guru Arjan's son, Guru Hargobind, reared horses and encouraged his followers to keep arms in their defence after his father's death. The assassination was a defining moment for the Sikh community. The days of eclectic religious preachers, Guru Nanak, Guru Angad, Guru Amar Das and Guru Ram Das, were over. The Sikhs were now led by Guru Hargobind, Guru Har Rai, Guru Harkrishan, Guru Tegh Bahadur and Guru Gobind Singh, all of them political leaders of a community along with being religious preachers. Guru Arjan's assassination gave birth to the need for the community to become a political body.

Earlier an amorphous religious group, it was now on its way to becoming a distinct community—the Khalsa.

The persecution of the Sikhs at the hands of the Mughals also had an impact on Muslim-Sikh relations. The urban Muslims have historically looked up to Mughal culture as representative of the Muslim culture. On the other hand, the Sikh community which suffered at the hands of the Mughals was vehemently anti-Mughal. During the riots in Punjab at the time of Partition, millions of people were killed, with an overwhelming majority being Sikhs and Muslims. Before the riots began, Tara Singh, a prominent Sikh leader at that time, took out his kirpan on the stairs of the Punjab Assembly in Lahore and said that the time to take revenge for the Gurus had come, implying revenge on the Muslims, the representatives of the Mughals. This was a result of a resolution presented in the Punjab Assembly for the creation of Pakistan. Master Tara Singh's call was received with a lot of fervour by the Sikh community, reflecting the pain they felt at being persecuted at the hands of the Mughals, all of which began with the assassination of Guru Arjan. Several Sikh demagogues at that time used the symbolism of the violence practised against them by the Mughals as being reason enough to attack the Muslims. Iqbal Qaiser, a Pakistan-based writer and author of the book *Historical Sikh Shrines in Pakistan*, is of the opinion that Guru Arjan's assassination was the starting point of trajectory, of which the violence between the Muslims and the Sikhs at the time of Partition was the last stop, four centuries later.

* * *

After the assassination of the Guru, a small structure was raised at the spot by his son, Guru Hargobind to mark the samadhi of the Guru and it is still present there to this day. Over the years, as the community grew in influence, so did the shrine dedicated to Guru Arjan. The present structure was first erected by Maharaja Ranjit Singh with further extensions made by the Sikh community in the early years of the twentieth century. After Partition, the gurdwara came under the control of the Pakistan Government which looks after it through the department of ETPB, created to take care of non-Muslim temples and shrines in the country. One of the most prominent Sikh structures in the country, located at such a popular tourist location, the ETPB regularly undertakes renovation work here. In 1996, rooms were built in the complex to accommodate the hundreds of pilgrims who come from India and other parts of Pakistan for special religious days. This new hostel was named after Mian Meer, the Muslim Sufi Saint of Lahore, a close associate of Guru Arjan.

While on the one hand, the antagonism between the Mughals and the Sikhs shaped Muslim-Sikh relations, there is another precedent which was set by the earlier Sikh Gurus and a few Muslim Sufi saints. Baba Guru Nanak, the founder of the Sikh religion, went all the way to Pak Pattan, the city of Baba Fareed, to collect his poetry from his descendants. This was later included in the Granth Sahib by Guru Arjan. Similarly, the friendship between Mian Meer and Guru Arjan is also the subject of several folk tales. Other Muslim Sufis whose poetry has been included in the Sikh holy book are Bhai Mardana, Pipa Ji, Bheekhan and Sata Balwand. The relationship of the Sikhs and the Muslims cannot only be seen through the prism of Sikh-Mughal rivalry.

* * *

A small door from the samadhi of Guru Arjan leads one to the langar hall, divided into two sections. Here, rows of mats have been spread out in four lines across the floor. Visitors take off their shoes before entering the hall and pick up the required utensils from a basket placed next to the entrance. The main langar hall is separated from the kitchen by a wall with some space spared on one side to act as entrance and exit. Here, the food is prepared by volunteers and employees of the gurdwara, an overwhelming majority of whom seem to be low-caste Nanak Panthis from southern Punjab.

Outside the langar hall, facing the gurdwara, is a big lawn with a beautiful white building, adorned with detailed frescoes and other art work. This is the samadhi of Maharaja Ranjit Singh, a grand structure compared to the modest building dedicated to Guru Arjan, more suitable for a king, as opposed to a spiritual reformer. A police official sits on top of the samadhi with his gun in front of him, looking at the activities taking place at the gurdwara. The lawn and the space around it have become a temporary camp for pilgrims who do not have rooms to sleep in, primarily Pathan-Sikh families who have come from Nankana Sahib, Hassan Abdal, Peshawar and the Tribal Areas. The Indian pilgrims and other important guests have been accommodated in the several rooms available in the complex.

At the time of the conclusion of Akhand Path, bhog (community prayer) is performed. All the devotees, who had earlier been resting on their mats, stand up listening to the priest chant through the loudspeakers. Occasionally, the audience says 'Waheguru', a term used to refer to God. At the end of the prayer, the entire community prostrates to the living Guru, the Granth Sahib, inside the hall.

* * *

In another part of the lawn, protected by tents covering them from the sun, a group of Sikh boys have set up a stall and are busy serving cold milk and juice to the devotees. Several pilgrims have thronged to the stalls, vying to get their share of drinks while another group of boys is serving freshly cut watermelons on paper plates.

Thirty-two-year-old Dr Manoj Singh is standing next to the stall attending to a few people. He is wearing a red turban and a red shirt with grey trousers. Writing on a small piece of paper, he hands it over to an old woman standing next to him who blesses him by putting her hand on his head, as he bends to seek her blessings. Dr Manoj Singh is the first MBBS doctor from the Pakistani Sikh community and is currently serving at the Ganga Ram Hospital.

'A lot of patients request to see me. They are fascinated by me,' says Dr Manoj. He belongs to one of the Pathan families at Nankana Sahib, who settled there after the unrest in the tribal areas. 'A lot of the Sikh families at Nankana Sahib are involved in *hikmat* (traditional practice of medicine); however, no one besides me has studied to become a proper doctor.' Now based in Lahore, he travels to Nankana Sahib regularly, where many old people come to him with their complaints whom he helps free of charge, today being no exception either.

Loud laughter is heard from behind the stall serving cold milk flavoured with Rooh Afza, turning many heads. This is the sound of Kartar refusing to let anyone else take charge of the bucket of milk, insistent on serving everyone himself.

He is the most highly qualified Pakistani Sikh. 'I remember once I was in class at Nankana Sahib during my undergraduate studies when a professor of mine commented that Punjabi is a language of the unrefined. His remark incensed me, but I kept my calm knowing that there is no point arguing with him. This is our religious language like Arabic is for the Muslims. This is the language of Baba Guru Nanak, Baba Fareed, Waris Shah, Bulleh Shah. That was the day I decided to do my PhD in the Punjabi language.'

These two men from the Sikh community are part of the next generation of the Sikh community in Pakistan, more aware of its religious, political and social rights. Whereas earlier members of the community were traditionally confined to a particular field, like *hikmat*, cloth trading and other forms of business, now as they acquire more education they are experimenting in diverse fields.

Next to them is twenty-five-year-old Premjeet Singh, the first Pakistani Sikh to have been commissioned into the Pakistan Rangers. Wearing his green ranger's uniform with a black turban, he is often sighted at the Wagah border during the daily ceremonial parade at the time of lowering of the flag. Premjeet has been allotted a room, as opposed to other local Sikhs, because of his social standing, which he is sharing with five other family members, a luxury at times like these.

'When I was new in the rangers, I remember once we were sitting at our checkpost near the Ganda Singh border.

Our in-charge walked in, lost in his thoughts. When he saw me, the colour of his face changed and he ran out. He thought he had walked into an Indian checkpost! His assistant told him that he was in Pakistan and asked him to come back,' recalls Premjeet with a chuckle. A religious man, Premjeet makes it a point to attend all the festivals around the year. 'My superiors are cooperative and give me holidays on religious occasions. I then volunteer to work on Eid when most of them are gone.'

With this rise in the education level, there is also a greater realization about the political rights that the elders of the Sikh community did not understand given their rustic backgrounds. Moving from tribal areas to the heart of Punjab, an overwhelming majority of them could not even speak the language. They remained confined to their little enclaves. However the younger ones, fluent in Urdu and Punjabi, have intermingled, leading to a greater socio-economic and political understanding of their community in comparison to the others.

* * *

'The PSGPC are cronies of the ETPB dominated by the Muslim community,' says forty-six-year-old Madan Singh, a former head of the PSGPC. A successful businessman from Nankana Sahib, he also runs a small school in the city called Guru Nanak High School, the only school in the country where the Granth Sahib is taught to Sikh children. 'What do the Muslims know about the Sikh religion? Even the priest (Granthis) and other employees are appointed by the government. I resigned as the head of PSGPC because they would not let me work independently. The current head of the organization is a puppet, someone who can be easily manipulated. No one from the local community respects him. He never visits the city. There is a conspiracy theory that he is not even a Sikh, but only posing as one.' Much liked in the community, a lot of Sikhs still approach Madan for any sort of political work.

All the affairs of gurdwaras in Pakistan, including arranging festivals, employment, cleanliness, property, renovation, etc., are managed by the Pakistan Sikh Gurdwara Prabandhak Committee (PSGPC) that functions under the purview of the ETPB. The PSGPC was formed in 1999 to look after the Sikh gurdwaras in the country and to collect the revenue generated at religious festivals like these, an amount that runs into several hundreds of thousands of rupees. Before 1999, the Shiromani Gurdwara Parbandhak Committee (SGPC), based in Amritsar, used to take the collection at the festivals back to India. The committee is also responsible for looking after the properties of the gurdwaras, most of which were allotted to the shrines at the time of Ranjit Singh. This is a vast amount of property, about 25,00,000 acres according to an official at the ETPB. With the growing political consciousness in the community, there is a growing resentment in certain sections of the community against the handling of all the gurdwara activities, revenues and property by the PSGPC.

In April 2012, Ghulab Singh, the first Sikh traffic warden in Pakistan, filed a case against the ETPB in the Lahore High Court, challenging the 'illegal' sale of land connected with Gurdwara Dera Chaal on Bedian Road, Lahore. The High Court ordered a stay on the sale of land. The Sikh community alleges that this is not the only case of corruption and several others are going unnoticed. There are claims of gurdwaras being rented out to fill the personal coffers of the officials.

For the past many decades, the local Sikh community has been aloof to these political matters. However, now, as the Sikhs gain greater educational and social independence, these issues are being discussed, setting the scene for a new battle with the authorities.

COMMEMORATION OF MAHARAJA RANJIT SINGH'S DEATH ANNIVERSARY AT LAHORE

Just behind the samadhi of Guru Arjan, a splendid building, white in colour, stands four floors from the ground with a small dome on the top. The minaret of the Badshahi Masjid, or the Royal Mosque, rises from behind this structure. Standing on the roof of this building, one can see the portal of the mosque, parts of the courtyard and three bulb-like domes, facing which is the Alamgiri gate of the Lahore Fort, named after the imperial title of the Mughal Emperor Aurangzeb. The Hazuri Bagh is situated in the middle of these monuments, with a single-storey pavilion placed symmetrically at the centre of the garden while four lanes lead towards it from all sides.

The Roshani gate, one of the thirteen gateways that lead into the ancient walled city of Lahore, is between the Alamgiri Gate and the Royal Mosque. This particular entrance was once reserved for the prince and the princess, who would go from the fort to the city through this entrance. In the night, lamps were lit all along the passageway for visibility and hence the name Roshani gate, or the gate of lights. Behind it is the Heera-Mandi bazaar, the area reserved for the prostitutes of the city before they dispersed all over Lahore, after a crackdown on them during the Islamist government of General Zia-ul-Haq. One would hear the sound of music, singing and dancing from the houses here in the evening earlier. Women standing on their wooden balconies would flirt with the passersby on the road, enticing them to come pay a short visit. Even though the prostitutes and dancers have been sent away, the musicians remain. This is still one of the largest markets for traditional instruments in the city, all of which are made here. Heera-Mandi is also famous for the food street that runs parallel to the wall of the Badshahi Masjid. These are outdoor cafes and restaurants that come to life during the night, as the floodlights of the Royal Mosque light its bulb-like domes.

The white building is the samadhi of Maharaja Ranjit Singh, the Sikh king who ruled Punjab before the British took over. The structure stands on top of another single-storey building, painted yellow in colour. The samadhi is in the middle of a courtyard with rooms for the pilgrims on its sides. The boundaries of the white samadhi are also painted yellow. The regal white structure stands prominently amongst its yellow background, differentiated purposefully by its architecture to stand out.

Two loudspeakers have been placed on top of the samadhi, facing the direction of the ground, erected opposite the mosque and the city, perhaps as a respect to the Muslim religion, a respect that is only expected of the religious minorities. They resonate with the sounds of two men reciting from the Granth Sahib. Standing on the ground, one can see colourful turbans popping from the balcony—red, grey and blue. These are Sikh men resting on the edge, all of them wearing white kurta-pajamas with a black belt that runs diagonally along their chest and back, holding a sheath for their kirpan. There are two staircases on either side of the yellow building. A few pilgrims rush out of the residential rooms at the base of the building as the final prayers of the ceremony are performed.

There is a sea of sandals and shoes at the base of the building, in front of the staircase that takes one inside the hall. These are only a few steps made out of granite stone. The hall is full of pilgrims, about 150 people, all men. There is a palanquin in the centre, constructed on a raised platform with its pillars made of white marble. The two men being heard all over the gurdwara are sitting here and reciting into the microphone. The pavilion is decorated with colourful frills and festoons, shining in the glare of a light bulb hanging from the roof. The rest of the room is dark, with only sunlight coming in from the entrances on the four sides of the square structure. This is the conclusion of the Akhand Path held in the honour of Maharaja Ranjit Singh, also known as *Sher-e-Punjab*, or the Lion of Punjab. The occasion is the death anniversary of the ruler and the date is 29 June 2011, twelve days after the death anniversary commemoration of Guru Arjan in the same complex. Those pilgrims have left and a set of new ones have arrived from India. For the city that the Maharaja once ruled, he is an alien, his memory kept alive not by people of the land he once ruled but by people from the other side of the border, a result of the division of history at the time of Partition.

* * *

Separated by twelve days, a huge historical and symbolic gulf separates these two events. Whereas Guru Arjan's martyrdom is a low point in Sikh history, at the time of Ranjit Singh's death, the Sikhs were arguably the strongest that they have ever been politically. Starting from a small fief around Gujranwala, a city 75 km away from the provincial capital, the Maharaja marched triumphantly into Lahore in 1799. Here he was greeted enthusiastically by a population sick of the lawlessness of that time. In 1801, Ranjit Singh was crowned as the ruler of Punjab by Sahib Singh Bedi, a descendant of Guru Nanak. At its peak, the empire extended from FATA (Federally Administered Tribal Areas) to Kashmir to Multan in the south and the River Sutlej. He struck a deal with the British government, which allowed each to govern their area without interference from the other.

The era of Ranjit Singh is now portrayed as a repressive time for Muslims in Pakistani historiography, whose entire purpose is to keep up a nationalist agenda, defined in opposition to Hindus and Sikhs. A Sikh ruler, no matter how loved by Muslims during his time, can no longer be appreciated. Different examples are cited to substantiate the claim. It is said that the Badshahi Masjid was used as a stable for horses. It is also said that he plundered other Mughal buildings. For example, he removed the top structure of Emperor Jahangir's tomb and placed it in the Hazuri Bagh. The pavilion, which now stands in the middle of the ground, was part of the structure of Emperor Jahangir's tomb. While it is true that these things happened during his tenure, but to use these examples in order to draw a universal principle is reductionist.

Like the third Mughal emperor, Akbar, Maharaja Ranjit Singh was a secular ruler who allowed freedom of religion. What Pakistani historiography generally does not cover is that he constructed a mosque at a mohalla called Gul Begum in Lahore in memory of his Muslim wife. Another Muslim wife of his, Jind Kaur, ordered the construction of a library at the shrine of the eleventh century Sufi, Ali Hujwiri, and gifted all the Qurans she had in her possession to it. The shrine near the walled city of Lahore goes by the name of Data Darbar and is one of the most popular Sufi Shrines in the city, revered by people from different religions. There were also a number of Muslim generals in his army, including General Mohammad Sultan, General Elahi Baksh and General Ghaus Mohammad Khan. The second most important man in his government, after the ruler himself, was a Muslim by the name of Fakir Azizudin. At one point, he held the two most important offices, that of prime minister and the foreign minister. His family still lives in Lahore in their ancestral house, located inside the walled city.

After the creation of a certain world view following the birth of a Muslim Pakistan and Hindu India, the religious syncretism of historical figures like Akbar and Ranjit Singh could no longer be entertained in Pakistan. The official history of the country treats history as a continuous process that inevitably led to the creation of Pakistan, instead of allowing it to be free of its contemporary prejudice and thereby robbed of its relevant context. Invaders and plunderers like Mahmud Ghaznvi and Ahmad Shah Abdali became national heroes due to their religious affiliation and local heroes became infidels, the ultimate form of disassociation in a Muslim environment. In the land of Punjab which was for over a millennium ruled by Afghans, Mughals and other non-Punjabis, Ranjit Singh was the first Punjabi to rule Punjab. However, as far as Pakistan is concerned, all his achievements and bravado is measured only in terms of his religiosity.

Whereas on the one hand, Pakistani historiography takes a religiously biased view of the Maharaja, some Sikhs on the other side of the border also elevate him to heights that would be difficult to substantiate empirically. Amanpreet Singh, thirty-five, is a trader from Ludhiana. He is one of the pilgrims who have travelled to Lahore to attend the death commemoration ceremony of Maharaja Ranjit Singh. This is the first time he is visiting Pakistan. As the religious ceremony taking place in the hall draws to a close, he loiters in the adjacent garden. 'The Maharaja was a great leader. People were happy during his time. There was justice, education, wealth and prosperity. There was no crime. People would leave their shops unattended as there was no concept of stealing. It was truly an era when the wolf and the lamb had water from the same river,' he says. This of course is another extreme view of the Maharaja, at the other end of the spectrum, very similar to the Muslim perception of the rule of the 'Rightly-guided Caliphs'. Both of these viewpoints are shaped more out of religious devotion rather than a historical reading.

However historically biased as it may be, such a devoted reading of Ranjit Singh's personality gives an interesting insight about the perception that Ranjit Singh's character projects. There is a view that Ranjit was a true follower of Guru Gobind Singh and founded an era of the Khalsa.

One reason why Ranjit arouses so much passion in the Sikh community is because of his work in the construction and renovation of many gurdwaras all over Punjab, considered a sacred duty and hence establishing his credentials as the upkeeper of the Khalsa. After years of civil war, he was able to bring stability in Punjab which lasted a good forty years. He was one individual who was able to keep the British at bay when the rest of India was coming under their control, directly or indirectly. The British treated him with respect and he was careful not to antagonize the British. The British took over soon after his death, as his descendants scrambled for the spoils. Punjab became a British colony almost immediately after his death, eventually leading to its division at the time of Partition.

* * *

Men, mostly in turbans, are sitting around the palanquin, most of them listening with their heads bowed in devotion, while others click pictures. This palanquin, right now occupied by the two men reading the Guru Granth Sahib, marks the spot where the last remains of the Maharaja were buried. His cremation took place in the ground accompanying the building. On a regular day, a portrait of the Maharaja is placed at the palanquin, dressed in a white robe, sporting a long white beard. Next to him is the portrait of his youngest son, Dalip Singh, who also happened to be the last Maharaja of Punjab, before the British took over. Today, the portraits have been removed.

The dome of the building from the inside is decorated with coloured glass. Small bits are intricately laid out to form geometrical patterns. Green, orange and red glass has been used to add to the aesthetics. The empty niches are decorated with colourful frescoes. There is a balcony here that looks down at the palanquin from the floor above, empty of pilgrims. Balcony walls depict different scenes from the court: attendants catering to the queen, or frescoes of religious drawings from Hindu mythology. There are depictions of Krishna, Ganesh, Ram and Sita, all important deities in the Hindu pantheon. The wall paintings have faded with time while a few have disappeared altogether. On others, people have noted down their names and numbers thereby disfiguring it.

One particular pilgrim, sitting at the end of the room, is dressed differently from all the others. He is wearing a long blue turban, with a yellow cloth in the middle. There are quoits of steel around the headdress. The Khalsa symbol is attached on the front and his entire dress is blue in colour, with a belt around his waist and his blue *chadhra* (something like a dhoti) tucked in such that it ends at his knees. Wearing a thick bangle on his wrist, his kirpan is a thick long sword, covered in a black sheath, resting on his shoulder as he squats on the floor, listening to the Akhand Path with his eyes closed. This devotee belongs to a particular Sikh order known as Nihang.

* * *

This order trains as warriors to protect the Sikh religion when the need arises. They are said to be the warriors of the Guru. The order was founded by Guru Gobind Singh as a fighting body of the Khalsa, forming the suicide squads of the Khalsa armies during the days of the Guru. A Nihang calls himself *sava lakh* (1,25,000), that is being equal to so many people or one person being the equal of an entire *fauj* (army).

Throughout his reign, Ranjit Singh used their services for political needs and showed deference to them because of the religious respect they enjoyed. In 1802, he employed a Nihang by the name of Akali Phula Singh to capture the city of Amritsar. Phula was largely responsible for the successful campaign. Phula Singh brought 2000–3000 Nihangs into the state army. In later years, the Nihangs, led by Phula Singh, played a pivotal role in turning battles in favour of Maharaja Ranjit Singh when uprisings led by Muslim leaders began in Kasur and Multan. As the rebellion by the Muslim commanders was given a religious colour against the infidel Ranjit Singh, the Maharaja employed the Nihangs to also give the battles a religious tone. In his book, *Ranjit Singh: Maharaja of the Punjab*, Khushwant Singh has this to say about the Nihangs:[1]

> *The word Nihang in Persian means crocodile. The order became very popular among the Sikhs. The Nihangs, also known as Akalis, wear blue and dedicate their lives to the service of the community. The order has degenerated into a sect of beggars notorious for the quantities of hashish they can consume. Nevertheless, they are an extremely picturesque lot — the Sikh version of Cervantes' Don Quixote with speech full of braggadocio.*

* * *

The door facing the main entrance leads to another hall: a double-storey structure with residential rooms on the ground floor, painted yellow from the outside. The hall adjacent to the samadhi is one big room, with a wooden door leading into it. A few pilgrims are standing here immersed in prayers facing a raised platform on one side of the room, on top of which there are thirteen small semi-spheres. These are the samadhis of the eleven women and two pigeons who also burned in the pyre of Maharaja Ranjit Singh. These include his wives and concubines. This practice comes from the ancient Rajput tradition known as *sati*, in which the widow also burns in the same pyre as the husband's.

As the religious ceremony draws to a close, people start moving towards the langar hall sitting in two rows facing each other, with volunteers distributing food to them. One of them pours dal, while another offers rice. They are followed by another boy, who offers pilgrims rotis. Another volunteer walks up and down the aisle carrying a large container of water, pouring into the empty glasses placed next to the platters of the pilgrims. Towards the entrance of the hall, an old man is sitting next to a table serving tea to the pilgrims who have eaten their food. Boiled with sugar and ginger, this form of tea is highly popular in East Punjab.

One of the pilgrims is fifty-four-year-old Jaswant Singh. Wearing a green turban and a white kurta, he is accompanied by a friend, a young man wearing a pink turban with a white shirt and brown trousers. Sitting on the floor, they are having lunch. Both of them are visiting Pakistan for the first time and belong to the city of Qadian in East Punjab. Situated in district Gurdaspur, this small city holds immense historical significance as the founding place of the Ahmadiyya movement.

* * *

In 1889, a Muslim man from the city, Mirza Ghulam Ahmad, founded the Ahmadiyya sect when he declared himself to be the promised messiah, thus inviting a backlash from the orthodox segment of Islam. Eventually, after the creation of Pakistan, a large proportion of the community migrated to the new country and settled in a city called Rabwah in Punjab. However, even the creation of a Muslim country did not appease the orthodox Sunni Muslims who continued to agitate against the claims of the Ahmadiyya community, which according to them are against the teachings of Islam. In the major cities of the country, one often runs into graffiti inciting violence against the Ahmadiyya community. Every other day there are instances of social discrimination against them. Ahmadiyya men are fired from their jobs and Ahmadiyya students expelled from school because of their religious beliefs. In February 2012, the lawyers' community of the Lahore High Court unofficially banned the sale and consumption of Shezan drinks in the premises of the court, the reason being that Shezan is owned by an Ahmadiyya family. The Ahmadis are also derogatorily referred to as Qadianis, as the movement began from the city of Qadian.

The Ahmadiyyas being allowed to live peacefully in India and persecuted in Pakistan is a strange irony of history toying with the lives of ordinary people for its petty pleasures. The Ahmadiyya community played a prominent role in the creation of Pakistan, a country where they thought they would be allowed to practice their religion freely.

Sir Zaffarullah Khan, a member of the community, drafted the Lahore Resolution which the Muslim League presented in Lahore in March 1940. This resolution is believed to be the basis for the demand of Pakistan. Zaffarullah was also the spokesperson for Muslim League when it presented its views to Sir Cyril Radcliffe, responsible for drawing the boundary between India and Pakistan.

Zaffarullah became the first minister for foreign affairs in independent Pakistan.

It was believed at that time that a 'Muslim' Pakistan would allow the Ahmadiyya community to practise its religion freely as opposed to a 'Hindu' India, which is why a large number of people migrated here and the headquarters shifted from Qadian to Rabwah. However, as the Islamic Republic of Pakistan becomes increasingly religious, it is becoming impossible for the Ahmadiyya community to practice its faith freely. Living in Pakistan, they struggle regularly against the social injustices meted out to them.

* * *

'The Ahmadiyya Muslims practice their religion freely in Qadian. We attend their annual festival at Qadian and they come to our gurdwaras as well. They are a prospering community there, part of the social fabric of the city,' says Jaswant. He refers to the Ahmadiyyas as Muslims, unaware of the fact that by doing so he is violating the laws of his host country.

'However, I have heard there are a few problems Ahmadiyyas face in Pakistan. Is that so?' asks Jaswant in all innocence.

SIKH NEW YEAR AT NANKANA SAHIB

Carrying a fly-whisk, Rajbir Singh stands in front of the palanquin that holds the Granth Sahib. His eyes are tightly shut and hands held together in prayer. There are a few other men around him, not all of them sporting a turban or a beard. Rajbir, wearing a white shalwar kameez and a blue turban, is concluding the bhog, the communal prayer. He has a saffron-coloured scarf around his neck; saffron being the colour of jogis and Sufis (saints in the Hindu and Muslim tradition). Guru Nanak is mostly depicted wearing saffron-coloured clothes. Rajbir is standing inside the room where Guru Nanak was born. Hundreds of devotees stand outside, following his lead. At seventy, Rajbir is one of the oldest employees of the Gurdwara Janamasthan. He moved here in 1978, following a passionate speech by Dr Jagjit Singh Chauhan, a fiery supporter of carving out a separate Sikh state within India, Khalistan.

* * *

'It was my first visit to Nankana Sahib,' Rajbir recalls. 'I had come with my cousin for the celebrations of Guru Nanak's birthday. I remember a speech made by Chauhan, in which he invited Pakistani Sikhs to move to Nankana Sahib to take care of the gurdwaras. I was living in Parachinar (part of the tribal areas in the north-western region of Pakistan) at that time. Within two months, my cousin and I moved to Nankana. For the first six months we lived alone, without our families. There were hardly any Sikhs here at that time. However, once we were able to set up a base, we brought our families along. We have been living here ever since.'

Rajbir moved to Nankana in one of the most tumultuous times in the city's history. This was the period when the movement for a separate Sikh state, known as the Khalistan Movement, was gaining momentum. Being arch-enemies of India, the Pakistani Government openly came out in support of Khalistan as revenge for what had happened in East Pakistan in 1971, eventually resulting in the creation of Bangladesh. The struggle, which gained popularity between the early 1970s and late 1980s became an aggressive movement with acts of violence on both sides. As a result, many Sikh expats living in the US, Canada and the UK, who were vocal proponents of the separatist movement, were banned from going to India. They started coming to Pakistan instead, on important religious festivals like Baisakhi and the birthday of Guru Nanak, which were attended by thousands of Indian pilgrims, most of whom were Sikhs. Because of the high-handedness of the Indian State, especially during Operation Blue Star, the cause gained popularity among the youth of Indian Punjab. Here, the political speeches at the conclusion of the religious ceremonies would find a sympathetic audience.

This was also the time when Pakistani Sikhs emerged on the national scene, as the expat leaders became vocal about their rights in Pakistan as well. Among other things, they highlighted the need to improve the conditions of the gurdwaras in the country. By addressing their needs, they thus gained popularity amongst the local Sikhs. That era defines the trajectory of the Sikh community in Pakistan.

* * *

After concluding the prayers, Rajbir bends and prostrates to the Holy Book with the entire community following him, after which they move to the other pavilion that contains the golden palanquin. Sitting inside the glass chamber, a young boy is reading the last pages of the Granth. He is the final reader of the Akhand Path.

The audience is a combination of Pathan Sikhs, based in Nankana Sahib and clean-shaven Sindhi devotees. There are about 300 people, half from each community. The clean-shaven Sindhi-speaking people are Nanak Panthi Hindus; Hindus who believe in Nanak.

'We are Sikhs but not Singhs,' explains forty-two-year-old Ajay Kumar from Sukkur, Sindh. Clad in a blue shalwar kameez, he sports a moustache and is wearing a purple cloth on his head. 'We came yesterday and will leave tomorrow. We have come to hold prayers in memory of Baba Thara Singh. He was a saint from our area. We are a group of more than a hundred people. The Akhand Path, which is concluding at the moment, is arranged by us. We have also arranged for langar after this.'

In the meantime, children bring packets of sweets, biscuits and other eatables and place them next to the glass chamber. These would be distributed after the conclusion of the prayer as prasad, also arranged for by the Sindhi believers. Children gather around the packets, unable to wait for the conclusion of the prayer. A group of women start unpacking them, collecting sweets and biscuits in a tray. Rajbir, sitting nearby, shouts at the children to go away, threatening them by pretending to stand up. A boy, sporting a kirpan and a dastar on his head, knows that Rajbir is only joking, sticks out his tongue, mocking him, before running away with the other boys. Rajbir, not amused by the gesture, grumbles under his breath.

Back at the pavilion, the reading of the Granth is complete. The community stands up and takes part in the prayer. Following the conclusion of the ceremony, the community moves back to the earlier pavilion. The stage has been set for kirtan. A pair of tablas are accompanied by a harmonium. There is a pulpit facing the stage. A microphone has been attached to it. Kartar Singh, wearing a green shalwar kameez and a matching turban, stands behind the pulpit.

The pilgrimage of the Sindhis coincides with a Sikh festival. They did not know about it when they decided to make the trip. This is the celebration of the Sikh New Year. However, unlike the other festivals, this is not publicized as it is not only a religious event but also a political one, with no precedent in Pakistan. The date is 14 March 2011.

After making the introductory remarks, Kartar quickly moves to the core of his speech. 'We Sikhs are a separate nation and we will not let the Indian *sarkar*, which is a Hindu lobby, take our identity away. They can block our way in whatever way they want, but we will continue striving,' he shouts into the microphone. Kartar perhaps thought his speech would evoke a strong reaction from the crowd, but they listen indifferently. Only a couple of young boys respond to his passion, by calling out *'Jo bole so nihal, sat sri akal.'* Sitting in the front row is Kartar's uncle, Madan Singh, a successful businessman and a philanthropist, whose family has been living at Nankana since the late 1970s and known to be one of the richest Sikhs from the city. He remembers one such fiery speech in particular.

* * *

It was the November of 1985, Guru Nanak's birthday, a year after Operation Blue Star, when sympathy for Khalistan was at its peak. Thousands of Sikh pilgrims had come to Nankana from all over the world. It was the final day of the ceremony. Akhand Path had been completed and bhog offered. Sardar Ganga Singh Dhillon, an American Sikh who is one of the most prominent proponents of Khalistan, took the stage and began a heated speech in favour of a separate Sikh state, and against the Indian government. The PSGPC had not been formed yet and the SGPC, based in Amritsar, was still managing the affairs of the Pakistani gurdwaras. At that time, the SGPC was represented through the Indian Government at the Indian High Commission in Islamabad, Pakistan. The representatives used to receive the pilgrims at the border and make arrangements for their stay inside the gurdwaras. That year was no different.

There were many representatives of the High Commission present during that speech. Two of them were Counsellor B. Jain and First Secretary K.K. Khanna. As the speech intensified, so did the emotions of the young people listening to it. At one point, temperatures rose so high that the gate of the gurdwara was closed and the two representatives were attacked by the attendees. They barely escaped alive, suffering serious injuries. One of the young men who were responsible for beating them up was Madan Singh, only nineteen at that time.

'The Pakistani government intervened,' Madan says as he recalls the events of that day. 'I was arrested along with twenty-five other people and held at Sheikhupura Jail for ten days.' Those were the days when banners reading 'Khalistan Zindabad' along with pictures of Sant Jarnail Singh Bhindranwale were found all over the gurdwara.

Today, the movement has lost its momentum after a crackdown on the separatists by the Indian authorities. Even though occasionally a few leaders speak about the discrimination in 'Hindu' India and the need for a separate state, the public support that the movement once enjoyed has fizzled away. The religious festivals at Nankana and other cities of Pakistan have gone back to being religious festivals.

The situation tonight is slightly different though. The Sikh New Year has become a controversial festival because of the complications involving the Sikh calendar. During the heyday of the Khalistan movement, a lot of Sikhs felt that there was a deliberate attempt on the part of the Indian government to incorporate the Sikh religion within Hinduism. At that time, the Sikhs were using the Hindu calendar, called the Bikrami calendar, causing problems for the Sikh community as the dates for their religious festivals would change every year on the Georgian calendar. This used to happen because the Indian calendar is calculated by combining solar and lunar movements. Along with this, the emergence of Sikh nationalism in the years of Khalistan was inspiring Sikhs to exert a separate identity, outside the fold of Hinduism.

To resolve the problem, a Canadian Sikh by the name of Pal Singh Purewal created a new calendar based on solar calculations. This pinned down the dates of the festivals according to the Georgian calendar. After sixteen years of calculations, he presented the calendar to the community in 1998, inviting reactions from them. In 2003, when no one found any major problem with it, it was implemented by the SGPC. The calendar was called the Nanakshahi calendar in honour of Guru Nanak.

However, once implemented, the calendar received a mixed response from the people. It was supported by a lot of expatriates, but within India there was opposition from a few Sikhs who held important religious posts. Puran Singh, the *jathedar* (priest) of Akal Takht (the throne of the God) in the Golden Temple, was one of them. The jathedar of the Akal Takht bears the highest spiritual post in the Sikh fraternity. To show his resentment, Puran celebrated the birthday of Guru Gobind Singh according to the previous calendar, whereas the SGPC celebrated it according to the new one. This caused a lot of confusion within the community, with most Sikhs not knowing which calendar to follow.

It is believed that under the pressure of the Indian government, in 2010 the SGPC approved amendments in the calendar, which once again brought it closer to the Bikrami calendar. Purewal rejected the changes. Passionate Pakistani Sikhs like Kartar believe that the move is a 'sellout' and they are determined to keep on using the original calendar devised by Purewal. The celebration of this particular event is in reaction to the step taken by the Indian authorities. This explains why 14 March was being celebrated as Sikh New Year here, while Indian Sikhs continue to celebrate New Year on 13 April.

* * *

'The Indian Government has banned this event all over India,' says Kartar. 'Otherwise there would have been large celebrations throughout the country. However, this event is being celebrated in places like the UK, the US and Canada. By making this event successful here, I would like to inform the Indian Government that we will not be pressurized by their tactics. We are a separate nation and will continue to remain so,' he concludes his fiery speech with this remark, managing to incite some fervor in the crowd. '*Bole So Nihal* (Whoever utters, shall be fulfilled),' Kartar makes a call. '*Sat Sri Akal* (eternal is the holy timeless God),' replies the crowd in a delayed humming sound.

Concluding his speech, Kartar sits at the end of the crowd and braces himself for the real function of the night. A group of qawwals make their way on to the stage. All of them are wearing brown shalwar kameez and have covered their heads with a Muslim cap. None of them have a beard, and almost all of them sport a thin moustache. This is a group of six people.

Qawwali is devotional spiritual music, popular in Muslim Sufi shrines. It was introduced by a sect within Sufi Islam. Called the *Chishtiyas*, this sect was founded in the tenth century CE in a small town called Chist in present-day Afghanistan. The sect promotes tolerance among members of different religious communities. The qawwals begin with a devotional song, expressing love towards the Muslim saint Baba Fareed. The Sikh community, which feels a strong affinity towards the Muslim saint, rejoices with excitement. 'This is the first time since Partition that Muslim qawwals have been invited to perform at Nankana Sahib. We have called them from Faisalabad,' whispers Kartar as they sing in the background.

If that is true, then this performance has immense symbolic value. The tradition of kirtan comes from Guru Nanak's Muslim companion, Bhai Mardana. Ever since his time, his descendants as well as other Muslim kirtan performers have performed at Sikh gurdwaras. However, this tradition was disrupted at Partition as the communities became divided, their individual identities and distinctions becoming pronounced and rigid. The performance of the Muslim qawwals at Gurdwara Janamasthan doesn't promise to revive that tradition, but is still a tribute to the years of interaction between the two communities at Sikh gurdwaras.

GURU NANAK'S BIRTHDAY AT NANKANA SAHIB

'I haven't been to the festival of Baba Nanak for a few years. This year I am thinking I should visit,' says Nadeem, as he pulls out his bag from under the holder of his bicycle. Having just completed his shift, he discards the cream shalwar kameez, now smudged with paint, and changes into a clean shirt and trousers. He turns his peak cap one-eighty degrees, bringing the shade side to the front. It reads, 'Silver Sand Paints'.

Nadeem, twenty-five, works as a painter in Lahore, Pakistan. He is a Muslim. Like the majority of the population of the country, he is not an orthodox believer, but practises the spiritual aspects of the religion. He does so by visiting Sufi shrines all over the country on the occasion of *urs*, which is an annual festival arranged on the death anniversary of the Sufi saints. He has been to the shrine of Baba Fareed, Data Darbar and Sakhi Sarwar, to name a few. For Nadeem, Guru Nanak is like a Muslim Sufi saint.

* * *

It is said that once Guru Nanak's companions, one of whom was a Hindu and the other a Muslim, asked him what religion they should adopt in order to follow his faith. He replied that if they were Muslims then they should strive to be true Muslims and if they were Hindus they should try to be honest Hindus. That would be Nanak's religion. The word 'Sikh' is a Punjabi word which means 'to learn'. An expert on Sikh religion, Iqbal Qaiser is of the opinion that anyone who is yearning to learn is a Sikh. 'I can be a Muslim and also be a Sikh if defined this way,' he says.

The movement that began with Nanak was a spiritual reformation movement, not bound by religious rituals and rites, as the incident narrated above testifies. In fact, if anything, Nanak's movement was a rebellion against institutional religion, as can be deciphered from various incidents from his life where he is quoted as speaking against the ritualized religion of Hinduism as well as Islam. But by the time of the tenth Guru, the movement that Nanak had initiated took up an institutionalized form, with rituals and rites in place, codified by the formation of the Khalsa, a distinct community, neither Muslim nor Hindu.

Guru Nanak did not appoint his son as his successor, but instead gave the honour to one of his pious followers, Lehna, who came to be known as Guru Angad Dev. Similarly, on his deathbed, Guru Angad Dev appointed one of his devout followers, Guru Amar Dass, to be his successor. From Guru Amar Dass, however, there was a paradigm shift. Guru Amar Dass selected his son-in-law, Guru Ram Das, as his successor. Guru Ram Das appointed his son, Guru Arjan, as the next Guru. All the subsequent Gurus were appointed from within the family until the tenth

Guru, Guru Gobind Singh, after whom the Granth Sahib became the living Guru for eternity.

As opposed to Khalsa Sikhs who believed in all the ten Gurus, there are several who call themselves Nanak Panthi Hindus or Hindus who follow the teachings of Guru Nanak. They don't believe in the Khalsa of Guru Gobind Singh. Similarly, many Muslims, acquainted with the teachings of Guru Nanak, are devoted to him too and visit his shrine.

* * *

This year when Nadeem returns to Nankana Sahib after seven years, he notices several changes. There is a heavy presence of police officials at all the entrances to the city. No car is permitted inside. The main gate of Gurdwara Janamasthan has changed. It was earlier made of iron bars, which permitted one to witness the activities inside. Now it is one big closed structure barring any view. One could enter through two smaller gates flanking it, both of which are now closed. The wall has been raised and protected by barbwire on the top. Police officials with guns stand at the gate, on top of walls and all the other higher structures at the complex. A new side entrance has been constructed at some distance from the main gate. There are two long queues to enter the gurdwara, one for women and the other for men. There is a small enclosure in the middle of the female queue; this is where they are frisked by female police officers. The men are checked in the open before having to pass through two other security checks; only then can they set foot inside the courtyard of the gurdwara.

Nadeem goes and stands in line, cursing the long queue. He takes out a handkerchief from his pocket and ties it over his head. A couple of Sikh men stand behind him. Just when Nadeem feels that the line is actually moving, a police official approaches him and asks for his national identity card. Nadeem, who like the majority of the population hates interacting with the police officials, takes out his worn-out brown wallet hurriedly. He sifts through numerous papers and cards before he finds his NIC. The official barely glances at the card before pulling Nadeem out of the line. He hands him his card and gestures him to leave without saying anything.

'What happened?' Nadeem asks, feeling humiliated. 'No Muslims allowed,' replies the official, not even bothering to look at him. 'But I came a few years ago.' He receives no reply. Nadeem, in no mood to be embarrassed any further, with his shattered ego, goes to the nearest shop for a drink.

Sipping his Pepsi, Nadeem is distracted for a little while by the logo on the bottle. Nankana still has Pepsi bottles with the older logos—the round yin-yang types, red and blue. One hardly finds these bottles in Lahore any more. Venting, he tells the shopkeeper that he will wait for the Nagar Kirtan, when the procession of Guru Granth Sahib will be taken out from the gurdwara for a round around the city. This will be the final ritual of the festival.

'That doesn't happen any more,' the shopkeeper replies, his eyes glued to a small television set placed on a wooden plank high up on one of the walls. He is watching Geo, the most popular Pakistani news channel. Nadeem notices a Geo van standing at the gate of the gurdwara amidst several other media cars. These channels are broadcasting live the proceedings from inside the gurdwara through their satellite antennas, fixed on the roofs of the vans. 'That hasn't happened for two years now. There is a security threat.

They will take out a small procession within the precincts of the gurdwara, where it is safe.'

Without saying anything, Nadeem pays the shopkeeper and steps out. He stands in front of the main gate of the gurdwara, keeping enough distance to ensure that he isn't noticed by any police official. He takes off his sandals and standing barefoot on the road, he raises his hand in the direction of the shrine and says, 'I will just say hello to the Baba from here then. Good bye, *Baba Ji*.' Wearing his shoes again and throwing his bag across his shoulder, he heads back to the bus stop.

* * *

Covering of the head and taking off shoes is a show of respect to the sanctity of a place or an individual in the South-Asian tradition. It is not permissible to enter a gurdwara without doing either. Entering a mosque or a Hindu temple also requires similar acts. While it is compulsory to take shoes off inside the main courtyard of the gurdwara, some people voluntarily walk barefoot in the entire complex as a sign of respect. Others go a step beyond that. One comes across several devotees, young and old, walking barefoot on the streets of Nankana. Nankana, because of its association with Guru Nanak, is considered to be one of the holiest cities in the world for the Sikhs, if not the holiest. The gesture of walking without shoes over here is a show of respect. And then there are a few passionate devotees who go even further.

Mahtab Singh, seventy-two, became a celebrity when his interview was broadcast on national television at the 2010 festival. He declared that he would not wear shoes throughout his pilgrimage in Pakistan as an act of respect to the land of the Gurus. Besides Guru Nanak, Guru Ram Das, the fourth Sikh Guru, was also born in present-day Pakistan, in the city of Lahore. Guru Arjan spent a lot of time in the same city, where he was assassinated and his remains interred. His son, Guru Hargobind, also spent a lot of time here.

* * *

Originally called Rai-Bhoi-Di-Talwandi, this city was rechristened Nankana Sahib in honour of Guru Nanak. Nanak spent the early years of his life here, which is why there are several gurdwaras in the city, paying tribute to different periods or interesting incidents from his life. Gurdwara Janamasthan is situated where he was born; Gurdwara Patti Sahib, where he received his earliest education; Gurdwara Balila, where he played as a child; Gurdwara Malji Sahib, where he encountered a snake; Gurdwara Kiara Sahib, where his cattle destroyed the fields of a farmer while he slept; and Gurdwara Tambu Sahib, where he hid after returning from the incident that came to be known as 'Sacha Sauda'. The entire city is full of his memories, preserved through his gurdwaras. For the entire duration of their trip, pilgrims travel to all the gurdwaras in the city, paying tribute to each one of them.

According to official estimates, 10–15,000 people come to Nankana Sahib for this festival every year, which is celebrated during the last days of November. This year (2011) however, the numbers have reduced because of the imminent security concerns in Pakistan. According to media reports, only 3000 people are attending. The festival, which is a celebration of Baba Guru Nanak's birthday, is referred to as Guru Nanak Jayanti or Gurpurab. This year it began on 8 November and will conclude today, on 10 November.

Several trains run from all over India to Nankana. Pilgrims from Delhi, Gujarat and Amritsar, amongst other places, cross over at the Wagah station, which lies on the outskirts of Lahore. After clearing Customs, the train travels to Nankana, where it waits for the pilgrims for three days as they perform their pilgrimage. At the Wagah station, the pilgrims are received by representatives of the ETPB and PSGPC. A langar is also arranged for them by the authorities.

The festival lasts for three days, during which Akhand Path is performed in honour of Guru Nanak. On the final day, after bhog (concluding prayer with distribution of prasad), the Nagar Kirtan is taken out. At the conclusion of the ceremony, pilgrims diverge to different cities to visit other historical gurdwaras. Richer pilgrims coming from the UK, the US and Canada arrive by chartered planes for this special occasion. They book buses here, which take them around. Unlike Indian pilgrims, their visa is not limited to particular cities, which allows them to travel freely. On the way to Nankana, around the time of the festival, one notices several buses with posters of travel companies promising to take one to 'all' the gurdwaras in Pakistan.

* * *

Most of the pilgrims from the developed countries stay at Gurdwara Tambu Sahib, which is a few hundred metres away from Gurdwara Janamasthan. Three hostel blocks have been constructed here with the help of donations from pilgrims coming from the UK, Canada and the US. A large amount has been donated by Kar Seva, a UK-based non-profit organization. One notices its name on yellow dustbins and other boards that have been placed in different gurdwaras of the city.

Compared to Gurdwara Janamasthan, the security at this gurdwara is lax. There are metal detectors and a few guards employed at the gate but it is fairly easy to walk in unnoticed, as most times there is no one monitoring the entrance. The area belonging to Gurdwara Tambu Sahib is the second largest in the city, making it the second-most popular destination after Janamasthan. This particular gurdwara is crowded with people; some are pilgrims passing through while others are camped here.

The shrine, which is a small yellow structure, stands in the middle of the ground with a white dome on the top. The ground around it is vacant, big enough to host an international cricket match. There is a newly constructed residential hall next to the entrance: a triple-storey building, with several rooms on each floor. There are two other much larger buildings for the residence of the pilgrims, constructed by the donations of the devotees. These stand next to each other, shadowing the shrine. There is a single-storey langar hall under the shade of one of the residential buildings. In the future, the Government of Pakistan plans to construct a Guru Nanak University in the vicinity of this complex. This has been one of the persistent demands of the expat Sikh community, with whom the government maintains close ties after their association developed during the years of the Khalistan Movement.

There is a bookstall here, set up by the Dyal Singh Memorial Trust, a pre-Partition trust based in Lahore.

Placed in the parking area, it is adjacent to the langar hall. Two Muslim boys sit behind the counter, playing on their phones. A Sikh woman, who has just come out of the langar hall, stops at the counter for a little while before slipping out of the complex. A group of men stand next to the counter, chatting with each other. These are three Sikh men, a Sikh woman, and a Muslim man. The latter is wearing a blue shirt and black trousers; his head covered with a saffron-coloured cloth and his shave unattended to for several days. His long white hair flows out of the cloth and touches his shoulders. Still talking, he picks up a blue book and holds it vertically. Opening a particular page, he points towards it for his companions. They all stare at the direction of his finger. The Muslim boys continue to play on their mobiles. The book is called *Historical Sikh Shrines in Pakistan*, and the Muslim man, its author, is fifty-eight-year-old Iqbal Qaiser. Every year on the occasion of this festival, he travels to Nankana Sahib. Being a Muslim, getting in is difficult but he manages because of his association with the expat Sikh community as well as the authorities.

'This is the only time in the year my book sells,' he says. 'All year round I sell a few copies. But here I sell somewhere between twenty to thirty copies, which keeps me going throughout the year. However, since the past few years, my sale has reduced. As this is an expensive book, it is usually bought by British or Canadian pilgrims. The Indian pilgrims, like us, are poor and not very keen on reading.'

A major chunk of pilgrims who have stopped coming because of the security conditions have been those from the UK, the US and Canada. This, of course, takes its toll on the religious tourism industry, as these people spend in dollars and pounds as compared to the weak rupee.

Behind the stall, a yellow board reads, 'This newly constructed building has been made by Kar Seva.' This is the langar hall. For these three days this, like the langar halls at other gurdwaras, would be occupied all day long. There is a police official standing at the top of the building, while others have been deployed on the roofs of the residential blocks.

Shaheed Hall, next to the langar hall, has also been constructed through the donations of Kar Seva. Recently completed, this is a clean place and the first choice of pilgrims from developed countries. However, since their numbers have reduced, a lot of Indian pilgrims are living here at the moment.

Walking into the building, one notices children playing in the corridors. Dirty clothes are left hanging on the railing in the middle of the hall, surrounding a hole that runs all the way through the building, from the top to the bottom. A few women are seen ironing clothes outside their rooms. Pilgrims who haven't been able to find any accommodation are sleeping on the floors of the corridor. Stairs take one to the roof of this five-storey building. No pilgrim is allowed here, says the police official sitting on a chair at one end of the roof, facing the ground of the gurdwara. He has put up his legs on top of the boundary wall, his gun leaning against his chair.

The roof provides a panoramic view of the city. One can see the tall minarets of the mosques rising high above all the other buildings, and small white domes of the gurdwaras, holding steady ground in their midst. There are remains of a few Hindu temples; cone-like structures rising from houses abandoned at the time of Partition, and the railway station, empty at the moment. On the other side, one gets a view of the open fields, green cultivation dancing in the November breeze. Also in sight are the neatly painted double roads coming into the city, bringing along more pilgrims. Arshad Malik, the thirty-five-year-old police constable, has been on duty here since eight in the morning. The time right now is almost two in the afternoon. It is a twelve-hour duty for him, after which he will be replaced by another official who will then sit here, out in the open all night. There is a glass of tea placed next to his chair, which he sips occasionally.

Malik belongs to a small village nearby and has been with the police for the past eighteen years. He says that the entire police force of the city has been deployed at the gurdwaras for these three days and extra officers have been called in from neighbouring stations for duty at other points around the city. Unlike the other two Muslims encountered earlier, Malik doesn't share any love for Guru Nanak or the Sikh religion. For him, it is the 'other' religion, separate from his own Islamic identity. Years of state propaganda after the creation of Pakistan has created a sharp division between different religions, which were non-extant or at least fluid prior to Partition. He has brought this tea from a local restaurant next to the gurdwara, whereas he could have had it for free from the langar. 'We are Muslims. We don't eat with the Sikhs or Hindus (from his religious nationalistic perspective, the difference is vague. Anyone who is not a Muslim can be put in this one camp, incorporating all non-Muslims),' he says, slightly offended at even the sheer thought of sharing food with the Sikhs. He would rather pay than have 'impure' food from an 'impure' utensil.

* * *

Outside, on the main artillery road that runs through the city of Nankana, Aslam Chaudary has been running his restaurant for the past ten years. Like Malik, he is also opposed to the idea of non-Muslims sharing utensils with Muslims. He doesn't allow Sikh pilgrims to eat from his hotel. In case an unfamiliar Sikh ventures into his restaurant, he tells him/her, 'We do not have your utensils,' and they get the point. 'The festival causes a lot of inconvenience to us,' he says. 'We can't bring in our cars. There are security checks at every turn. We become prisoners within our own city,' he finishes off with a sigh. However, not all shopkeepers and traders are resentful of the pilgrims who bring a lot of money with them, giving an impetus to the local economy.

From a small obscure city, Nankana has turned into an important city in the past decade. During the Musharraf era (2001–08), newly constructed roads and other government facilities made their way into the city. In 2005, Nankana Sahib was separated from Sheikhupura and made into an independent district, with this city becoming the district headquarters. Sikh expats are now demanding that a hotel of international standards be opened here for the pilgrims and the city be declared a holy city with no visa requirements. At the moment there is no progress on that front, but one can hope for such developments in the future.

One can see several pilgrims sitting at local shops, buying souvenirs and gifts for their relatives and friends. As the gurdwaras are spread all over the city, several pilgrims can be seen walking from one end to the other. During these three days, the city is flooded with pilgrims. There are more men wearing turbans than those who aren't. A majority of the women are wearing mangalsutra and *sindoor*, identification of a married woman. One notices banners reading STD outside shops in the market. One sees several pilgrims sitting on a bench, waiting for their turn. In Pakistan, this facility is referred to as PCO, STD being an Indian term. However, since the majority of the pilgrims are unfamiliar with the term PCO, the local traders just use the Indian term to facilitate them. The entire city looks like a mini-India during these few days.

* * *

About 200 metres from Gurdwara Tambu Sahib, in the direction of the railway station, which is opposite the Gurdwara Janamasthan, one comes across a brown board on the left reading, 'Gurdwara *Panjvin* and *Chevin Patshahi*,' meaning the gurdwara of the fifth and sixth Guru. This gurdwara is the only one in the city which is not in memory of Guru Nanak. Once, the fifth and the sixth Sikh Guru, Guru Arjan and his son Guru Hargobind, made a pilgrimage to the holy city of Nankana Sahib. They decided to leave their horses a little outside the city and walk to the shrine (Gurdwara Janamasthan) as a mark of respect. They tied their horses at this particular spot to a *waan* tree and covered this journey of about 700 metres on foot.

This is a fairly small gurdwara. The main shrine, a double-storey building in the traditional mango yellow colour, is on the left. The Nishan Sahib stands next to it, proclaiming the presence of the Khalsa. A few pilgrims have gathered underneath it, praying. One of them, an old Sikh man wearing a black turban, notes down his name with a pen on the platform on which the flag is standing. A single-storey building, divided into several rooms, is spread out horizontally behind the flag. These rooms have also been allotted to pilgrims. One of the doors of the shrine opens towards the side of the flag. There is a Thara Sahib in the middle, which holds the Guru Granth Sahib, wrapped in a white sheet, a fly-whisk resting nearby. Pilgrims walk in and prostrate before the Granth Sahib, after which, taking a clockwise direction, they come to stand behind the Thara Sahib. Picking up the fly-whisk, they fan it over the Granth Sahib before moving on.

Outside the shrine, there is a staircase leading to the first floor from the side of the residential block. There is a small room on top of the shrine, also regarded as sacred by the pilgrims. A rectangular glass showcase is placed in the middle of the room, containing a piece of the waan tree that was used by the Gurus to tie their horses. A few devotees who are present here touch the glass for blessings and pray. Some linger at the balcony outside the room, enjoying the view of the city. Similar acts of devotion are being practised at all the gurdwaras of Nankana Sahib. All year round most of them remain locked, only to be opened at the time of the festival. There are security guards employed at the entrance to all of them.

* * *

The main focus of the pilgrims is Gurdwara Janamasthan. A sea of people has swamped the area beyond the highly secure gates. More police and security officials are present inside the complex than at the entrance. Everyone has been allotted a pass, even representatives from the media. There are several blocks of hostels here, constructed during various eras. Most of the pilgrims are accommodated in these blocks. Pilgrims look at the proceedings below from the balconies and windows of their apartments.

There is a separate building for communal washrooms on the left side of the main shrine. Several stalls have been set up next to it, providing services to the pilgrims, including laundry, public telephones, juices and other eatables. Only the pool at this gurdwara is filled with water out of all the gurdwaras of the city. The weather is changing; hence a lot of people are avoiding taking a dip. A few children, oblivious to the harmful effects of the changing weather, are bathing here wearing only their shalwars, underwear or trousers, while their heads are covered with a cloth. A few men, brave enough to take a dip, are standing next to the water covered in towels. From far away, one can see them shiver. A child sitting on the top stair, which is above the water level, trembles as water drips from his body. Some women stand nearby, keeping an eye on their children, instructing them to remain towards the edge. The pool gets deeper at the centre as the stairs descend gradually. A couple of police officials have been deployed at the entrance of the pool.

A web of lights is cast all over the façade of the main shrine. These would be lit in different colours in the night. There is a banner at the main entrance, which has a picture of Guru Nanak on one side and one of Guru Gobind Singh on the other. All the other Gurus are depicted in between them. This series of pictures also shows the transition of the religion from a spiritual reformation group to an institutionalized religion; Guru Nanak is portrayed wearing a saffron-coloured cloth, dressed like a mendicant, whereas the last Guru, Guru Gobind Singh, is wearing a shiny dress with a pearl necklace around his neck and a turban that looks like a tiara.

A blue bus decorated with yellow flowers stands at the base of the entrance. This would take a round around the green belt at the centre of the complex during the procession called Nagar Kirtan. Pilgrims pose in front of it for photographs. There are more tents here, both on the left and right side of the shrine. They are for the traders who have come from other parts of the country.

Meena Kumari, fifty-four, sits on a white polyester sheet spread on the ground. Sitting underneath Block 1, a residential hostel, she is one of the several vendors who are seated all the way till the end of the apartments. She has laid out jellies, chips, sweets and other eatables on the floor in front of her, struggling to keep track of her sales with so many children thronging her. Trusting most of them, she receives the money according to what they say they have taken.

'I have been coming to the festival since the past many years,' she says. 'My husband has been setting up eatable stalls here, whereas I would watch the festival along with my children. However, this year I thought that I should also set up a stall. So I bought these things in bulk from Mardan, and now I'm selling them. Back home, I can never imagine running a shop of my own.' Facing her, joined to the building of the gurdwara, are the offices of the gurdwara administration. Further ahead there are stalls of T-shirts, similar to the ones being sold at Hassan Abdal. '*Never Forget 1984*,' '*Singh is King*,' '*Raj Karega Khalsa*,' read a few. Vishal Nasir Chand, the boy from Multan who studies in Quetta and was selling religious paraphernalia at Hassan Abdal, has also come here with his brother and cousins, selling shirts this time. Sitting next to a huge bundle of shirts, a few of which have been laid out in front for the perusal of the customers, he tries to entice the pilgrims to take a look.

The alley takes one to the newly created langar hall. Like Gurdwara Tambu Sahib, food is served here around the clock. The floor of the hall has become wet due to the slushy mixture of water, food, tea and mud. Everyone is barefoot, their soles blackened. As the langar hall fills up to the brim, the volunteers suggest that newcomers sit in the corridor next to the building. Most of the volunteers are local Pathan Sikhs. Police officials have been deployed here, patrolling the area. The hall is the last building before the boundary wall, beyond which lies the Guru Nanak Government College. A wall has been raised from here as well, with barbwire on the top. There is a large brown gate, which is a recent addition. Contingents of police officials have been positioned here. A couple of pilgrims argue with the officials at the gate to allow them to leave from here, but they refuse. Besides the officials, no one is allowed to come or go from this gate. Behind the langar hall, there are two large tubs filled with water. Several men and women are busy washing dirty utensils here. They do this by putting them in the water for a little while and then wiping them with a cloth. The utensils are then collected in a large bucket and taken to the hall for the pilgrims. Meanwhile, buckets of dirty utensils come from inside to be washed. All of these people are volunteers, performing sewa.

A local Pathan Sikh asks a group of women to give way as he tries to squeeze through this crowded narrow space while carrying several cartons of milk. He is heading towards a small room next to the washing area. Watching him arrive, another Pathan Sikh unlocks the door and swings it open. The man carrying milk rushes into the room. Quickly coming out, he locks it again and both of them disappear into the crowd. This room stores raw material for langar.

There are two entrances into the courtyard of the main shrine. One of them is from the front and one from the right side, facing the langar hall. The entire courtyard is covered with tents and the floor with carpets. Pilgrims, who have brought their own bedding, have made themselves comfortable on the floor. Families, men, women, children, old and young, are spread out all over the courtyard. This is where they sleep at night, using their bags as pillows. The majority of these pilgrims are locals from Khyber Pakhtunkhwa and Sindh; however, there are a few Indian families as well. Some are sleeping, others listening to the kirtan being performed; some read the Granth, while others socialize.

Kirtan is being performed from the stage next to the shrine. This is a group of three men, all wearing white shalwar kameez. One of them is on the tabla, while the other two are on the harmonium. The one seated in the middle is also the singer. They have short black beards and have covered their heads with a loose turban, a popular style in the villages of West Punjab. They appear to be Muslims. There is a screen placed behind the stage, being monitored by a clean-shaven man in a blue shalwar kameez. It plays different scenes from the activities taking place at Gurdwara Janamasthan as they unfold. These are being broadcast live through the Internet and viewed by millions of people the world over. This is the first time it is being done from here.

A long queue of pilgrims stands behind an orange robe that blocks their way, waiting to pay their tributes to the shrine of Guru Nanak. A local Sikh stands at the helm, making sure no one crosses it. The line originates from the main entrance. After those performing the darshan have moved away, a few more people are allowed to prostrate in front of the Guru Granth Sahib, after which, going in a clockwise direction, they enter the shrine through a small door on the left. Here they seek the blessings of the Granth Sahib, which is being read at the moment. A few Sikhs are sitting inside the room reading their pocket Granths, or simply watching the Granthi perform his rites. Some wait for the fly-whisk to be vacant and then take their turn of fanning it over the Holy Book. Completing the rite, they leave the room from a similar door on the right side of the shrine. Outside, there is a man with a bowl of *sujji ka halwa*, offering prasad to the pilgrims. As the devotees exit, he puts a little halwa in their palms. The devotees receive it with both hands and eat it.

There is a Sikh family sitting at the edge of the pavilion on this side, listening to the kirtan. They have come from the Indian state of Gujarat. Ajay Singh, eighty-two, is accompanied by his wife, Amrinder Kaur and his son, Ghulab Singh. This is their first trip to Pakistan. 'I was seventeen at the time of Partition. We used to live in Sargodha city (currently in Punjab, Pakistan). I remember a sweetmeat shop at Kucheri Chowk,' says Ajay in a Punjabi accent which is still similar to the one that one hears in that region. His son, on the other hand, doesn't have the same accent. 'I long to go back to my city, but I can't. My visa doesn't allow that. I don't think I'll ever be able to see Sargodha again.'

By now, the readings of the Akhand Path have been performed. The pilgrims prepare themselves for the final ritual of the event, that is, Nagar Kirtan, and start gathering at the courtyard outside. People push and shove each other for a better view. Some climb on to the roofs of adjacent buildings. Heads peek out of several windows, which dot the façade of the gurdwara. People scatter all over the courtyard, wherever they can find a suitable place. Most of them remain on the track that the bus would be travelling on. Cameras are taken out of their covers and settings adjusted to take into account the overcast weather. The bus has moved in front of the entrance, ready to complete its lap. Thousands of pilgrims stand in front of it. Volunteers shout and ask people to move out of the way. Some do, clearing a few immediate steps, but move back to their previous positions when they realize that the bus is not moving as yet.

A decorated pickup honks from the alley to the right of the gurdwara, as it fights its way through the people. There is a dhol-wala sitting on the stop, wearing a red kameez and a dhoti. He has a maroon turban on his head, in the traditional rural Punjabi style. Squatting on the roof, he has placed his dhol in front of him and plays as the pickup makes its way through the crowd, honking and threatening to drive over people who fail to move. Young Sikh boys, with a weakness for the beat of the dhol, jump in front of the car and start dancing. They lead the car as it makes its way through the people. Four to five young boys hang from the back of the pickup, distributing packets of juice to the people standing on the sides. The free distribution causes havoc and a mob of people rush towards the moving car, snatching and pulling the hands of the volunteers. The young boys tell the crowd to act civilized, but in vain.

In the meantime, a group of Sikh men gather in front of the blue bus. It is covered with yellow flowers, with a few peacock feathers on top. They stand in a formation of two lines of five each. The front row is dressed in white *cholas*, a loose piece of cloth worn like a kurta. They wear saffron-coloured turbans and have tugged up their dhotis such that their calves are bare. Garlands of yellow flowers encircle their necks. All of them are holding the Nishan Sahib with both their hands, on a pole that looks like a hand from the top. The formation behind them is holding swords (kirpan) instead of flags. Their uniform is a saffron chola with a blue turban. They have quoits of steel and the Khalsa symbol on their turbans. People climb over each other to get a peek at this procession.

The bus starts moving slowly as the crowd around it also starts to walk along, while the formation of the five-five leads the procession. People click their cameras, eager not to miss a moment. Journalists scramble through the crowds, lifting their cameras high up to get a better view. Some climb poles and trees to get superior shots. The side door of the bus is open. Two men sit here, attending to a golden palanquin where the Guru Granth Sahib is resting. People rush towards this opening to seek the blessing of the Living Guru. The man sitting inside gives them prasad while the bus continues to move. When the bus takes a turn from the main gate of the shrine to head back towards its resting place, a group of devotees sitting on top of the gate throw red rose petals. Another dhol-wala waiting here plays celebratory beats. Flowers keep falling from the sky, as youngsters dance to the rhythm of the dhol. Reaching its starting point, the bus comes to a halt. This concludes the Nagar Kirtan, marking an end to the religious rituals of the festival.

Things in Nankana Sahib will soon calm down. At least till the next year . . .

AFTERWORD

While this book is about the experience of being a minority in Pakistan, it is important to understand a little bit about the context in which material for this book has been gathered. As has been emphasized at various points throughout the book, the minority experience in Pakistan is fraught with danger. Interacting with minorities and gaining their trust therefore took some doing. Based as I am in Lahore, much of my fieldwork took place in the city itself and its vicinity. This is bound to have had its limitations. While acknowledging these limitations below, it is my view that these do not detract from the relevance and the appeal of the book as a whole.

Hindus

My research with the Hindu community primarily remained confined to the city of Lahore. All the structured interviews that I have used are of people from here. I did interact with members of the community from Multan, Bahawalnagar, Khyber Pakhtunkhwa and Sindh but that was within the framework of festivals, which meant that they were short interviews. Whereas there are certain themes that are uniform to the Hindu experience all over the country, there are likely to be variations according to the region.

The majority of the Hindu community is based in Sindh and southern Punjab, where they have a proportionate representation from the lower and upper castes. For the course of this particular project, I could not delve into much detail about the experiences of the community from these regions, where they are a part of the social fabric of the area, unlike the 'ghettoization' they experience in central Punjab where I conducted my research. My perception is that the conditions under which members of the Hindu community live in central Punjab are the harshest compared to the other regions. Almost all the interviews I conducted were of Hindus belonging to the lower castes because there are hardly any high-caste Hindus in this region. This is a limitation in my research and I would like to point out that in no way can my observation and analysis from central Punjab be construed as being reflective of Hindu communities in areas where there is a considerable population. My accounts are merely a few snapshots. Perhaps in future, I will have the opportunity to 'take' some more.

Christians

The majority of the Christian minority is based in Punjab and so unlike the Hindu community, my work with them can be generalized to be reflective of the larger Christian community in the country. However, having said that, I would like to point out that one of the basic purposes of this book is to highlight that the experiences of the different religious minorities in Pakistan which cannot be generalized into one. This would also hold true for every individual part of the religious minority. Within the Christian community, I have interviewed people whose houses have been burnt down because of religious persecution, whereas on the other hand, there are people who said in their interviews that they don't think being a Christian is a hindrance in Pakistan. I feel that my pool for Christian interviews due to its different socio-economic conditions was much more diverse than the Hindu group and so the accounts of the Christian community are able to give a better sense of the social conditions of the Christian community all across the country as compared to the Hindu accounts.

Zoroastrians

The majority of the Zoroastrian community of Pakistan is based in Karachi. But for the purposes of this research, I limited myself to the members of the community based in Lahore. I conducted only three structured interviews from the community, but interacted with a number of Parsis during the Navroz celebration, observations from which are part of the account. Through these interviews, I have tried to understand the differences between the communities in Lahore and Karachi, but I would like to state that these aren't my personal observations, but provided to me by my sources in Lahore.

Baha'is

The Baha'i community is a small minority group in the country, and like the Parsis and Sikhs are referred to as 'others' in the census reports because of their tiny number.

They are evenly scattered throughout the country, with Lahore and Islamabad being two of the important cities as far as Baha'i representation is concerned. For the purpose of this book, I interacted primarily with the Baha'is in Lahore.

Sikhs

My research on the Sikh community was limited to the Sikhs based in Nankana Sahib. As was recounted in the accounts, these are not indigenous people from the city, but recent migrants from Khyber-Pakhtunkhwa (KPK) where there is a considerable Sikh population. Given that most of the people I interviewed remember this internal migration from KPK to Punjab, one gets a good picture of the different socio-economic conditions in both of these provinces.

ACKNOWLEDGEMENTS

I would have never been able to complete the book without the encouragement and the support of a number of people and I would like the opportunity to thank them here. The greatest inspiration has been Sharmeen Obaid Chinoy. She has to be the best boss I could ask for, who believes in allowing an individual to grow to the fullest. Having said that, I must add that she also pushes one to the fullest, making one outperform oneself. She was always open to my ideas regarding the project and gave me all the freedom that I could ask for. Thank you, Sharmeen.

I would also like to thank members of my family, who have tolerated me patiently, listening to me talk about the book for hours. I would like to thank my sisters, Sana Khalid and Nida Umer, who allowed me to use their room for writing. I would like to thank my parents, for bearing my expenses when I was 'unemployed' and writing this book. On days when I felt that I was wasting away my life, my father would reassure me that writing was the greatest job in the world. Thank you, Abu.

I would like to thank my mother for never giving up on me, even when all the odds were against me. I would like to thank my mother-in-law, Ms Neelofar Zakaria, for her support and encouragement. I would like to thank my colleagues at Citizens Archive of Pakistan (CAP) — Faisal Saeed, Maryam Altaf, Humayun Memon, Rida Arif, Samra Noori, Bilal Aijaz, Abrar Ali and Owais Rana. I would like to thank Iqbal Qaiser, my mentor, who inspired me to take up this field. He is my eternal guru and I can never be grateful enough for all that he has done for me.

The journey of this book began with a series of rejections from publishers and agents. I happened to come across the email address of Kanishka Gupta by chance. He replied within minutes and, at the end of the day, was my literary agent. Where I had received rejections prior to his service, Kanishka turned things around, making my dream a reality. Thank you, Kanishka, for making this happen.

I would also like to thank my publisher, Paul Vinay Kumar, for taking the risk of signing a first-time author. *A White Trail* would have not have come about without his support. After acceptance began the long process of editing which was done by Karthik Venkatesh. I am grateful to him for patiently bearing with my numerous grammatical errors. The editor is the unsung hero of any manuscript. Thank you, Karthik for such an amazing job.

Finally, I would like to thank my fiancée and my former colleague, Ms Anam Zakaria, for reading all the chapters with me and giving me the inspiration and motivation to go on, when I faltered.

I would like to dedicate the book to you, Anam. You wrote each and every word of this book with me and have felt for it as much as I have.

NOTES

Holi at Multan

1. Hindu devotion towards Guru Nanak is explained in the chapter 'Guru Nanak's Birthday at Nankana Sahib'.
2. This concept is explained in detail in the chapter 'Shri Valmiki's Birthday'.

Shivratri at Killa Katas

1. Iqbal Qaiser, *Historical Sikh Shrines in Pakistan*, p. 174.

Baisakhi at Ram Thamman

1. The religious identities of Hindu and Christian overlap for certain Hindu communities. This phenomenon is explained in detail in the chapter 'Shri Valmiki's Birthday'.

Commemoration of Guru Arjan's Martyrdom at Gurdwara Dera Sahib, Lahore

1. *Sikhism: Origin and Development* by Dalbir Singh Dhillon, Atlantic Publishers and Distributors, New Delhi, 1988, p. 108.

Commemoration of Maharaja Ranjit Singh's Death Anniversary at Lahore

1. *Ranjit Singh* by Khushwant Singh, Notes for Chapter 4, published by Penguin India, 2001, New Delhi, p. 275.

The historical temple of Katas Raj with its emerald pool.

Gurdwara Tambu Sahib at the time of sunset.

Celebrating Holi in the city of Hiranyakashipu and Prahlad Bhagat.

A pilgrim placing his hand on the handprint of Guru Nanak on the sacred rock at Gurdwara Panja Sahib, Hassan Abdal, on the occasion of Baisakhi.